$ELLING Goodness

ADVANCE PRAISE FOR SELLING GOODNESS

"Levine's case is put in clear, simple, compelling prose: People doing good works can and should do a better job of selling their causes to the public. His purpose is not merely to inform, but to motivate. He alternately chides, teaches, and exhorts America's army of citizen activists to effectively use the media to convince our fellow citizens to join up."
ROGER L. CONNOR,
Executive Director, Center for Community Interest

"As the head of a small organization with a limited promotional budget, I heartily concur with Michael Levine's belief that goodness must be sold."
GERRY CORNEZ, *Executive Director, WAIF*

"This is an important book that will serve as a guide for all charities and non-profit organizations in helping to promote their important causes."
MARGOT ANDREW, *President, Camp Laurel*

". . . [Selling Goodness] is obviously of interest to charities and non-profit organizations." COLONEL JOHN M. BATE,
National Chief Secretary, Salvation Army

"I certainly agree with the premise that the continued good work of the nation's charities requires an unprecedented approach to public relations."
JOHN J. MAHONEY, *President, National Hospice Organization*

". . . your book was quite interesting and provided a solid rationale for promoting one's philanthropic work." JOHN H. GRAHAM IV,
C.E.O., American Diabetes Association

"States the case for selling goodness convincingly."
JOEL FOX, *President, Howard Jarvis Taxpayers Association*

"Mr. Levine's approach is as focused as a bullet in flight."
USA TODAY

$ELLING
Goodness

MICHAEL LEVINE

RENAISSANCE BOOKS
Los Angeles

ACKNOWLEDGMENTS

Grateful acknowledgment is made for the permission to use the following: From "How to Ignore Charitable Appeals with a Clear Conscience," copyright © 1997 by Ardian Gill. From "Black Philanthropy Is Growing," by Lori Sharn, copyright © 1997, *USA Today*. Reprinted with permission. From "Company's Use of Its Employees To Get Publicity Suits Them to a T." Reprinted by permission of the *Wall Street Journal*, © 1995 Dow Jones & Company, Inc. All rights reserved worldwide.

Library of Congress Cataloging-in-Publication Data

Levine, Michael.
    Selling goodness : the guerilla P.R. guide to promoting your charity, non-profit organization, or fundraising event / Michael Levine.
      p.   cm
    ISBN 1-58063-009-X (alk. paper)
    1. Public relations—Social service. 2. Mass media and social service. 3. Promotion of special events. 4. Fund raising. 5. Charities. 6. Nonprofit organizations. I. Title.
    HV42.L48   1998
    659.2—DC21   97-52572
                                             CIP

10 9 8 7 6 5 4 3 2 1

Design by Susan Shankin

Distributed by St. Martin's Press
Manufactured in the United States of America
First Edition

CONTENTS

DEDICATED TO WISE VIRGINS EVERYWHERE.

ACKNOWLEDGMENTS

"All these people had their moments.In my life, I've loved them all."

My encouraging associates at Renaissance Books

My father, Arthur, step-mother, Marilyn, and sister, Patricia

My loyal and hardworking office staff:
Kristina Bullard, Sharma Burke, Michelle Dolley, Jill Henry,
Phillip Kass, Kelly Kimball, Kelly Pieropan, and Jennifer Trauth

My long-time friends: Bill Calkins, Richard Imprescia,
Karen Karsian, Nancy Mager, and John McKillop

Wise council on this bookwas provided by the following caring
people:Howard Ahmanson, Joel Engel, Joel Fox, Harold Johnson,
Rabbi Harold Kushner, Candy Lightner, Allen Mayer, Julian Myers,
Dale Olson, Scott Peck, Dennis Prager, and Tom Provenzano

Special thanks to Harold Johnson for his invaluable help
and support in developing this book

PREFACE

CHARITIES and nonprofit organizations fulfill very noble purposes, whether it is feeding and clothing the poor, spearheading the funding of important medical research, or leading the cause for justice or peace. There is no question about the social value of charities and nonprofits in this country or anywhere in the world. Nonprofit charitable enterprises are often the only unconditional source of assistance and aid to help the sick, the poor, and the war-torn. Whereas governments often play politics with lives and causes, and businesses usually have a profit motive for direct charitable actions, charities and nonprofits are usually dedicated to helping people without regard to political, religious, or economic beliefs. They simply want to save lives, restore happiness, and sow the seeds of freedom wherever needed.

Unfortunately, I have seen too many of even the most noble and vitally needed charitable nonprofits fade into obscurity, never having accomplished the laudable goals they set out to achieve. In most cases, the reason for their demise is that they did not promote themselves with vigor and assertiveness. They either failed to learn to use public relations (PR) to their advantage or they did not avail themselves of the services of professionals who could have launched their causes into the limelight and helped them get the momentum, manpower, and funds they needed to stay alive.

These early deaths are disappointing, unsatisfying—and tragic. They could have been prevented if the right steps had been taken. As a public-relations professional, I strongly believe that the world cannot afford to lose the efforts of so many charities and nonprofit organizations which help solve the never-ending problems that plague our fragile planet.

This book is therefore dedicated, with passion, to helping these charities and nonprofits learn to use pubic relations of all kinds to accomplish their important goals. Drawing on my background as the founder of one of Hollywood's most prominent public-relations firms, and having represented hundreds of the entertainment industry's biggest celebrities, I wrote *Selling Goodness* to show you how to take advantage of professional public-relations techniques on a fledgling charity's often-impoverished budget. The book describes how the media operates, and how you can make it work for your charity or organization.

In the following chapters, you will find advice on such matters as pitching a story, writing a press release, and giving an interview. I guide you through the critical steps of a PR campaign, from initial contacts with the media through follow-up, special events, and dealing with a PR crisis should one happen to you.

Throughout the chapters, you will also find two types of "boxed features." One contains special hints about PR techniques or additional elaboration on a topic. The other presents case histories of inspiring PR stories from my personal files. Indeed, one of my joys in writing this book is that I get to recount some of the great stories I've collected over the years of promotional techniques used by many different businesses and nonprofits.

THE MORAL CASE FOR PROMOTION

But *Selling Goodness* is much more than a practical handbook on skills and procedures. It is also a moral manifesto. If you are a humble

THE TIFFANY THEORY REVISITED

If you give someone a present, and you give it to them in a Tiffany box, it's likely that they'll believe that the gift has higher perceived value than if you gave it to them in no box or in a box of less prestige. That's not because the receiver of the gift is an idiot; but rather, because we live in a culture in which we gift-wrap everything—our politicians, our corporate heads, our movie and TV stars, and even our toilet paper.

Public relations is like gift-wrapping.

do-gooder with qualms about seeking either attention or special promotion, this book presents a powerful case for promoting yourself and your charitable cause. I believe the moral argument is especially compelling now that government is trimming outlays on social services. Nonprofits are being called to fill in the gaps. They will need more resources—and they therefore must do whatever it takes to get them, especially vigorous promotion of their vital cause.

If after reading this book you are able to take your cause more seriously, and promote it with greater vigor and intensity, you will not only be contributing to your individual charity, but to the broader purpose of promoting goodness. It may sound quaint but the truth is that the promotion of your charitable work can assist all living beings. This is a grand vision, to be sure. But imagine the potential of a planet that is better nourished, both in substance and in spirit. I believe this is our potential.

My plan in this book is direct, and the process doable. It can make you an ally in the grand project of selling goodness, and, through that alliance, a portion of paradise can be regained.

MICHAEL LEVINE

1

The Moral Case for Promotion

Charity and personal force are the only investments worth anything.
WALT WHITMAN

IF you grew up in the late 1950s or early 1960s, you probably share my memory of a popular admonition that was delivered at many family dinner tables. "Finish your meal," parents would say. "There are children starving in China. It's a sin to waste food."

A sin to waste food? As teenagers, we were usually tempted to roll our eyes when we heard that lecture over and over.

But on deeper reflection, it really isn't absurd or even a melodramatic statement. If you think about the poverty and depth of deprivation in some parts of the world, it is not hyperbole to say there is something immoral when those of us with more food, more wealth, and more resources, waste them.

I suggest that the same logic applies to charitable work. If you have a project that can make the world a better place, reduce unjust suffering, or eradicate sadness, then surely it is wrong—in fact, sinful—to waste it. Not only is there a moral argument for promoting humanitarian projects, *it is immoral not to promote them.* Why not promote your charity or nonprofit so that it becomes as strong and effective as it can be? Indeed, if the good works of the world were publicized as much as the activities of the Mafia, I believe the world would be transformed.

Unfortunately, in my profession as a public-relations expert, I see nonprofit organizations and charities wasting efforts and precious resources all the time. I have watched dozens of charity executives, fund-raisers, and volunteers with the noblest of character and generous motives plow time, money, heart, and soul into life-affirming pursuits—food banks, battered-women's shelters, scholarship funds, and AIDS walks—only to sabotage their well-intentioned efforts by refusing to promote their good work. Their undue modesty, humility, and naiveté become a unexpected barrier to achieving their altruistic purposes.

This attitude is wrong both practically and morally. Please remember: *A well-planned and well-executed public-relations strategy is as essential to the success of a charitable venture as it is to our largest corporations, or the careers of our politicians and movie stars.*

To support my conviction, I have developed a "PR moral manifesto" for charities and nonprofit organizations, to guide you on your way to greater success. My moral manifesto contains ten commandments, or maxims if you prefer. These maxims are summarized on the next page, and we will review them one by one in this chapter. I implore you to photocopy this page and hang it on your wall. "Bind it as a signpost on your doors," as the Bible instructs. Whenever you are uncertain of your path, or feeling downtrodden or tired, I hope you will refer to this PR moral manifesto for inspiration and guidance. I will feel victorious in writing this book if this moral manifesto helps you obtain the funding and manpower you need to make your organization a success.

THE PR MORAL MANIFESTO
for
CHARITIES AND NONPROFITS

1. Thou shalt overcome neurotic humility about promotion.

2. Thou shalt get thy head out of the clouds.

3. Thou shalt remember that people love to give—and give to love.

4. Thou shalt ask at every opportunity for promotion of good works.

5. Thou shalt believe that one person or one idea can make a difference.

6. Thou shalt teach businesses that charity improves profits.

7. Thou shalt lead by example.

8. Thou shalt raise consciousness, which is as important as raising money.

9. Thou shalt seek "good reality" and "good perception."

10. Thou shalt not be afraid to think big.

Thou Shalt Overcome Neurotic Humility about Promotion

C. S. Lewis said, "Every virtue, taken to extremes, has the potential to become a vice." So it is with humility about promoting good deeds. I am constantly astounded that so many good people pursuing charitable works need to be reminded that what they are doing is worthy of being promoted—and in fact is necessary to promote.

This maxim challenges many of you to forget about personal blocks and neurotic humility if you seek to publicize your organization so that you can help others as effectively as possible. We are born into a variety of cultural and psychological inclinations, many of which are rooted in the Judeo-Christian ethic that implores us to be humble and modest, even about our good deeds. However, excessive humility and modesty serve no purpose in charitable work; they needlessly prevent many nonprofit enterprises from realizing their full potential. It is necessary to apply critical and moral logic to these cultural stumbling blocks in order to move beyond them and embrace the moral case for promotion.

Having neurotic humility about promotion is ironic since much of our Judeo-Christian ethic actually endorses promotion for good work. Jesus said, "Let your light so shine before men, that they may see your good works, and glorify your Father in heaven." Judaism, too, teaches that altruism should receive public recognition, and that there is no shame in advertising one's generosity. Quite the contrary. Putting your name on the side of the hospital wing you have helped endow is considered perfectly appropriate in Jewish tradition.

Father Richard John Neuhaus, a prominent Catholic priest and editor of *First Things*, a journal of religion and society, says "It is a great and needed thing to be actively promoting volunteerism. In the encyclical, 'Centissimus Annus,' John Paul II talks about the importance of intermediary institutions such as private, voluntary charitable organizations. They give individuals an opportunity to be active agents of change in their own lives and in the lives of their neighbors. This enhances the dignity of individuals—and anything that promotes these possibilities and encourages more people to answer the challenge is to be welcomed."

"There is indeed a moral case for self-promotion," says America's perhaps best-known rabbi, Harold Kushner, who is also the best-selling author of *When Bad Things Happen to Good People*. "If the purpose you have in mind is to do a good deed, then you do the public a favor by bringing it to their attention."

Rabbi Daniel Lapin, a business consultant and president of the Seattle-based educational foundation, Toward Tradition, agrees. "The Rabbinic and Talmudic wisdom down the centuries teaches us that there is a positive mandate to advertise your charitable deeds, to put your name on that hospital, for instance," he says.

Hugh Hewitt, a Los Angeles law professor and television personality, and host of the 1996 Public Broadcasting Service (PBS) TV series, *America's Search for God*, struggled with the promotion issue and concluded that there is no conflict between Christian belief and an intelligent use of the media to illuminate good works. For his PBS series, Hewitt interviewed a number of prominent people of faith representing a wide range of views. He spoke with the evangelical writer Charles Colson; the inner-city African-American pastor, Reverend Cecil Murray; and the contemplative Roman Catholic priest, Father Thomas Keating. All of them saw religion as involving not just worship, but service to others. Hewitt's talks with them strengthened his belief that advertising good works is itself a good work.

"Jesus did some of his most famous miracles very publicly," Hewitt reminds us. "There was his feeding of five thousand people with but a few fish and loaves of bread; his turning water into wine in front of a wedding throng—not to mention that small thing about walking on water."

I like to use the following parable from the Book of Matthew to exemplify the fine line between appropriate humility and smart promotion. Called "The Tale of the Wise and the Foolish Virgins," this story is quite curious, but as you will see, its message cannot be understood in any other way than to endorse the value of taking care of your own business. This important but unfortunately obscure parable goes as follows:

> There were ten virgins who took their lamps and went out to wait for the arrival of a bridegroom. Five of the virgins were wise and five were foolish. The foolish ones brought their lamps so that they could see and be seen once it became dark. Trouble is, they brought no oil with which to light them. The wise ones did not make that mistake. They had plenty of oil for their lamps.
>
> Night came, and all the virgins fell asleep. But they were awakened when a cry went up: "The bridegroom is coming. Get ready to meet him." When the foolish virgins attempted to light their lamps, they were unable to do so. Their lamps had no fuel. They asked the wise virgins for help: Would you share some oil with us? No luck. The five wise virgins answered that they did not have enough oil to allow them to share some and still keep their own lamps burning. The foolish virgins were therefore compelled to go out in the darkness in search of oil.
>
> While they were gone, the bridegroom arrived. He greeted the five wise virgins and took them inside a great hall for a marriage festival. The foolish virgins eventually returned to find the door of the hall closed to them. They knocked frantically. But when the bridegroom came to the door, he refused to let them in.
>
> "I don't know you," he said. And so they went away sorrowfully.
>
> MATTHEW 25:1-13

On first glance, this parable suggests a harsh sermon—that, because of some unexplained lack of thinking, some women were kept out of the bliss of marriage. An upsetting story, or so it would seem. What of charity and Christian compassion? Don't human beings have an obligation to share and to support each other? Why should the other five women be rewarded for being selfish with their resources?

When I first read this story, I was confused. However, on reflection, I came to a deeper level of meaning. I began to understand that the parable actually carries a different message. It imparts a powerful lesson when the oil in the lamps is seen as a symbol of promotion. The wise virgins had readied themselves for a life-changing encounter; they took their own causes seriously and did not worry about appearing vain for having prepared themselves. Meanwhile, the foolish virgins, out of laziness or sloppiness, had not the courage to make themselves ready, and so they lost out on the life-changing experience.

In my view, the conclusion to this story is clear. No one can give you the gift of promotion. We can encourage others to speak up for themselves, but the act of doing so for ourselves ultimately has to be accomplished by each of us individually. It takes self-confidence, pride, and commitment. You cannot get promotion in a bottle, nor from your closest friend, just as the foolish virgins could not borrow it from the wise ones.

Another lesson also shines through the parable: the value of shining a light on yourself when you want to stand out. After all, what is a lantern's purpose, but to illuminate the person holding it and the surrounding area? The wise virgins were able to see the bridegroom in the darkness—and get the bridegroom to see them in return—not by being shy and hiding under the dark night sky, but by lighting their lamps and lifting them high. If this moment of life-changing opportunity was not going to pass them by, they had to think ahead, and be willing to illuminate themselves.

The great Jewish philosopher Hillel said, "If I am not for myself, who, then, will be for me?" In a lighter vein, a friend of mine in the publicity business says, in mock-biblical style: "*He that tooteth not his own horn, the same shall not be tooted.*"

THE REVEREND ROBERT SCHULLER: A DUTY TO GET YOUR MESSAGE ACROSS

In the words of the Reverend Robert Schuller, pastor of the Crystal Cathedral in southern California: "We live in a world where people are overwhelmed with messages. You have to take special steps to make sure yours gets through. You have a duty to do so—if you truly believe in your cause. You are shirking your duty if you are keeping your charitable pursuits under wraps."

Reverend Schuller knows something about the art of promotion. He started his career as a clergyman in the 1950s by preaching from the roof of the concession stand at the Garden Grove, California, drive-in theater. People listened from their cars. The attention he got from reaching out to spiritual seekers in this unorthodox way catapulted him into the newspapers and into public consciousness.

The trajectory of his personal fame—and the effectiveness of his ministry—has been on a steep ascent ever since. His *Hour of Power* television program, originating from the Crystal Cathedral in Garden Grove, is broadcast internationally. His books advocating positive, "Possibility Thinking," have sold in the tens of thousands. President Clinton introduced him, during the 1996 State of the Union address, as a man offering hope to Americans in search of uplift and guidance. And countless people have benefited from his message about the power of the individual to overcome adversity.

Randall Wallace, for instance. A few years ago Randall was a member of a vast army within the greater Los Angeles area: the legion of frustrated screenwriters. Well into his forties—with a family to support—he had spent years writing scripts and trying to get them considered by movie-studio executives. To no avail. His chosen path in life—his vocation of love—seemed to have led into a cul de sac. And into a valley of frustration and emotional turmoil.

During this dark period, when he was considering giving up on his dream, one morning he happened to hear Reverend Schuller on television. He had never been an admirer of Schuller. In fact, Randall Wallace will tell you that he was cynical about the man and his seemingly sugary platitudes. But this particular morning, something in the speaker's words grabbed Randall's soul and shook it. The sermon revitalized him, giving him renewed energy and commitment. The eventual result was a script about a thirteenth-century Scottish freedom-fighter who carried the same surname as the scriptwriter: William Wallace. Mel Gibson played the title character in the film, and the Academy of Motion Picture Arts and Sciences honored the production with the Best Picture Oscar of 1996. *Braveheart* stirred millions of moviegoers, offering an ennobling example of love of liberty and sacrifice for others.

I recount this story because it fits in so well with the moral manifesto of this book. Dr. Schuller's influence would not have been possible without his savvy use of promotion. He was not put off by our culture's admonition on the one hand to do good, but on the other hand to be humble. He has come to terms with this apparent contradiction, and risen above it.

Dr. Schuller sees a very practical case for being a promoter. "Some universal principles apply to charitable works as much as to any other kind of enterprise," he says. "I'm talking about basic rules of management and business. You don't go into a business enterprise, be it secular or religious or charitable, unless there's a need to be filled.

"Second, you have to have a response to that need.

"And third, you've got to be willing and able to let people know that you're there, that you've got what they need. That's promotion, and it's as much a part of a suc-

cessful enterprise as good motives and smart management." Public relations "is so extremely important, that to
neglect it is to allow yourself to be delinquent, to under-
perform for those you're supposed to be serving."

Thou Shalt Get Thy Head Out of the Clouds

Given the nature of their work and their lack of resources, many
charities and nonprofits are forced to rely on the efforts of "people
of good heart" to accomplish their mission. This often means that
these organizations don't truly have consistent professional management or financial guidance to help them maximize their effectiveness. Using a bevy of volunteers and sometimes a revolving door
of leadership, these organizations seem to succeed solely by keeping
their eye on the cause, without regard for their operational efficiency. Unfortunately, this is why so many charities and nonprofits fail
or achieve only a portion of what they set out to accomplish.

This maxim is therefore intended to convince charities and nonprofits that they should stop working "with their head in the clouds."
I borrow the phrase from Father Robert Sirico, a Catholic priest and
president of the Acton Institute, a think tank studying the intersection between social values and economic issues. Father Sirico talks
about the failure of small charities to market themselves effectively in
these terms: "I think some nonprofits are so intent about their mission that they neglect the practical necessities of finance and promotion. Their heads a bit too much in the clouds, you might say."

I agree with Father Sirico. Although you are a nonprofit organization, you must pay as much attention to your operational efficiency as any business if you are to survive. And one major element
of this is learning to use public relations to your best advantage.
There is no point keeping your head in the clouds by pretending
that PR is beneath your organization or that PR exists only for
celebrities and politicians.

Father Sirico's Acton Institute knows well the value of good PR. To keep their name in the limelight, they founded the Samaritan Awards to identify, publicize, and support worthy but little-known altruistic organizations around the country that needed a boost. The director of the Samaritan Awards, Barbara von der Heydt, summarizes the goals of the institute by saying, "We look for charities that genuinely change lives." She notes that the program's criteria follow an alphabet soup of "effective compassion," as identified by Marvin Olasky, a historian and sociologist at the University of Texas at Austin. The elements of effective compassion include the following:

+ *Affiliation.* Does this organization build relational bridges from the recipient back to family, friends, and the community?
+ *Bonding.* Is there a direct bond between giver and receiver? Is there a mentor to work with the recipient over time?
+ *Character.* Does this group build good character, fostering the virtues of self-restraint, honesty, and reliability?
+ *Discernment.* Does this organization distinguish between people looking for a hand-out, and those who need temporary help to get on their feet? Are services and expectations tailored to fit the individual?
+ *Employment.* Do recipients receive marketable job skills and learn a work ethic that will empower them to get a job and keep it?
+ *Freedom.* Do recipients learn to use freedom to make choices responsibly? Do they learn to take responsibility for their actions?
+ *God.* Do recipients come closer to knowing their Creator, loving him, serving him? Is this work building his kingdom?

Operating with these criteria, the Samaritan Awards have assisted groups that serve "not so much as safety nets but as trampolines, helping people who have hit hard times get themselves back up and regain their bearings," according to Ms. von der Heydt. Examples of groups they have helped include

- ✦ Step 13 in Denver, which has transformed the lives of hundreds of formerly homeless alcoholics who are now sober and productively employed;
- ✦ The Interfaith Housing Coalition in Dallas, which guides homeless mothers toward self-sufficiency;
- ✦ Caphas-Attica, Inc., in Rochester, New York, a counseling program for prison inmates and former inmates in residential facilities, boasting a 70-percent rate of readjustment without recidivism; and
- ✦ Enterprise Mentors International, based in St. Louis, which sends entrepreneurs to developing countries where they help people start businesses and build an economic base for themselves.

As you might guess, these awards serve two purposes: they draw attention to the winners and, at the same time, they expand the name and reputation of the Acton Institute as a leader in its field.

As a public-relations professional, I am convinced that all charities and nonprofits can learn to avail themselves of the incredible wealth of opportunities for promotion just as the Acton Institute does. Through better and more consistent promotion, you, too, can come closer to fulfilling your goals. It's time to stop working with your head in the clouds of naiveté and come down to reality: Promotion is necessary.

CHARITY IS ENTREPRENEURIAL

Victor Kiam, the well-known owner of the Remington Apparel Company, asserts that charity work requires an entrepreneurial mind, much like starting a new business or marketing a new product. He offers the following maxims about doing charity work.

- ✦ Motivating charity workers is different from motivating people in business, but in both cases, money can be the key. He offers his paid charity workers a bonus of 5 percent or so from whatever they save from the fund-raising budget.

✦ Businesses should get their employees involved in charity work. They get to know the needs of others and learn to be supportive, qualities that tranfer back to the workplace.

✦ Setting goals is a vital fund-raising technique. A high goal energizes people and makes them work harder.

✦ Don't badmouth other charities. You may end up someday requesting a donation from someone who likes another charity, and your denigrating it could insult the person.

✦ Never give up on a donor. You never know when an alternative approach will finally get the donation you were seeking.

✦ Be passionate about your good works. They are good for your community, the nation, and the world.

Thou Shalt Remember that People Love to Give—and Give to Love

People working for charities and nonprofits can sometimes forget that the human spirit soars high from time to time. This is understandable, given that many of you are faced day after day with constant rejection as you seek money or assistance from individuals and businesses. When continuous rejection happens, it's easy to become disappointed, disillusioned, and cynical.

However, one of the greatest teachers of love, and a personal hero of mine, Dr. Leo Buscaglia, reminds us that charity is one of the most important gestures humans can make to experience love. He says, "Only when we give joyfully, without hesitation or thought of gain, can we truly know what love means. To learn how to give is one of the most important aspects of human behavior and human development."

Buscaglia is therefore adamant that charities have an obligation to make themselves known so that the world at large can see that they are there. "How can we get the joy of giving if we don't know they exist, when we don't know how wonderful is their potential to brighten the world?"

For Buscaglia, giving doesn't just benefit the recipient. The giver also gains—perhaps even more powerfully—because, as Buscaglia says, "when you give, you get a sense of your own worth. You come to understand that through your own actions you are bettering the world. You also gain insights into others and, ultimately, into yourself."

To prove his point, Buscaglia started the Felice Foundation (pronounced Feh-LEE-chay), a vibrant organization that supports charitable ventures. *Felice* is the Italian word for peace and joy—and it also happens to be Dr. Buscaglia's first name. The seeds of his effort were planted many years ago while Buscaglia was traveling in Hong Kong. He met a Chinese refugee, Wong, who with his family lived in extreme poverty. Wong needed to learn English if he was going to be able to find work. Dr. Buscaglia paid his tuition to an English-language school. Years later, Wong was working and had earned enough to move his family out of the refugee camp. He wrote to Dr. Buscaglia offering to make good on his "debt." Instead Buscaglia urged Wong to assist another determined person such as himself, and to give that person the money "with love from Wong and Leo, with the hope that in this way it might continue to touch many lives."

So, the next time you become discouraged, I ask you to remember Leo Buscaglia and this maxim. You cannot help the thousands of big-hearted people who seek to engage in your charity work if you insist on anonymity. You might even think of your public-relations effort as a good deed in itself, a charity you perform for other people who desperately desire to help you through their donations. In this sense, there is really no difference between the giver and the recipient: we are all recipients. Indeed, the Felice Foundation states in its manifesto, "The roles of helper and helped are constantly interchanging."

In short, promotion is required if you want to give others the opportunity to give to you, to enlarge their souls by exercising their charitable "muscles," as Rabbi Daniel Lapin reminds us.

GIVING CREATES HEALTH, TOO

Here's a curious fact you should consider whenever you feel uncertain about promoting your cause. Research indicates that people who routinely help others, through charity work or simple kindness on the job or generosity at home, are more healthy.

So reports Ervin Staub, professor of psychology at the University of Massachusetts in Amherst. "That's because being nice fosters a critical sense of connection with others," he says. Helping other people creates bonds. "You also gain a boost in self-esteem, which reinforces the desire to be nice again," Staub says.

David Rosenhan, professor of psychology and law at Stanford University, says, "research indicates that giving is the key to deriving benefits." There is a quantifiable, positive change in the immune system that comes with a positive interaction with other people, he says.

Martin Selifman, author of the book *Learned Optimism*, attributes this phenomenon in part to the fact that people who get involved in helping projects tend to be optimists. "Optimists have better-functioning immune systems," he says, "and that helps ward off disease."

In his book *Living Life on Purpose*, Greg Anderson, founder of the American Wellness Project, says that altruism is actually quite good medicine. He quotes physician and psychologist George Vailliant, director of a forty-year study of Harvard graduates: "[Service is] one of the qualities that helps even the most poorly adjusted men of the study group deal successfully with the stresses of life. It's service that makes the difference."

By contrast, selfishness can exact a price. Larry Scherwitz, a social psychologist at the Medical Research Institute of San Francisco, says that in a study he conducted, "The more self-centered people were much more likely to die of heart attack than the less self-centered."

So, remember that being a hero of charitable endeavors is good for society, good for our soul and psyche, and—now we learn—good for the body.

Thou Shalt Ask at Every Opportunity for Promotion of Good Works

People doing good works often become comfortable with the idea that they need to wait to be seen before asking, like a child in an old-fashioned household. But times have changed, and so have our cultural mores. In today's world of information overload, you will definitely get lost if you don't speak up loudly and clearly at every opportunity for promotion.

In my view, charities and nonprofits must learn to show more pride in themselves, to "beat their chests" often and loudly through a combination of efforts including publicity, promotion, and fundraising. One reason for this is that everyone else is doing it, too, and so those who don't ask for attention, don't get it.

Hugh Hewitt, whom I mentioned above as the host of the 1996 PBS TV series, *America's Search for God*, frequently consults with charities and nonprofit organizations about their programs and strategies. "It's absolutely true that many of these organizations are lost when it comes to promotion," he says. "I'm talking about very competent nonprofit professionals, people who are aware of community needs and committed to moral causes. Time and again I meet leaders in charitable organizations who have no idea how to translate their message into a form that will reach the public, seize attention, and build the base of support they need.

"It's a fiercely competitive world for nonprofits. They must learn that the media is not their enemy, that it can be their friend if they know how to approach it. And they need to accept that promotion is a positive good, not a dubious indulgence."

Think of it this way: The public is swamped with messages, coming at them in thousands by the week. A typical commercial enterprise, such as a local grocery store, sends their customers one or two mailers per week. The typical major product company advertises their product on television from five to hundreds of times per week on television.

Why shouldn't charities and nonprofits aim to obtain the attention these companies get? Obviously, an important difference is money; charities and nonprofits are not purchasing advertising time the way businesses do. However, there are literally thousands of avenues for free publicity and promotion that can be followed to get attention focused on you.

Here's a powerful example demonstrating how promotional shyness affects one group of nonprofits. In Orange County, California, one of the nation's wealthiest counties, you would normally think that the regional charities and nonprofits might take advantage of the excellent opportunities for fund-raising. Of course, some of them do. The Second Harvest Food Bank of Orange County, for example, has become one of America's largest privately operated food banks, through energetic courting of local donors.

But their example is apparently not emulated very widely in Orange County. In a 1996 poll conducted by the University of California at Irvine, Professor Mark Baldasare discovered a curious fact. When asked, "How often do charities (excepting churches) ask you for money?" fewer than half the Orange County respondents answered "very often." This was true even among respondents with incomes above $80,000, a prosperous group that philanthropies arguably should be wooing with special vigor.

Clearly, promotion and fund-raising don't need to be a part-time or halfhearted commitment for charities that seek to be full-time successes. Professor Baldasare's research seems to indicate that the public can withstand plenty of promotion from nonprofits—and they won't complain.

To be blunt, the public can stomach hearing your messages more often. So why not aim to get all the publicity you can take? If you don't ask, you won't get.

DON'T BE SHY: THE MEDIA WANTS YOU

You may not know it, but the media craves your news. In fact, without news, the media couldn't exist. It is their nourishment. They need people and organizations to feed them.

Southern California publicist Gloria Zigner points out that, by one estimate, "eighty-five percent of what you read in the printed media, hear on the radio, or see on television has been planted there." Stories come from public-information officers, government-relations professionals, investor-relations specialists, volunteers working with nonprofit groups, and so on. The dynamic is shared, notes Zigner. "People call up the media and say, 'Here's an idea for a story that we think your readers or viewers will like.'"

So don't be shy about promoting your cause. Your news is wanted.

THOU SHALT BELIEVE THAT ONE PERSON OR ONE IDEA CAN MAKE A DIFFERENCE

Several of the best success stories I know about charities and nonprofits revolve around the intense promotional efforts of a single person who did not balk about promoting his or her organization's cause. Such individuals are shining lights for all of us, proving that when you stand up and shout, you can make a difference in the world.

One of the most touching stories I know to exemplify my point is the work of Mary Jo Copeland. A champion of good works for the poor, her kindness and concern for everyone she meets has helped her create a phenomenal charity success story, and earned her the nickname the "Mother Teresa of Minneapolis." Mary Jo founded the organization Sharing and Caring Hands in 1985 in downtown Minneapolis to help those who had exhausted all other avenues of hope.

April 1994 article in *Good Housekeeping*. Reporter Kim Ode described Mary's Jo's work in:

> Mary Jo Copelan washes the blistered, bleeding, stinking feet of the poor. She kneels before them, stripping off shoes and socks that have trudged too far, gingerly probing skin stretched shiny and throbbing where thick toenails burrow in. She immerses the feet in hot, sudsy water, then scoots over to another pair, now wrinkly pink, which she dries and slathers with cream. Her hands traverse the blisters and calluses, bestowing comfort, acknowledging pain, offering love . . . .
>
> Fifty-one-year-old Mary Jo—who has been married for thirty-two years and is the mother of twelve, three still at home—provides solace to about ten thousand people a month who visit her charity. [Her foundation] operates solely on private donations [and has] about one thousand volunteers who work each month at the charity.

Mary Jo grew up in an abusive home—her father beat her mother. Her house was run-down and dirty to the point that she couldn't bathe properly, and she was taunted by her classmates. She began to do volunteer work for Catholic Charities, but she was soon frustrated with the bureaucracy. To have more impact, she started handing out food and clothing from her own car, which she would park behind a bar in the inner city. Her break came when she was awarded a $2,200 grant from a TV station for her efforts. She gave away half to a church and used the other half to start her organization, Sharing and Caring Hands, in a rented storefront in downtown Minneapolis.

But Mary Jo has a head along with her heart. When I called her, I learned quickly that she practices something akin to my moral manifesto when it comes to recognizing the value of aggressive promotion. "You can be a wonderful person full of caring and compassion," she says, "but if you don't have the business smarts to see the need for promotion, you can end up irrelevant to the solutions for our social problems."

Mary Jo continued, imploring me to let others know: "When people think about opening a charity or other kind of nonprofit, they had better be prepared to get out in public and promote it, or they don't have any business opening it in the first place. They had better be prepared to have a full speaking schedule, and to be dealing with the media continually, or they don't belong in charity work. I've seen too many groups stagnate for two reasons: one is too much bureaucracy, the other is not enough energy or interest in telling people about [the charity]."

For this reason, Mary Jo spent forty-three weekends in one recent year speaking at churches and private groups, raising the $150,000 a month needed to run her organization. Indeed, she is always giving speeches—to Kiwanis, Rotary, Lions, any organization that hosts speakers. Her marketing verve—her eagerness to interact with the public—has had staggering results. She has raised more than $7 million in only three years, all from private sources, allowing her to build temporary housing for the poor as well as to operate her daytime shelter. Furthermore, 95 percent of the what she collects goes to her "customers," the poor. Mary Jo takes no salary or government assistance.

Her marketing tenacity even extended to my own interview with her. I called her on a Thursday, during which she graciously talked to me about her background and program for about half an hour. The next morning, a Federal Express package arrived at my office with a video and news clippings on Sharing and Caring Hands.

There are many stories like Mary Jo Copeland's, of people who know how to sell goodness. Perhaps, you, too, can become one of them.

CANDY LIGHTNER—DON'T GIVE UP, GET MADD

Candy Lightner is a powerful shining light in marketing goodness who deserves special mention in my book.

Before the 1970s, juries were widely sympathetic toward drunk-driving suspects. All that changed beginning around 1980. Why? Because that was the year Mothers Against Drunk Driving (MADD) was formed. It is now the nation's largest organization helping victims of drunk driving and lobbying for stiff laws to deal with the offense.

Was MADD the first organized effort to change the climate of opinion about drunk driving? By no means. But it was the first that made a difference. "For most of the twenty-five-plus years I've been in law enforcement," Huntington Beach, California police chief Ron Lowenberg says, "drinking and driving was the social norm. Now it's not, and MADD has been a major reason why it's unpopular."

MADD was founded by Candy Lightner, a woman who can sell goodness perhaps better than anyone in the late twentieth century. She came to the drunk driving issue out of her own personal tragedy when her daughter was killed by a drunk driver. Candy linked up with Cindi Lamb, whose daughter had become a quadriplegic when a drunk driver smashed into the family pickup. Together, these two, along with other mothers who'd experienced similar tragedies, didn't stop at lobbying legislators for tougher laws. They told their wrenching stories to the media. The publicity they generated put heat on the politicians. Paul Snodgrass of the National Highway and Traffic Safety Administration said that federal traffic studies had long called for tougher laws against drinking and driving. But "MADD made it happen."

In 1980, about one million drunken drivers were arrested. In recent years, that number has risen dramatically to around 1.8 million. Meanwhile, alcohol-related deaths are down by a third. MADD now has more than four hundred chapters worldwide, and more than 2.8 million members.

Little of this would have happened if Candy Lightner had been reluctant to get publicity for herself, or if she had not made herself a master of the art of the press release, the television interview, the radio public-service announcement. But Lightner didn't consider herself above trafficking in media messages and images. She understood the imperative of promotion to save lives and to change society for the better.

THOU SHALT TEACH BUSINESSES THAT CHARITY IMPROVES PROFITS

It seems logical to think that getting donations from businesses means that they lose money. After all, their money is now out of their account, and into yours.

However, this thinking turns out to be erroneous. In a strange twist of logic, I have learned that asking businesses for contributions actually builds their bank accounts rather than draining them. This means that you should encourage businesses to give as generously as they can—and not worry that you may be draining them financially.

How does altruism promote profit? you may be wondering. To answer this, I turn to Rabbi Daniel Lapin again, who explains the logic this way.

Business, if it is to be dynamic and growing and successful, requires a willingness to risk, to put capital at risk in the belief that an investment in an idea or resource or human being will pay off eventually in larger revenues and a more vibrant business operation. This means that someone in business cannot horde his holdings, but must be prepared to part with them in the service of the business's growth.

Philanthropy is thus a wonderful vehicle for exercising this psychic muscle, the muscle employed when one willingly, gladly surrenders some of what has. Philanthropy offers practice in the discipline of not holding on tight to all one's assets. So entrepreneurs should be on their knees giving thanks for the opportunities presented by philanthropy, and by the chance to use some of their resources to help other people.

This sleight of thinking may seem ludicrous, but it is as true as the color of gold. I therefore urge you to promote this thinking among the businesses in your community. Tell them with conviction that the more they practice philanthropy, the smarter they will operate and the greater their fortunes will be.

There is another benefit in getting businesses to promote charity, especially when it is done very publicly. When philanthropic efforts are advertised in public, they are more likely to be emulated. It's like a traffic jam: As soon as one person starts honking, the others can be easily convinced to follow. By announcing the gifts and donations that one business gives you, many others will likely follow suit so as not to seem less worthy than the next donor.

As you will discover, public announcements of donations from businesses can create a very dynamic society of contributors to your cause—and you can rest assured that none of them will go bankrupt because of you.

THOU SHALT LEAD BY EXAMPLE

Expanding the previous idea that publicly announcing donations leads to a form of competition among donors, this maxim focuses specifically on the process of intentionally making examples out of your best philanthropic assets.

In the words of Rabbi Daniel Lapin, "If a giver wants to give anonymously, every effort should be made to dissuade him from doing so, because an anonymous gift brings only half the potential good. It doesn't offer others the example of a named, identifiable person doing charity and getting deserved credit. Such examples prod others to emulate them."

Rabbi Lapin illustrates the argument by recounting a conversation he had with a minister in his community who was complaining about his congregation's meager donations to the church. "I asked him how he was trying to improve things, and he said that every Sunday he berates the congregation for not giving more. I said, 'Why don't you try a different strategy? Why don't you tell them how grateful you are for their large donations to the church?'

"He replied: 'But they aren't giving large donations.'

"I said, 'Even if it's not true, every person will think he or she is the only person who isn't giving substantially. You will have prodded them into generosity by encouraging them not to be outdone by others.' "

Public giving, with public credit going to the giver, has that same effect: It can get the best kind of competition started—a competition to see who can fill the most stomachs and clothe the most children and comfort the most sick. Ted Turner understood this when he challenged other wealthy giants of the business world to give more to charity. You might recall that Turner even proposed that the world should have an "Ebenezer Scrooge Prize" for the wealthiest individuals who failed to contribute sufficiently to charity, and a Heart of Gold Award to honor the most generous. Turner's chiding is credited with prompting several extremely wealthy individuals such as Bill Gates and George Soros to award hundreds of millions of dollars to various good causes.

If Turner's prizes did exist, it is likely that Turner would be the first recipient of the Heart of Gold award, as, in 1997, he pledged to give away $1 billion over the next ten years to fund United Nations humanitarian programs. In declaring his donation, Turner said,

"What I am trying to do is set a standard of gallantry. The world is awash with money, with peace descending all over the earth. We can make a difference in the future direction of the planet."

The philosophy of "leading by example" was also what spurred Arianna Huffington and the Center for Effective Compassion, which she chairs, to ask members of Congress to identify which charities they personally help. "Reading through the responses of House Members and Senators," Huffington wrote, "a patchwork emerged of home-district groups, diverse in their means and missions, but stitched together by a common thread of compassion.

"We could almost hear in the names of the local groups the authentic tones of Americans taking matters into their own hands to turn lives around: The Gleaners Community Food Bank in Detroit, the Baldwin House Soup Kitchen in Pontiac, Angel's Place in Southfield, the Burton Manor Seniors' Center in Livonia, Palmer House for Children in Columbus, the Country Life School in Piney Woods, the Queen of the Valley Hospital in West Covina, and the City of Hope in Duarte...clearly this is how to make an American quilt."

Given the results, Huffington asked, "In 1994, a total of $724 million was raised for House and Senate races across the country. What if Members of Congress tithed their fund-raising time to raise money for groups fighting poverty in their districts?"

Thankfully, she notes, there are wonderful examples already available. Former congresswoman Pat Schroeder of Colorado reported giving $35,000 in contributions, from speaking fees in 1995, to thirty charities in her state. Senator Tom Daschle from South Dakota "not only leads Senate Democrats but, together with his wife, is out front on charity fund-raising as well, from the National Organization for Fetal Alcohol Syndrome and the Luther Place Homeless Shelter in Washington, to the annual March of Dimes dinner and the MS Foundation. Some Members such as Representatives Steve Largent (R-Okla.), Jim Talent (R-Mont.), and (former Representative) Andrea Seastrand (R-Calif.) donate 5 to 10 percent of their income directly to the needy without taking a tax deduction."

As you can see, leading by example is another significant element in the *Selling Goodness* moral manifesto, another reason why promotion is vital for charities and nonprofits. The examples you choose to highlight can be perhaps the best testimony to others that your cause is worthwhile and good. The publicity you create around those you've chosen as your examples can trigger others to become active in altruism.

There is another wonderful story I use to illustrate the idea of leading by example. The story concerns a young monk who was asked by the great Francis of Assisi to accompany him to the local village where Francis was going to preach. The monk was thrilled at the opportunity to hear a great and generous man impart his wisdom.

They set out on the journey, traveling down country roads and village streets and alleyways. All along the way they passed poor and needy people, to whom Francis invariably offered help and quiet expressions of love. By day's close, they were still walking, but Francis had not yet delivered a speech. Finally the monk could contain his frustration no longer. "I've traveled with you all day, and you did not did not give a single sermon to the crowds, as you'd led me to believe you would."

Francis responded: "On the contrary, we preached all along the way. Every time we helped someone, our actions were noted by many observers. There is nothing to be gained by traveling somewhere to preach unless one preaches as one travels."

WHEN ANONYMITY MAKES SENSE

I believe in leading by example as much as possible, However, there are the occasional sensitive situations that require anonymity among donors or participants. For instance, consider the work of Richard A. McDonough.

You haven't heard of Richard McDonough? I'm not surprised. The fact that he does his work of protecting battered women and others in need of shelter who are essentially unnoticed by the general public is, I believe, a reason for sadness. However, Richard's work is one of those sensitive situations that makes publicity and disclosure difficult.

You see, Richard is president of America Responds With Love, an organization that finds hotel rooms in communities around the nation for people "in economic need or in imminent danger," as he puts it. The group serves crime victims, battered women, and families who have been homeless. "As best we can tell, we're the nation's largest safe-home network for battered women," Richard says. Close to 700 hotels and motels in around 280 cities now participate in his program; 6,800 people were served in 1996 alone.

The necessity to keep the location of these facilities secret—because of the security risk for many of the people being housed—is one of those rare instances that creates a hurdle for promotional efforts. "We can't give the participating hotels publicity for their participation in the program, or we'd risk tipping off men who've been abusing women we're sheltering, or the perpetrators of the other kinds of crimes whose victims we're protecting," Richard notes. "And because our program isn't concentrated to any great degree in one community, we go where there is a need and where we find hotel proprietors willing to help."

As seemingly valid as the arguments for anonymity are, Richard may have created some obstacles that weren't needed. In fact, to some degree he's shunned publicity when he probably needn't have. Consider the fact that Richard McDonough was the third recipient of the Points of Light designation during the administration of President George Bush. The Points of Light program brought public attention to inspirational examples of people giving of themselves for others. Richard McDonough was near the top of a long list of worthy recipients. Moreover, in 1990 he won the national Good Neighbor Award from the Red Cross for his heroic program.

Did he send out press releases announcing either of these honors? No. "It would have looked egotistical," Richard says, noting that the awards were to him as an individual, and he didn't want to be seen crowing about his personal achievement. But such modesty might finally have to give way to a more pragmatic outlook. "We're getting to the point where promotion will probably have to take place," he says, noting that his organization's budget hadn't been fully paid for as of the middle of 1997.

Ultimately, I believe that Richard should increase his publicity to let more people know about himself and his own great work. You're a hero, Richard. So please, don't disdain press releases. Don't deprive the rest of us of the opportunity to be uplifted by your example.

Thou Shalt Raise Consciousness, Which Is as Important as Raising Money

I consider this maxim to be extremely important because those who have experience working in charities and nonprofits well know that getting monetary contributions is only half the battle. The other half is getting the world to hear your message—and to assimilate it into their hearts.

This maxim hits on the same distinction that the well-known aphorism about "giving a man a fish" versus "teaching a man to fish" addresses. A nonprofit's goal is to retrain the world to think like them. A dollar today is worth just one dollar. But acquiring a devotee to your cause can return a lifetime of dollars and other devotees.

Listen to the words of Julie Jaskol, communications director for the Los Angeles Free Clinic, an exceptional organization that offers no-cost medical care and social services for indigent individuals and families. "We work very hard to market our program and our services. We do so, obviously to strengthen our donor base and to draw in more volunteers. We're heavily reliant on volunteers; we have six hundred of them right now, and we estimate that the cost of our services would be four times higher if it weren't for our large volunteer participation.

"But marketing is important for a larger reason as well. It's important as a way of raising public consciousness about the issues we're dealing with: poverty, homelessness, AIDS, and other illnesses. We're helping educate, we hope, the larger community about the troubles that are out there and the need to get involved."

Ironically, a campaign to raise consciousness can often prove more profitable than one aimed strictly at raising cash. This is because getting the public behind an idea can often attract the support of increasingly large donors and high-powered movers and shakers. "The name recognition we build through our promotion is crucial in getting supporters of a high stature," says Jaskol. For example, the L.A. Free Clinic has been able to land a number of high-powered entertainment-industry supporters, including David Hoberman, head of Mandeville Films; entertainment attorney Tom Hoberman; Gary Marshall, producer of the TV series *Happy Days* and *Laverne and Shirley,* and director of such films as *Pretty Woman*; Bernie West, a writer for *All in the Family* and other classic shows; rock promoter Lou Adler; and Ted Harbert, former president of ABC Entertainment.

In my own life, I have used PR to raise consciousness on an issue that was dear to me. Several years ago, I founded a prominent monthly dinner called the L.A. Media RoundTable. My purpose in hosting these functions was to respond to the unfair label that Los Angeles has had as a place devoid of intelligent life and thought. I was born in New York. Since moving to Los Angeles, I had been offended by the image of the city as an intellectual desert. For example, in Woody Allen's movie *Annie Hall*, released in 1977, the same year I arrived in Los Angeles, Woody says that the only cultural advantage to living in L.A. is the ability to make a right turn on a red light.

Sure, this was funny, but it's not my experience of the reality of life in the nation's second largest city. Los Angeles is filled with bright, dynamic, even scholarly people. Hence the purpose of my dinners: to highlight and foster intellectual dialogue in the city. To that end, I've had dinner guests from major media, entertainment, cultural and political institutions. My speakers have been among the most noteworthy names of the day: former L.A. police chief Willie Williams, for instance; L.A. district attorney Gil Garcetti; Charlton Heston; to name a few. Future speakers will be just as stimulating, including Oliver Stone and others of his prominence.

Although they're off the record, these dinners provide the assembled opinion-makers with opportunities to test and expand their ideas and perspectives. In fact, they may be more valuable as a learning experience for the guests precisely because everyone agrees that nothing will quoted. (Ironically, I have to admit that our discussions are much more candid and freewheeling when we don't need to worry about press coverage.)

The L.A. Media RoundTable dinners are the product of a vision—a goal that went beyond any promotional motive for me. I submit that this is why they have also been an effective promotional tool—because of the intrinsic meaningfulness of the idea. I was seeking to raise consciousness more than to toot my own company's horn, the equivalent of raising money.

However, be aware that we live in an age of heightened consciousness about everything, and so working this maxim requires careful planning and strategizing. This is one unfortunate consequence of living in today's red-hot media world, where everyone seeks to raise the public's consciousness about an issue. As an experienced communications expert, I always counsel my clients to be respectful and honest about the approach they take in raising consciousness. Generally, today's savvy consumers can see right through a manipulative campaign that tries to take their consciousness where it doesn't want to go.

A Saint by Any Other Name...

For the past thirty years, one of the most effective leaders in the world for raising consciousness was the late Mother Teresa. She died while I was writing this book, but her reputation shall live on for centuries.

Mother Teresa founded her Missionaries of Charity in Calcutta in 1950. For years she and her order toiled in relative obscurity, their care for the poor and dying little-known beyond Calcutta's ghettos. All that changed after the mid-1960s, when a British journalist, Malcolm Muggeridge, produced a TV documentary on her work, *Something Beautiful for God*. She and her order went on to become famous. Her charitable accomplishments won her the Nobel Peace Prize in 1979.

I cite Mother Teresa because she sparked, perhaps more than any other soul in the twentieth century, a new worldwide awareness of the poverty and sickness yet to be eradicated in many parts of the globe. Her work inspired millions, and her order now boasts 4,400 nuns and brothers in 600 facilities around the world. Mother Teresa is another shining example of how goodness grows when goodness finally gets promoted to the awareness of the world. After all, it wasn't until she received the notoriety of the Nobel Prize that her blessed work took on worldwide significance.

Thou Shalt Seek Good Reality and Good Perception

I'm an advocate of vigorous promotion as a way of business and a way of life—but not for promotion for its own sake. In other words, PR should only be done when the entity has meaningful purpose or message to put before the public.

Guy Kawasaki, the prolific writer on computers and business strategies, is right when he says that, for a PR campaign to have integrity and long-term promise, you have to be marketing something with substance. "The first step is to create a 'good reality'" he says. "This means that your organization has to have a worthwhile mission and be executing it."

Obviously, in many instances, an established nonprofit group automatically earns good reality, without needing to lift a finger. They are well-accepted in their community and everyone respects their work. But in some other cases, such as with new nonprofit organizations, the group must build its good reality deed by deed. For example, in my community, the L.A. Free Clinic mentioned above needed time to establish itself and win praise for their incredible work. Joel Kotkin, a bright urban-affairs professor at Pepperdine University and a contributing editor to the "Sunday Opinion" section of the *Los Angeles Times*, hails the clinic for how it established itself as strong on both compassion and cost-effectiveness. "They are helping so many people—and doing it at substantially lower cost per unit of time and medical service than the public health-care system of Los Angeles County. That means there is more bang for the buck, more medical aid for the dollar—and more people can be served." This is the kind of nonprofit success story "that cries out to be publicized and promoted—and I'm glad they're very serious about doing so," says Kotkin.

Similarly, Jacqueline Canter of the famous Canter's Deli Restaurant, a landmark gathering place in the Fairfax District of Los Angeles, learned the same lesson. She has been part of an effort to revitalize this colorful, historic section of town where her business is located, and she says that promotion and publicity have been indispensable to its success. "We're making things cleaner, safer, more attractive—and we're also putting a major effort into getting the word out that this is what we're doing. If you brighten up a neighborhood, make it cleaner and safer and give it a better image—and no one knows about it, well, what a waste of energy that would be." Through hard work to improve the neighborhood, Canter and her friends have achieved the "good reality."

So, if you are involved with a nonprofit organization with a wonderful mission, dedicated people, and a serious plan for making things happen, pay attention to what Guy Kawasaki talked about. Make sure you either have "good reality" or that you are working on earning it.

With that said, I hasten to add that having a good reality is also only half the battle. You must also have what I call "good perception." Today's world is based so much on appearances and thrives so much on hearsay, rumor, and distortion that, however good your reality is, if it is not perceived the right way, your cause is lost.

A comment by Don Burr, former CEO of People Express Airlines, exemplifies the interplay of reality and perception. "In the airline industry," he once said, "if passengers see coffee stains on the food tray, they assume the engine maintenance isn't done right." That may seem utterly irrational, but in the PR business, image conveys a truth of its own. Is it really illogical for people to wonder whether there might be some connection between how meticulous a company is toward its customers and how detail-oriented it is in other areas of business? Maybe so, at least where airplane coffee stains are concerned, but if you have a product or service—or charity—to market, the last thing you have time to do is to argue with human nature.

The point is: perceptions count—a great deal, probably more than you'll ever know. But understanding this fundamental truth is just the tip of the iceberg.

As a PR professional, I also must tell you that perceptions are finicky, fickle, wily creatures that are hard to catch. A single individual, organization, or event can actually evoke many perceptions, all of them dancing around like so many dervishes at a midnight ritual. Because of this, the goal of the savvy promoter is to control which perception the public dances away with.

A PR pundit once pointed out to me, "We don't persuade people. We simply offer them reasons to persuade themselves." His comment cuts to the heart of the perception dilemma. Because of the vagaries of perceptions, the most you can hope for is to massage or reorient the public's perception of something so that it corresponds closely to what you want perceived.

Consider a major political scandal, for example. The same story told using the same information can actually create a wide array of beliefs, depending on the means in which the story is delivered. Which perception the public ends up with often depends simply on who had the best PR agent.

A recent survey of more than one thousand Americans confirms that perception is quite relative. In this poll, people were asked to identify which conveyors of information they most trusted. Not surprisingly, the least believable sources were company spokespeople. Fewer than half of those questioned (46 percent) found corporate PR staffers "very" or "somewhat" believable. Spokespeople for an entire industry or trade group were deemed believable by a slightly larger number of people (49 percent), while 50 percent found word of mouth from friends to be "very" or "somewhat" trustworthy.

The most believable messengers—with a 92-percent favorable response—were eyewitnesses. Next-most-believable were independent experts (just under 90 percent), followed by a victim or the family of a victim (84 percent). Reports from journalists were considered highly believable by 65 percent, while 71 percent were prone to believe consumer advocates.

The moral of this poll? The same information carries different weight in the public's eye, based on who is reporting it. Beyond showing how perceptions can shape reality, this survey argues strongly for charities and nonprofits to rely on public-relations savvy because it can make a world of difference in how you get your message reported in the media. You will likely have a higher believability quotient if your message is delivered straight to the public by someone perceived as being an organizational spokesperson rather than someone with a vested interest.

One more point about the perception dilemma in our society: In today's world, perception has a way of becoming its own "fact" once it gains enough momentum. No matter what the truth is, how the public *perceives* an issue becomes the accepted truth.

Consider this example. According to a Gallup Organization survey reported in *Heart Info Navigator* in 1996, 82 percent of American women believe that breast cancer causes more deaths among females than does heart disease. However, the truth is that around 233,000 women die annually from heart disease, much more than the 43,000 or so who die from breast cancer. To be fair, it should be noted that the charities fighting breast cancer have not intentionally distorted the facts in their publicity campaigns. To the contrary, they have rightly hammered hard at the grim fact that breast cancer is a major killer of women—more of a threat than was long recognized. But for the women who hold the mistaken belief that breast cancer kills more than heart disease, that belief has now consumed its own truth, and many women doubtless act on it by getting themselves tested, and by donating funds to help combat the disease. All that is well and good, but the real truth has actually gotten lost in the PR.

My comments about perception are not intended to suggest that you should practice dishonesty or that people are easily fooled. The marketing perceptions you should seek to create, should themselves reflect the high standards you hope to promote—the better to build on the "good reality" at the heart of your venture.

THE TIFFANY THEORY REVISITED

With so many people feeling negative about publicity, I created the Tiffany Theory you read about in the preface to this book.

While our culture's emphasis on appearances is regrettable, it is a reality that PR professionals live with and fully accept. For this reason, I urge my clients to package themselves in the most colorful, pleasing boxes they can find. Such wrapping does not negate the noble gift you have inside. You must have a good reality (your underlying product or service must be reliable) but that's just the start when you're selling goodness. You must also have good perception.

Public relations teaches you how to package your reality so that it attracts the interest and enthusiasm of the people you need as supporters. It's about enhancing the perceived value of what you have to offer. Much of this book is designed to show you how to gift-wrap your charitable cause so it has the greatest possible perceived value in the eyes of the public. I will give you tools to fulfill your "good reality," and "good perception" needs so you can do your duty as the caring person you are—and let the "better angels of nature," as Abraham Lincoln referred to our highest human instincts, sing their sweetest song for all to hear.

THOU SHALT NOT BE AFRAID TO THINK BIG

Many charities and nonprofits attempt to use promotion and publicity, but they do so in ways that are small and lackluster. I commend any attempt, but in today's media world, minimal efforts provoke only minimal response.

What the leaders of today's nonprofit groups need are grand visions for their organizations. This requires thinking big—and bigger and bigger. When you are creating a press release, shout from the highest mountain, not from the little hill around the corner. When you have a radio interview, tout your organization's strengths loudly; there is no reason to whisper. When you manage to get on television, wear your best suit and speak as best as you can, so that millions of people will know the full story behind your group.

The rules that even small, fledgling charities and nonprofits should live by include the following:

✦ *Don't be afraid to think big.* This includes both finding major supporters and planning the scale of any special events you sponsor. If you are not a socially prominent person in the community, identify some who are—and who have social conscience—and try to recruit them to your cause. A local hero can bring you energy, connections, and overnight credibility.

✦ *Take your projects seriously.* Go for pomp and grandeur as much as you can. Formality and glitter impart a sense of importance and seriousness about your cause. Avoid halfway measures that belittle the importance of your goals. Your attitude toward your own projects should be as dedicated and regal as you can make them.

✦ *Go for mass appeal.* Fund-raising works well when you can bring the masses into it, such as sponsoring a run, a walkathon, or a weekend competition of any kind. Mass appeal also helps give everyone a sense of camaraderie in a larger cause.

Here is a wonderful example of a charity promotional effort that won praise for its big thinking—much to the surprise of its guests. This excerpt is taken from the February 9, 1997, issue of the *Orlando Sentinel*.

> The 2,100 guests at the Susan G. Komen Breast Cancer Foundation's charity gala in Dallas in October expected a luncheon. What they got was an extravaganza. First, the chandeliers in the huge ballroom dimmed, leaving the spotlighted dais looking like an oversized movie screen. Then the trumpets of the 14th Marine Naval Air Station color guard blared, and a local ROTC saber corps snapped to attention, weapons aloft in an arc over the steps leading from the stage.
>
> As an announcer boomed their names, representatives of corporate America marched under those crossed swords to their tables. JC Penney. Pier 1 Imports. Tiffany. Ford. Each stared solemnly ahead. A few looked slightly mortified. Most wore a pink ribbon pin on their blouse or lapel.

Later in the program, many of those executives would bow their heads slightly, as medals of appreciation were placed around their necks.

A bit much? Perhaps. But all part of what it takes to become THE CAUSE in the competitive world of causes, to remain *the* disease in an era when everyone is trying to get attention for his or her disease.

"This is our moment, and we have to make it work for us," says Nancy Brinker, founder of the Komen Foundation, which has raised more than $65 million for breast cancer-research, education, screening, and treatment since 1982, most of it during the past five years. It didn't happen overnight, and it didn't happen by itself.

As the article suggests, the vision behind this gala belongs to Nancy Brinker, the wife of a Texas businessman. Brinker's sister, Susan Komen, had died of breast cancer at age thirty-six, and in 1984, Brinker herself was diagnosed with the disease. She became a woman with a mission: Breast cancer deserved much wider attention than it was getting, and breast-cancer research needed more dollars. Brinker knew she had to have a high-profile campaign to achieve those goals. So she started the Komen Foundation in her sister's memory and she aimed high in looking for sponsorship. A breakthrough came in 1988 when Vice President Dan Quayle and his wife agreed to become honorary chairs of the five-kilometer Race for the Cure in Washington D.C., which Komen created.

Through Brinker's efforts, the level of awareness about breast cancer grew exponentially in succeeding years. In 1996, there were seventy-seven Race for the Cure events around the country, with more than 324,000 runners. One index of heightened public consciousness: Government spending for breast-cancer research rose from $45 million in 1989 to more than $550 million today.

So what does it take to think big? You will find the answers in the rest of this book.

ALTRUISM ON-LINE

Although this book is addressed at people who already work for charities and nonprofits, you might perhaps be interested in knowing that the World Wide Web can steer you to many other organizations that welcome your participation. Here is an article from *Home PC* (October 1, 1996) to inform you of how to find more opportunities.

Although many nonprofits have been slow to take advantage of the Web, thousands now have their own home pages. Some sites, such as the one for the American Red Cross (http://www/crossnet.org), are little more than electronic billboards with 800 numbers to call if you want to volunteer. But others make full use of the technology. For instance, Amnesty International (http://www.amnesty.org) helps members send e-mail to authorities on behalf of political prisoners.

[A] good starting place is the Internet NonProfit Center (located at http//www.nonprofits.org), where you can search for all the community service groups in your zip code, as well as organizations devoted to particular causes in your state.

ACHIEVING FAME AND FORTUNE FOR YOUR CAUSE

I hope my "PR moral manifesto" inspires you to action. As I indicated in the beginning of the chapter, it is your imperative to shine light on your organization whenever you can. And this means learning about and developing promotional skills, without feeling guilty or embarrassed or naive about using them.

More than a decade ago, the savvy financier Felix Rohatyn put it colorfully but accurately: "Everything in this world has turned into show business," he said, as quoted in Thomas Whitside's *The Blockbuster Complex*. "Politics is show business. Running Chrysler is show business—look at Lee Iacocca trying to get the attention of Congress by running full-page ads in the newspapers.... Sports is show business.... That's the reality of the marketplace. If you're not in show business, you're really off-Broadway."

Yes, it's true that today's hungry mass media seems to raise just about any mediocre thing to the pinnacles of fame. No one can deny that. But don't let this thought stop you from participating in the process. The people and the organizations who do noble deeds deserve to get their due share. So, go for fame and fortune. "Fame is the spur," Milton wrote—and it can spur the best among us along with the not-so-great.

It is fame that I wish for the life-giving charity providers of the world. But in order to gain fame and thereby advance your cause, by definition you cannot shun the media marketplace, even though you might find much of its fare and its celebrities less than edifying. Quite the contrary: You have to master its tools—and prepare yourself to take advantage of its power.

One last point. Our culture is short on heroes. We need all the inspiration we can get. In that sense, our charity workers owe it to the psychic and spiritual health of society to let their stories be told and to let their light shine. Mary Jo Copeland is a hero. Likewise are Candy Lightner, Nancy Brinker, Richard A. McDonough, and the good people at the L.A. Free Clinic. So, of course, was Mother Teresa. How grateful we should be that we know about their precious work and can profit from their examples. That's promotion—and thank goodness for it.

2

Thinking Like a Publicist

Only in men's imagination does every truth find
an effective and undeniable existence. Imagination, not invention,
is the supreme master of art as of life.

JOSEPH CONRAD

OFTEN you don't need to hire a professional firm to get your organization all the publicity, promotion, and attention it deserves. You simply need to begin to think like a publicist.

So, before delving into the nuts and bolts of doing your own public-relations work, this chapter is devoted to showing you how to develop a PR mind. Thinking and strategizing are actually the most important elements in the publicist's art. They precede all the other skills of writing press releases, setting up radio and television appearances, or creating fund-raising events.

How does one develop the ability to think like a publicist? This chapter breaks the challenge down into seven basic skills. As you read each one, think about how much of the skill you probably already have, and you will begin to realize that you are not far off from being able to handle all or most of your organization's needs.

SKILL 1: DEVELOP YOUR CREATIVE THINKING

It was a creative person who came up with the following rhetorical question that has perplexed students in high-school and philosophy classes over generations: If a tree falls in the forest, and no one is around to hear it, does it make a sound? So it is with your nonprofit organization: If your good work remains little-known, how much impact can it make?

For this reason, I place creativity at the top of the list in learning to think like a PR professional. My deepest personal philosophy is that each of us is blessed with boundless creative potential. We simply need to unlock our creativity and put it to good use.

"Be brave enough to live creatively," says actor Alan Alda. "The creative is the place where no one else has ever been. You have to leave the city of your comfort and go into the wilderness of your intuition. You can't get there by bus, only by hard work, risking, and by not quite knowing what you're doing. What you'll discover will be wonderful: yourself."

Fortunately, the creative ability to imagine a great work is a talent that most readers of this book probably already have, at least to some extent, if they're working in the fields of philanthropy and altruism. But a more systematic development of creativity is necessary if you're going to give your good work renown and ultimate success.

In the old days, the proposition that people could systematically develop their creativity was considered impossible, if not flaky. Not today, though. Nowadays, developing one's creative thinking is as mainstream as power ties and button-down shirts. Creativity is now a staple of business training in the nation's largest companies, including Du Pont, IBM, Nestle, Alcoa, and Prudential. All these firms send their top employees to creativity-training classes, and many belong to the International Creative Forum, a project founded by one of the world's top creativity consultants, Dr. Edward de Bono.

De Bono is one of the pioneers of teaching creativity, and author of two best-sellers on creativity, *Six Thinking Hats* and *Six Action Shoes*. One of his leading-edge concepts is learning how to force your mind to go places where it would not normally go if left to its own devices. "From there," as *Fortune* magazine described the process, "the mind, mouselike, scurries back to familiar territory. The path between something random and something known may provide the insight you seek. Example: Newton's apple. Newton had a mass of information in his head awaiting something to order it. The apple fell, and—bingo—a random stimulus yielded the theory of gravity."

Obviously, forcing your mind to match a random idea with a known one is the difficult part. To counteract our natural resistance, de Bono therefore developed a number of techniques. "Why wait for apples?" he asks. "Why not shake the tree?" To shake the ideas out, de Bono throws out to attendees at his creativity conferences random words, provocative statements, and exaggerated claims—all in the spirit of getting people to free-associate, to link old ideas with new.

One reporter recounted his own experience of de Bono's process as taught in a creativity workshop: "Five people at my table are given a word, *party*. Our challenge: to use it to generate ideas for a new type of computer keyboard. After a moment we begin tossing out associations: keyboards that can be used only by persons 'invited' (authorized) to use them; keyboards with 'surprise' (pre-programmed) keys." As you can see, the forced links between party and *keyboard* seem to have led to some unique ideas that could develop into the stuff of creative inventions.

Since de Bono, many teachers of learning styles and creativity experts have developed a wide range of other provocative activities that can be used to spur your creative thinking. In my experience, I have found that the best ones for creatively promoting nonprofits and charities are based on six easy techniques:

Convert an Everyday Item

Look for an item that has a use all its own in everyday life, and harness it for a marketing purpose. For example, during the autumn, you might challenge people to donate a certain amount of money for every pound of leaves that is raked and bagged by volunteers for your organization.

One great campaign was based simply on the piano key. Shirley Beard of Georgia's Gwinnett Council for the Arts came up with an idea for tickling the ivories on behalf of the council's fund-raising project to buy a concert grand piano. The council "sold" the eighty-eight piano keys to donors for $100 each, carrying the group a long way toward the purchase price of an instrument.

Juxtapose Two Items

Place a person or an object in a context that is jarringly inconsistent with its image. You will be amazed at how powerful this technique is.

For example, one of the most challenging PR assignments I've ever faced was enhancing the image and career of the great tablet-giver himself: Charlton Heston. How could this superstar possibly be more famous? He already had epic status, due in no small part to the epic themes of so many of his films.

But that's what gave me a thought: Why not put him in a context that showed a much different side to him, the down-to-earth Chuck Heston that his friends knew? After all, he is among the wittiest gentlemen I have ever met. A lightbulb went off in my head: Why not have Mr. Heston guest-host *Saturday Night Live*? Selling the concept to the show and to Mr. Heston took some doing. But in the end, he did the show and it was a big hit. Many critics called it "a PR masterpiece."

Or consider these two disparate themes: insurability and the legs of one of my clients, *Entertainment Tonight* host Mary Hart. I helped come up with the idea to have her gorgeous legs insured with Lloyds of London for $2 million. Mary is one of the brightest people in

Hollywood, and she saw the potential in the idea immediately. It became a big feature story in the media as soon as we announced it.

In San Diego County, fund-raisers for a mental-health facility combined a couple of images you don't connect with each other every day: top socialites and car-washing. The "Black Tie Car Wash," in which some of the community's most prominent movers and shakers spread suds on automobiles while clad in formal evening clothes, was a success at generating money and publicity.

USING POLITICS FOR PROMOTIONAL FUN

The PR firm Hill and Knowlton came up with an innovative idea to promote its client, Bumble Bee tuna, during the 1992 presidential campaign. According to officials in the George Bush administration, a Hill and Knowlton representative called the White House to ask for Mr. Bush's favorite tuna recipe for use in a bake-off against Bill Clinton's favorite recipe. Alas, President Bush's aides declined the request, not wanting their man to appear unpresidential.

But the concept remains a good one you can apply to your situation. How about asking two candidates in your own home town—or two community officeholders viewed as friendly rivals—to participate in a chili cook-off or some other lighthearted contest, with the proceeds going to your nonprofit?

Use Humor

Humor is one of the most surefire ways to get attention, but it is also one of the riskiest, as each of us has a different sense of what is funny. While there is no foolproof formula for hitting the funny bone, one approach that usually has potential is exaggeration.

For example, seize on some characteristic about your service or product, and take it to comical extremes. Oscar Mayer did that with their fleet of six Wienermobiles, twenty-three-foot-long hot dogs on wheels, which travel the country provoking people to laughter—and to joining in spontaneous choruses of the company's famous jingle, *"I wish I were an Oscar Mayer wiener...."* Indeed, it was probably inevitable that this marketing idea would appeal to the wacky humor columnist Dave Barry, who devoted a column to his pleasure in tooling around in the elongated vehicle:

> "Rob," I said to my thirteen-year-old son, who was—this being a school morning—sleeping, face-down in his breakfast. "How would you like it if I picked you up at school in the Oscar Mayer Wienermobile?"
>
> "DAD!" he said, coming violently to life, horrified. "NO!"
>
> So right away I knew it was a good idea. Your most important responsibility, as the parent of an adolescent, is to be a hideous embarrassment to your child.
>
> Recently Oscar Mayer offered me the opportunity to drive a Wienermobile, no doubt hoping this would result in favorable publicity (although of course I'm far too ethical to promote Oscar Mayer meat products, which are known to cure heart disease)....
>
> But the highlight of the day was picking up Rob at school. He was out front, with all his friends, when I pulled up, broadcasting on the PA system.
>
> "ROB BARRY, THIS IS YOUR FATHER," I said. "PLEASE REPORT TO THE WIENERMOBILE IMMEDIATELY...."
>
> That's what makes this country great: An older generation passing along a cherished tradition to a younger one, in very much the same way that a row of people at a baseball game will pass along those tasty Oscar Mayer wieners, which by the way also have been shown in laboratory rats to prevent baldness.

REAL RACING WEINERS

"The dog days of summer came early to the Los Alamitos (Horse) Race Course as twenty-four dachshunds tore up the track at the inaugural Weiner Nationals. Saddled with racing numbers, the jockey-free 'weiner dogs' scooted out of a starting gate and down a fifty-yard straightaway, into the waiting arms of their owners. The event raised $4,000 through ticket sales and donations for the Seal Beach Animal Care Center, becoming the center's largest fund-raiser ever."

The Orange County Register

Devise an Image

Another way to spark your creativity is to conjure up vivid images rather than thinking only about facts. Images can often convey a message much more memorably than a mere listing of facts and statistics.

For example, the Tax Foundation, a straightlaced economics think tank in Washington, D.C., used to put out a press release every year stating what percentage of the gross domestic product went to taxes. Their expectation was that people would realize that taxes cost too much and start a groundswell to reduce them. But how many people remember a statistic an hour or even fifteen minutes after they hear it? Very few.

Something clicked in the Foundation's PR department, and they had the brainstorm of creating an image representing the amount of taxes we pay. Therefore starting in 1972, the Foundation took to demonstrating our tax burden by announcing "Tax Freedom Day." This day represents how many days the average American must work only to pay taxes, and the day changes each year depending on the tax rate.

For example, in 1997, the Foundation's economists projected that the nation's effective tax rate, when applied to the calendar year, required people to work only to pay taxes until May 9, 1997.

This meant that the average American had to work 128 days to pay off his or her tax bill, earning "tax freedom" only on the 129th day. The announcement of Tax Freedom Day now gains widespread publicity every year. As you can see, the Tax Foundation people created a powerful image, and they've reaped powerful publicity as a result.

Another wonderful story to exemplify the power of an image deals with a anti–teen drinking campaign that Candy Lightner (the woman who founded Mothers Against Drunk Driving) worked on. Candy relates that a California legislator once asked her to appear at his press conference introducing a bill to color-code teenagers' driver's licenses, in order to cut down on the sale of alcohol to minors. She agreed to go, but she feared that the proposal, as important as it was, wouldn't draw much media interest.

"Then, at two A.M. of the day when the press conference was to take place, I woke up with an idea," she says. "We needed to graphically show how easy it was for someone under the legal drinking age to buy liquor by altering the driver's-license date of birth. My seventeen-year-old daughter would make the purchases. I called the sheriff's office, and got them to agree to help. When day broke, we met with an undercover agent who was ready to help us. He visibly altered the birth date on my daughter's license so that it indicated she was twenty-one. Then, he went with her to four liquor stores. She was able to buy alcohol at two of them— even though she was a young-looking seventeen. At the press conference, we propped the booze up for the media, and let my daughter tell the story. It was front-page news the next day."

MAKING USE OF YOUR DREAMS FOR CREATIVITY

One lesson to learn from Candy Lightner's story: Keep a notepad by your bed. Many successful people say some of their best ideas have come to them when they were in bed, either right before falling asleep or in a dream. Indeed, it is a well-known phenonmenon that dreams, which arise from your subconscious, are a powerful gateway to creativity.

Author William Styron says he had a waking vision one morning in the mid-1970s that convinced him he should drop the book he was working on and start another project—the one that became *Sophie's Choice.*

Sue Grafton, the phenomenally successful murder-mystery writer, finds subject matter in scary dreams. "A frightening dream is wonderful for me," she says, "because it re-creates all the physiology that I need in describing my private-eye heroine, Kinsey Millhone, in a dangerous situation. For instance, I remember one night I dreamt that there was a child in a room across the hall playing with a dog. At a certain point, I, in my half-waking state, understood that it was not a dog at all but something very dangerous. And the fear and the horror that rose up in me from the information about this vicious creature in the room with the child created such heart-thumping and sweating that I immediately started cataloging my physical symptoms so that later, in describing Kinsey in a moment of great terror, I could use that information. I loved it."

Stephen King finds dreams and dreamy meditation an aid to his memory. "In a story like *The Body* or *It*," he says, "which is set around the late fifties or early sixties, I'm able to regress so that I can remember things that I'd forgotten. Time goes by and events pile up on the surface of your mind like snow, and it covers all these other previous layers. But if you're able to put yourself into that sort of semi-dreaming state—whether you're dreaming or you're writing creatively, as the brainwaves are apparently interchangeable—you're able to get a lot of that memory back."

Charitable works turn our noblest dreams into reality. So why not try to employ the insights of your inner mind to make your waking actions more creative and powerful?

Brainstorm with Others

Brainstorming is one of the most effective techniques to get your creative juices flowing. Invented by creativity pioneer Alex Osborne in his classic book *Applied Imagination: Principles and Procedures of Creative Problem Solving*, brainstorming is the technique of allowing a roomful of people to think creatively together. More specifically, the goal of brainstorming is to play ideas off of each other in an effort to generate as many ideas as possible. Quantity is what counts at first, not quality. In a brainstorming session, participants do not pass judgment on other ideas; they simply let everyone think and invent whatever they want, be it ridiculous or bizarre or seemingly impossible. Then, after as many ideas as possible are generated, the group can begin to edit and condense ideas, seeking to find either a single leading concept or an intersection between concepts that provides the needed solution.

Here's how to have an official brainstorming party: Set your agenda and the goal. For example, let's say you want to coin a name for your nonprofit organization. Hang a large, display-size sheet of paper on the wall or on an easel, and have magic markers on hand. Encourage everyone in the group to spontaneously speak up with ideas. As each idea is spoken, one member of the group writes it down. No one comments or critiques any idea while the "storming" is going on; every idea gets written down uncritically, in large print so everyone can see it. People are then encouraged to build on ideas already mentioned, or to speak up with new, unrelated statements, whichever approach sparks their imagination.

After fifteen or twenty minutes of throwing ideas on the wall, the group must take a five-minute break. During that time, the person who recorded the ideas on the paper, rewrites them in a formal, numbered order. The reassembled group then discusses each idea in turn, and spontaneity gives way to orderliness, as people begin to pick and choose among the ideas and develop a consensus about the best one.

Meditate on Your Own Life

Creativity can also be inspired simply by meditating on your own life experiences and applying them in an innovative way to help others. For example, *Time* magazine, March 10, 1997, saluted R. David Smith of San Diego as a "hero," because of his creativity in surmounting a disability and lifting up others with his success. "As a child," *Time* reported, "Smith was taunted by playmates because he was born without a left forearm. In his early twenties he won an acting scholarship for disabled persons sponsored by Paramount, which led to a career as a stunt man. Four years ago, he began training [many other] disabled persons to perform stunts and helping them get gigs on TV shows. As he tells new amputees: 'You're going to feel better about yourself than before your accident. I'm living proof.' "

Like Mr. Smith, if you're engaged in charity works, you inevitably confront many difficult obstacles and hardships, both in the lives of the people you're trying to help, and in your own efforts to make your helping project succeed. This is all the more reason to work at developing the habit of thinking creatively. Indeed, charity providers probably need a bigger reserve of optimism than the average person, and I believe creativity can help supply it.

Walt Disney coined a word for utilizing imagination to the max: *imagineering*. That's the title he gave to a whole division of creative people in his company—the visionaries who come up with the theme-park designs and rides. If you can learn to think creatively, I truly believe you will become your organization's best in-house "imagineer."

SKILL 2: BE CARING AND CURIOUS

One of the strongest traits of the best publicists is that they are extremely curious people. Fortunately, if you're working with a nonprofit organization, chances are you already have some of this trait. After all, you cannot be selfishly absorbed in your own private world, oblivious to the condition and feelings of people around you, and be an effective philanthropist.

Public relations has been called the craft of forging bonds between an entity and the constituencies important to its success. For a business, those groups include its customers, employees, shareholders, and suppliers. For a charity, they include volunteers, fundraisers, donors, and, of course, the people the nonprofit directly serves.

Showing care is one of the primary ways to forge bonds. In this sense, the public-relations profession and the world of charity actually share common goals. Both are "other-focused," concerned about the welfare of other people. Both the charity provider and the professional publicist make it their business to pay attention to other people's needs, concerns, expectations, habits of thought.

Similarly, curiosity is a major trait of a good PR professional. If you want to fashion a promotional message that has real power, you cannot be someone who tunes out fellow humans. PR and marketing require a passionate interest in other people—in what stimulates their minds and souls, what they're worried about, what makes them happy, what makes them sad.

In my own life, I have been described as an intensely curious person. I am curious about just about everything, especially other people—what they're thinking, doing, saying, and why. I am almost addicted to questions. If I'm in a restaurant, I'll often ask the waiters about themselves, and we can get into some very searching conversations about issues in their personal lives. Often people are just waiting for an opportunity to open up in the most personal and revealing way to someone who is interested.

Not long ago, a prominent national magazine called me one of the country's half-dozen best networkers. I don't know exactly what that signifies; maybe it says something about how little other people, even in my profession, cultivate networking in an energetic way. For me, cultivating people is a way of life. And, returning to the value of creativity, I am certain that my creative abilities are honed as a result of my curiosity.

While perhaps I was born with a prominent curiosity gene, I

believe that anyone who isn't naturally curious can at least develop the capacity. Studies now suggest that somewhere around 30 percent of our human individual characteristics are not genetically conditioned—i.e., the result of nature—but rather are somehow developed by environmental influences or our own force of will, called nurture. Now, 30 percent is smaller than half of all our characteristics, but it's considerably larger than 5 percent.

What these studies suggest is that you have the power to increase your capacity for curiosity. And many people have a strong need for just such an upgrading in this department. If you were to go to any city in this country and randomly pick out a shopping mall, and at that mall pick out the first 100 people—of any race, age, gender, sexual orientation—and ask them, "What's the opposite of love?" 95 percent would answer, "Hate."

And 95 percent would be wrong. The opposite of love is apathy, indifference, a lack of caring about others. Not living an engaged, passionate life is a form of not caring about the world. It diminishes the experiences of anyone who has such a habit of passivity. But it is especially fatal to someone who acts as a publicist or marketer.

Public relations is about communication, and communication is important for anyone who cares what others think, who sees other people as important and valuable. And it's from this mental alertness and vitality that vibrant ideas, or robust creativity flows.

The good news is that if you're a charity worker, you probably have a head start when it comes to caring like a publicist. You're not imprisoned by a preoccupation with yourself. You've already made the commitment to reach out to others.

THE FUND-RAISER THAT NEVER TOOK PLACE

Here's an example of a humorous approach to fundraising:

"You wouldn't expect a mental health organization to ring the cleverness gong. But the Mental Health Association of

> Montgomery County has done so in a big way—with its fifth annual Druthers Ball.... The ball is scheduled for April 31.
>
> "We'll pause for a second to let that sink in. Right. No such date. Which is precisely the point. This is the only fund-raiser on your social calendar that doesn't exist.... The non-ball is advertised in a way that will appeal to all harried Washingtonians. You won't have to wear black tie. You won't need a baby sitter. You won't need to battle traffic. Or eat rubber chicken. Or be bored. Or persuade your spouse to attend. All you need to do is make a donation, and you'll be eligible for several nice prizes...."
>
> *The Washington Post*, April 12, 1988.

How to Show You Care for the Media

Part of your role as a publicist is therefore to exercise plenty of curiosity to find out about the journalistic "gatekeepers" in your city. These are the people who will determine whether stories about your organization get into the media, and how your organization will be portrayed.

Just as with any business relationship, with marketing and publicity there is a buyer and a seller. You are the seller, and you have an obligation to find out what different buyers—the media gatekeepers—want, and how to get it to them. You have to be curious enough to ask. For instance, some editors prefer e-mail and love to communicate by computer. Some don't. Get curious. Find out.

One of the best ideas in the nonprofit world is to get journalists involved firsthand in your organization's work. How? Simple: Ask a journalist to sit on your nonprofit's board of directors, or establish a public-relations task force within your nonprofit and have a journalist serve on it. Los Angeles lawyer Hugh Hewitt says, "If you're involved with a nonprofit in a relatively small community, the universe of press people whom you'll find yourself working with over the years is very small—maybe one or two each at the local TV and radio stations, and a couple of people at the newspaper. Build friendships with these people, friendships that go beyond office hours. Too many people in the community tend to put journalists warily at arm's length on a social level. If you take a different approach and give a journalist an opportunity to become active in a community organization, on his or her off-time, you'll be doing that person a service and earning their gratitude."

WHAT THE PROFESSIONALS SAY ABOUT WORKING WITH THE MEDIA

Here's a rundown of what a variety of my colleagues have to say about working with the press and other media.

Los Angeles lawyer and public-television host Hugh Hewitt:

"I believe that creating long-term personal rapport with key media people in your community is a more important PR strategy than all the media kits and press releases you could create in a lifetime. Treat them as individual human beings, develop a relationship with them."

Erin Brady, a spokeswoman for the American Heart Association:

"Proactive involvement with media people is crucial to intelligent public relations. Call them before they call you. Let them know you want to help them do their job."

Helga Luest, communications director for Goodwill Industries International:

"Get to know the journalists covering your organization as human beings. Develop a reputation as a straight-shooter with the facts, open and honest, and willing to go the extra mile to help them get the information they need. The bonds you build can help ensure the organization gets balanced and thorough coverage."

Business and computer writer Guy Kawasaki, author of *Selling the Dream:*

"Do right by the press, opinion leaders, and pundits. Build a relationship before you need it. Assume that you are going to need help, so build up credit in advance. Don't try to manipulate the press. Think of these people as your wife—you aren't going to fool them. If you try to, you will lose credibility.

"Be courteous. Return phone calls quickly. Make time for them on your schedule. Give them stories and scoops. This way you will endear yourself to them. If you become a good source of stories, they probably won't burn you.

"Treat every relationship as a long-term investment. This week's *Podunk Gazette* reporter may soon be writing an article about your cause for *People.* Or, he may be the author of a best-selling book about evangelism. As a corollary, don't ignore or abuse freelancers. This week's unemployed freelancer who begs you for an interview could be next week's West Coast editor of the *New York Times.*"

SKILL 3: APPEAL TO THE SOUL

Here's another element in the publicist's bag of skills: Seek ideas and images that strike a deep chord in the soul of your audience. You don't have to boast a degree in psychology to come up with these ideas. All you need is careful observation of your own soul and that of other caring people.

Just as images are more powerful than statistics, appealing to the soul is more meaningful than appealing to the mind. Some of the most powerful campaigns I know are those that focused around a very personal human story. Statistics—even statistics about human poverty or some other widespread human problem—only touch the intellect; it's hard for them to stir the soul. In contrast, the flesh-and-blood troubles of just one person can rivet an entire nation—if her situation is presented to the public on an intimate basis.

Perhaps you remember Jessica McClure, the toddler who became trapped in a well in Midland, Texas, in 1987. As it happens, my firm donated public-relations services to her family. The press coverage made her trauma a personal concern for millions of Americans—as if she lived right next door. For thirty-seven hours leading up to her rescue, the nation was fixated on this little girl and her family. CNN's ratings had never been higher. One might say that there was a sense of oneness among Americans that had seldom been stronger.

Ultimately, a TV movie memorialized her story. What an awesome impact, all because the power of mass communications was married with a compelling image—of a solitary, scared little girl.

Admittedly, some people have trouble with such stories. For instance, the brilliant L.A. author and radio talk-show host Dennis Prager has criticized the media for the attention they focused on little Jessica. I agree he has a point. As he wrote in his book *Dennis Prager—Think a Second Time:*

> I was overjoyed several years ago at the successful conclusion to the drama of little Jessica McClure. Still, the... nationwide anxiety over one girl's fate prompted me to ask: Why, with all the horrible suffering in the world, was so much attention devoted to the suffering of one family in Midland, Texas?
>
> The answer, of course, was the inherent drama of the rescue. Another was the joy of seeing many people working heroically to save a little girl. It does us good to see goodness in action.
>
> There is an additional answer, however, that does not speak as well about human nature and conduct. Most peo-

ple do not empathize with other people's suffering unless they actually see it. Between visible and invisible anguish, the visible nearly always wins, even when the invisible suffering is far greater. Whenever I see a crowd of candle holders standing vigil outside a prison where a murderer is about to be executed, I wonder why these people never do the same at the home of the murdered person's family. And then I realize that one reason is that the murder victim is invisible—as was the murder itself—while the murderer and his execution are visible.

Prager goes on to urge that we "regain some balance in the sympathy we apportion to those who suffer, [to] become conscious of our natural tendency to care more about the suffering of those whom we see, and consciously sensitize ourselves to concern ourselves with the suffering of those whom we cannot see."

There is truth in his concern and advice. But for the publicist— and the nonprofit seeking a place in the public's attention—it is also necessary to deal with the real world. This means that, public preferences for drama being what they are, commanding attention for a good cause requires seizing on the power of the media and getting the attention of the vast proportion of the population.

Skill 4: Learn to Differentiate Your Cause from Others'

The need for charities to become more adept with the tools of publicity has actually never been stronger. Statistics on donations to the philanthropic sector reveal a challenge in the making. Although more money is being donated overall, the number of people not giving, while still a minority, is going up. In 1989, 25 percent of American households didn't contribute to charity; that compares with 31 percent who didn't in 1995.

But more importantly, while the number of people who do not

give to charities is rising, the number of charities asking people to give is increasing as well. That situation leads to a conundrum for charities: There's competition out there for dollars and attention. It seems altruism has company these days.

The attention-getting competition is so severe for charities and nonprofits today that even being a famous cause is insufficient protection against failure. Consider the venerable Smithsonian Institution. In early 1997 it announced that its 150th-anniversary traveling show, "America's Smithsonian," was being put on hiatus for several months because of a lack of funds. The project had drawn substantial numbers of visitors, up to two million in its first year of operation, to see some three hundred choice items from the Smithsonian's holdings in its Washington, D.C., museums, such as Thomas Edison's lightbulb, Abraham Lincoln's hat, the ruby slips worn by Judy Garland in *The Wizard of Oz*, and the *Apollo 14* space capsule. But the fund-raising numbers weren't as encouraging. The goal of raising $100 million from large donors had not been met. The show's difficulties stemmed in part from the fact that increases in federal dollars can no longer be assumed. But the private sector had also not produced the outpouring that had been hoped for.

To illustrate how many charities are vying for public attention and money today, here's an tongue-in-cheek column from the *Wall Street Journal*, Feb 18, 1994 by writer-photographer, Ardian Gill about the race for donor dollars.

Like many Americans, I contribute to a number of charities, museums, environmental groups and educational institutions. As a result, I am plagued daily by solicitations in numbers that numb the soul—they even exceed the Chinese restaurant menus under my door.

Last year I decided to count them. I started on July 1, figuring the count for the balance of the year could be doubled for approximating an annual "mailfall." By year's end I had filled two shopping bags with 429 pieces of mail weighing 22 pounds, making my estimate for the year nearly 900 pieces at almost 45 pounds.

I then sorted by sender. Heavy hitters were the Wilderness Society and the Sierra Club (hey, these guys are supposed to preserve trees) with 11 each, matched by Planned Parenthood and CARE. There is an irony here: All four have received contributions from me for many years, so they don't need to solicit from me at all. There is also an unhappy equation: If a mailing's total costs are a dollar per piece, then the first twenty bucks or so of my contribution was eaten up by expenses.

The mail itself demonstrated considerable ingenuity in inducements for opening the envelope. Some are stamped "Second Notice" in red, as if they were overdue bills, putting me in mind of the old gag, "Merry Christmas from your mailman, Second Notice." Other envelopes have messages such as "Documents Enclosed," "Urgent News," "Free Gift Enclosed" (what kind of gift isn't free?), "Mailgram," "Hand Deliver," or my favorite, "Last Chance." There are also "Have you overlooked?"; "We are disappointed, etc."; and "Your membership is about to expire"—six months ahead of time.

Some send Christmas cards I don't want, note cards I wouldn't send to my dog, decals and return address labels, most often with my first name misspelled. Others are heavily underlined to emphasize certain passages, rather like those unsettling italics in the King James Bible. Some include photographs: vivisected dogs, dead elephants, beaches with bloated fish bodies, everything but the *Harvard Lampoon's* "If you don't buy this magazine, we'll shoot this dog" cover.

Once you become a contributor, you become a target of techniques designed to increase your contribution. The Sierra Club, the National Organization for Women and

the NAACP, as examples, split themselves in twain, forming "legal defense funds" or "education funds," seeking
thereby to double up your contributions, a trick I've fallen
for more than once. The museums favor membership categories, inspiring a cartoon by Roy Delgado, which
appeared in the *Wall Street Journal*, showing a panhandler
with a hand-lettered sign reading, "Benefactor $5, Patron
$2, Friend $1."

Give money to one charity and you soon will receive
mail from other, similar charities, since they trade or rent
their lists. The most prolific are the Indians: Give to the
Native American Rights Fund or the American Indian
College Fund and you will receive requests from the Red
Cloud Indian School, the Little Sioux Indian Mission, the
Sinte Gleska University, the American Indian Relief
Council, the Native American College Fund and the
Navajo Health Foundation; the list goes on (I received
twenty-one such requests in six months). A donation to
Friends of the River will produce mail from American
Rivers, Southern Utah Wilderness Alliance, Save-the-
Redwoods League, Scenic Hudson, Grand Canyon Trust,
Rainforest Action Network, Defenders of Wildlife, the
Trust for Public Land and Mohonk Preserve. This swap-
ping of lists leads to multiple solicitations (three in one
day from UNICEF) because no attempt is made to elimi-
nate duplication.

It's impossible to stop this sorrowful waste, but there
are defenses. I now avoid multiple contributions to the
same organization by lumping my giving in a single month,
December, near the close of the tax year (October for
museums, because membership renewal is likely to be
assigned to the annual appeal, and you will be hit again).
While this helped, my conscience wouldn't let me overlook the mail that continued to pour in. Then my bank

came up with a bill-paying service that liberated me. Now I make up my list of donees, select the amounts and dates for the contributions and set up recurring annual payments, which I'll review and edit each year.

A postscript: In a moment of weak resolve, I went outside my system and sent some money to the Asia Society to support a particular event. I wasn't able to attend the event, but it happened to include a raffle, and I won a fourteen-day cruise. There's a moral here, but it eludes me. Perhaps it lies in the cruise being a circumnavigation of Greenland.

The lessons for all charities and nonprofits in this column are significant. First there is a very practical message: Save stamps by making sure no one is on your mailing list more than once. But there is also a strategic message to heed: Don't get so cute with your promotional ploys that they risk turning off people who might otherwise be well-disposed toward your group. Sending an envelope disguised as a collection agency's letter isn't creative, it's counterproductive and dumb.

The point should be clear by now. Thousands of national, state, and local charities are vying for the public's attention and money. If you are handling the public relations for your organization, make sure you tell your constituencies why they should give to you more than another group.

SKILL 5: DARE TO BE BOLD

Another skill of the effective publicist is letting go of normalcy and learning to be daring. Ordinary ideas are just that; ordinary, but a daring idea can help you break out of the pack of solicitors vying for your potential donor's attention. If you can be daring, you don't need professional help to become a charity that succeeds in fundraising and getting all the publicity you need.

Here are three promotions that in my book are wonderful

examples of a daring PR ploy. Although some of these stories come from the business world, they are nevertheless good examples of the type of thinking you need to do.

Case Number 1: Wet Seal Clothing

The owners of the California clothing firm, Wet Seal, wanted to make sure consumers knew their firm was a woman's retailer, not a new version of the boating store Marineland.

The PR firm, Gloria Zigner and Associates rose to the challenge. Zigner proposed holding an eight-hour kissing marathon in the college town of Chico. Everyone has heard of a letter "sealed with a kiss," after all. The PR team started by making sure kissing marathons were allowed under California law. It turned out they were. (But forget about dance contests; they aren't.)

Next the Zigner group thought up rules, got all the needed equipment together, and developed plans for the layout, food, and restrooms. Wet Seal offered a $1,000 shopping spree to the winning female. The guy puckering with her would receive $500.

To advertise the event, Zigner employees went all over Chico distributing posters, flyers, counter displays, T-shirts and entry forms. They made sure to hit both commercial and campus radio and TV stations. They got the local Top 40 radio station to give an on-air mention and to provide emcees. They handed out flyers during class registration at California State University at Chico.

And the kissers came in throngs, making the promotion a lip-smacking success. "Ideas have consequences," a famous scholar once said. In this case, a daring idea helped define Wet Seal in the public mind as a leader in fun, sporty attire for women.

Case Number 2: Bruce's Bakery

Meet Joel and Bruce Zipes, "two shameless self-promoters," as a *New York Times* article humorously described them, who own Bruce's, a bakery and restaurant in New York City. Joel and Bruce turn out to be two great imagineers of their own publicity.

Their story begins with a bold audacious letter, which they wrote and mailed to people all over their neighborhood:

My name is Joel Goldberg. I will be hosting a meeting of "Fight ALL Discrimination Against Left-Handed People" (FADALP). This is not a joke or a prank. Left-handed people are tired of being the world's fools.

What happened next was a great PR coup for promoting their bakery. As Michael Norman excerpted in the *New York Times:* April 4, 1985

One day, Joel was having coffee with Danny Frank. Mr. Frank is a professional pitchman with an unbridled imagination. He runs a concern called Cosmopolitan Concepts— public relations, advertising and so forth. "We make things happen," his letterhead promises.

Joel was complaining about living in a "right-handed world." Danny Frank looked around the restaurant and was inspired. Here was a nifty conceit.

Lefties are a minority. Lefties have problems. If some of them were gathered together in one place—Bruce's bakery and restaurant, for example—reporters and camera crews might follow.

They would go through the front door, past the delicious-looking mandel bread and macaroon layer cakes. They would sit at the tables and drink the rich coffee. And, of course, they would have a chance to get to know the hale and hearty fellows who run the place.

The letters went out, experts were summoned, and today FADALP met. Joel [told the crowd] about a left-handed deli man who struggled to cut his lox correctly in a right-handed world.

The program that followed had all the classic elements: a developmental ophthalmologist, who talked about hand muscles and finger stress; a retired professional baseball play, who proclaimed that lefties had a "natural slider"; a representative of the State Human Rights Division, who assured the audience that her agency would guard against discrimination, and one Patricia Siegel, a handwriting analyst who teaches a course at the New School for Social Research, in Manhattan.

The schtick went over well—except with a dean from Great Neck South High School, who had brought a group of students in the belief, she said, that "this was going to be an educational meeting. It turned out to be a lesson in how to get publicity for your restaurant."

And what a lesson. The event got big huge play in the press. Scores of people who'd never previously heard of the restaurant would now be coming back for the mandel bread and macaroon layer cakes.

Like Bruce and Joel, charities must dare to promote themselves—and even dare to be impish about it.

Case Number 3: Orange County Red Cross

A *Los Angeles Times*, June 30, 1992 story by Jodi Wilgoren reported this wonderful, daring PR coup.

It was ten A.M. Monday, and Union Bank manager John Baker was expecting to meet with one of the company's attorneys. But the attorney never showed. He sent a goat in his place.

"A goat, huh?" a puzzled Baker said when two teenage girls arrived with the stand-in. "Why are we getting this goat? What are we supposed to do with this goat?"

Employees watching, Baker tried to remain calm as he met Nancy, the 135-pound Alpine goat, in the parking lot.

"I have an idea what kind of deposits she might make—and I might have to clean that up," Baker said, positive that he did not want Nancy behind his desk. "Take this goat back, quickly."

Nancy is among about thirty-five goats traveling through [Orange County] to raise money for the Red Cross. People pay $25 to send the goats to friends and colleagues, and the lucky recipients pay $10 more to make the goats go away.

"I'll have to call and thank him," Baker said, chuckling once he got the joke. "I'll have to call and do something to him."

Goats visited law firms, ad agencies, and a construction site. They stopped by the Municipal Courthouse in Newport Beach, a county government building in Santa Ana and a local police station. They romped around at an elementary school and a Girl Scouts meeting.

One marched into the lobby at the Four Seasons Hotel in Newport Beach, and another was the featured guest at a fiftieth birthday party. A third was hired to meet a group at the Goat Hill Tavern in Costa Mesa.

About seventy-five volunteers, mostly teenagers who had attended a Red Cross leadership camp or are otherwise involved with the chapter, took the goats on the road in loaned cars and minivans. But first they had to attend goat school.

At a three-hour seminar Saturday, volunteers said they were taught how to calm a goat (massage its back), how to move a goat (tweak its tail) and how often the goats need a roadside break ("often," according to Nancy's driver, Connie Lu, sixteen, of Huntington Beach.

"I never thought that in Orange County we'd have goats, we're so conservative here!" said volunteer Priscilla Schoch, who brought the "Get Your Goat" concept to California after visiting a Red Cross chapter in Louisiana last summer. "But here we are."

Daring imagination. The truth is, you currently possess all you need in order to conjure up clever and effective promotional ideas. You simply have to work at it in an organized, thoughtful, diligent way.

WHAT TO DO WITH A SPARE BOEING 727

Here's an example of a creative and bold fund-raising event for a charity, the Virginia Special Olympics, as described in an article from a Virginia newspaper.

"Musclebound twenty-member teams threw their collective power into raising money for the Virginia Special Olympics on Saturday, straining to pull a seventy-ton airplane twelve feet down the tarmac faster than their opponents.

"Chesapeake sheriff's deputies came in first, clocking 6.07 seconds and besting Chesapeake police by only .02 of a second.

"In another heat to see which team could pull the plane with the lowest combined body weight, Hampton police pitted 1,130 people-pounds against the big Boeing 727 and took first place, outpulling the Muscle Beach East Gym team, whose members weighed in at 1,200 pounds.

"But the real winners of the innovative fund-raiser were Virginia's Special Olympians. The mentally retarded children and adults will benefit from the effort by more than $12,000."

The Norfolk Virginian-Pilot, September 29, 1996

SKILL 6: DEVELOP A LONG-RANGE PLAN OF ACTION

Confucius said: "In all things, success depends upon previous preparation, and without such preparation, there is failure." Oprah Winfrey agrees. "Luck is a matter of preparation meeting opportunity." The Boy Scouts put the thought straightforwardly: "Be prepared."

Publicity is not a spur-of-the-moment profession. It takes thinking and planning, often months in advance of a campaign or promotion, if not years.

The problem is, many people fail to plan a carefully laid-out map to success. They depend on lucky breaks or on the help of others. When they fail, they will often say of those who are more successful: "They just happen to know the right people," or "They get all the lucky breaks." But planning for success has no more to do with luck or knowing the right people than does planning carefully for a cross-country trip.

Sir John Marks Templeton, a world-renowned investor, writes in his book, *Discovering the Laws of Life*:

> To develop a plan of action, mentally visualize the thing you want to accomplish, jot it down across the top of a sheet of paper, then list the steps needed to accomplish it…. If your goal is composed of many levels, you might want to prioritize them. Make a list, giving them a rating of A, B or C. Then tackle the A's first….
>
> The following six rules may help you to achieve your goal:
>
> 1. Think of your goal not as something vague but in specific terms.
> 2. Write about your goal in detail.
> 3. Keep your mind on your goal by reviewing it every day.
> 4. Learn everything you can relating to your goal.
> 5. Be willing to work as hard as you can when the opportunity comes along.
> 6. Remember, "Failing to plan is planning to fail." Just as a road map is an indispensable tool for travel, a plan is an indispensable tool when you travel toward your life goals.

Dreams without plans are sinfully worthless.

SKILL 7: MEASURE YOUR EFFECTIVENESS

Beyond the above skills, you also need to learn to constantly measure whether your ideas resonate and excite people. Successful promotion means you've got to hit the mark more often than not, but unless you follow your campaigns and see how they work, you won't have that information.

For instance, I've seen a number of campaigns that have used humor in an effort to attract attention. Unfortunately, the humor backfired on the nonprofit. The problem is, humor is a very, very subjective thing. Especially in charitable promotions, humor that makes fun of individuals has to be very carefully crafted, something designed to provide good fun for all, including the person who is the subject of the joshing. This is a fine line to walk, and often not worth the risk.

For a yardstick to judge the worth of ideas before you act on them, I refer to two important points made by Steve Fiffer in his book, *So You've Got a Great Idea*. He was addressing inventors primarily, but the approach can be translated quite readily to PR people:

+ First, the need. Does your idea fill a need, serve a purpose, provide a benefit to others? The charity publicist should ask: Will it promote our organization by forging a link with the media?
+ Second, the freshness quotient: Is your idea new and exciting, original and likely to stimulate a response? This is a central concern for people who want press attention: Journalists aren't looking for the same-old-same-old. They want new twists, new angles, and new stories.

Using these two questions as your yardstick will always help you stay in the ballpark of effectiveness. Nevertheless, the professional publicist always follows up on campaigns to assure that all the arrows launched have hit their target as close to center as possible.

SUMMARY: GOODNESS GUIDE

1. Ideas and passionate creativity are the publicist's stock-in-trade. You can learn to develop your idea-generating capacity, and be your own publicist. Ways to improve creativity include utility, juxtaposition, humor and images. Learn to use them all.

2. Keep a notebook by your bed—sometimes the best ideas come just before the Sandman arrives.

3. Intense caring and curiosity about people, places, and things is another key to the publicist's art. Use your "other-oriented" instincts as an activist in altruism to help you think like a publicist. Listen to other people, and figure out what concerns are important to them, and what kinds of images and messages move them.

4. Work to build a relationship with selected members of the local media. Take them to lunch or dinner. Suggest additional opportunities for socializing. Invite a journalist to join your non-profit's board of directors. Or form a publicity committee for your nonprofit, and ask a local journalist to join.

5. Appeal to the public's soul. The heart speaks louder than the mouth.

6. Set yourself apart from others; there is competition for the public's mind and soul.

7. Using daring ideas to get attention. Avoid boring, run-of-the-mill PR tactics that we've all heard or seen before.

8. Plan ahead. Don't think that you can build a successful PR campaign overnight or in a few weeks. It takes months of careful planning.

9. Keep measuring how you are doing. Ask others what they thought of your campaigns or media events. Keep an ear and an eye on how the public views you.

3

Getting Your Cause
in the Papers

What is the difference between advertising and P.R.?
Advertising is saying you're good.
PR is getting someone else to say you're good. PR is better.

JEAN-LOUIS GASSEE,
former director of product development for Apple Computers

When the circus comes to town and you paint a sign about it,
that's advertising. Put the sign on the back of an elephant and
march him through Beverly Hills, and that's promotion.
If the elephant walks through the mayor's flower bed,
THAT'S *publicity! And if you can get the mayor to laugh or comment*
about it, that's public relations.

POPULAR SAYING IN THE PUBLIC-RELATIONS BUSINESS

BOTH quotes above contrast advertising and public relations, and
come down clearly in favor of the latter. While advertising gives

exposure, public relations-generated coverage yields credibility. Advertising is what you pay for. PR is what you pray for. The difference lies in the fact that the public doesn't see news coverage as paid-for promotion, even when a public-relations campaign triggered the story. This is the beauty of the PR process.

The good news is, you don't have to be an official member of the PR profession to get reporters to listen to you or plug your nonprofit organization. You simply need a willingness to learn the basics of writing press releases and creating compelling media kits to make editors eager for your news. That's what this chapter will accomplish.

First Step: Establish a Filing System

In their guide to publicity for small businesses, journalists Tana Fletcher and Julia Rockler talk about the need for a command and control center. The same idea applies to charities and nonprofits for creating a unified and organized promotional effort.

Your command and control center basically consists of a permanent "publicity planning system." This is actually nothing more than an organized filing system for tracking and storing all the paperwork you will generate in developing a PR campaign and keeping up with the news on your organization.

Your filing system can be large or small, depending on your needs, but remember that it is likely to grow with each success. This is where you will store all your files for press clips, media lists, publicity photos, and other paperwork that becomes part of your nonprofit's promotional efforts. If you are tight on space, you can even get away with a small filing cabinet, suitable for storing twenty-five or thirty file folders.

Find a space that works though, a permanent space such as a desk drawer or a cabinet in a closet that offers you stability and easy access. You can even use a portable file container, if you think you will need to transport them frequently.

Organizing Your Files

What kind of files do you need to create? Tyrone Vahedi, executive director of Children's Rights 2000, a Los Angeles advocacy group that lobbies for educational improvement and has successfully placed an education-funding initiative on the statewide California ballot, lists eight categories for which you will need folders:

1. *Letters to the media.* Vahedi reminds you to keep copies of everything you send to any editor, producer, or on-air talent coordinator. Also file any letters you get in return.

2. *News clippings about other organizations that give you ideas applicable to your own project.* "This is your inspiration file, supplying you with creative concepts," says Vahedi. "Also, it's a way to keep tabs, in an organized way, on what the 'competition'—other nonprofit groups—are doing to market themselves."

3. *Clippings of news articles about you and your project.* You can either photocopy the articles or quote from them in the promotional material you send out. You can include news clips in media packets you send out to reporters and editors. Such clips prove that your organization is already "press-worthy," which helps when you are trying to get a new media source to give you some coverage. Reproducing clips is also useful for showing to your board of directors as a reminder of the impact your group has in the community.

4. A *log recording broadcast coverage you've received.* From experience, Vahedi knows how useful this log can be. He says, "Keep a record of when stories ran about your group on TV or radio. This information is something to cite to supporters as an indication of your impact. You can also refer back to it if you need to contact a station about getting a tape of the report. Television stations will usually provide a videotape (sometimes at a small charge), and radio stations will usually provide an audiotape, also sometimes at a charge."

5. *Your organization's brochures.* Brochures are an effective tool for introducing your organization to donors, volunteers, media, and recipients. The best-size brochure is 4"x 9", a size that fits easily in a purse or coat pocket. Keep your brochure slim, between four and twenty pages. Use graphics if possible to keep it interesting. Graphics might include photos of people your organization has served, and perhaps some pie charts or graphs illustrating the size of the social problem your group fights against. The copy should clearly indicate where you're located, who operates your organization, what it does, whom you serve and how many, and how you've improved life for individuals or the community at large.

6. *An idea folder, with results from brainstorming and creativity sessions.* "Since new developments are the products of a creative mind, we must therefore stimulate and encourage that type of mind in every way possible," said George Washington Carver in 1910. This folder is thus a structured system to help you generate more ideas for promotion and for other aspects of your business and life. "Regular brainstorming sessions should be part of your nonprofit group's schedule," Vahedi advises.

7. *A media list.* We will cover this in more detail later in the chapter, but your media list is your holy grail. It is a listing of all the people in the newspapers, magazines, radio and TV stations whom you hope to contact in order to spread the word about your organization.

8. *Publicity photos.* It is very worthwhile to keep some photos on hand of your group "in action," so to speak. You could have photos of your volunteers and/or clients, but be sure to emphasize how you help people. Vahedi reminds us, "People photographs have more impact than photos of buildings."

In addition, you should also make sure you have room to store a supply of stationery and business cards. When you design your business cards, get a designer to help you develop a logo for your organization. As discussed in the last chapter, a visual image of who you are helps people remember your organization. You don't need to get elaborate in designing your logo. In fact, simple logos often have elegance all their own, but whether your logo is simple or detailed, it should be consistently printed on all your stationary and business cards.

No Doughnuts, Please

Hillsborough County Sheriff's Department officer Jim Gaczewski acknowledges some people don't have a good impression of police officers. Most interact with them only after breaking the speed limit.... Tampa Bay law enforcement officials are prepared to crush that mean, doughnut-dunking image while wearing a different uniform.... The Tampa Bay Guardians, a full-contact football team composed entirely of police officers, will play against the West Palm Beach Bandits in Badge Bowl IV.... The purpose of the game is to raise funds for the Suncoast Children's Dream Fund, which grants wishes to terminally ill children; and the Gold Shield Foundation, which helps provide college scholarships for children of slain officers.

The Tampa Tribune, March 22, 1997

COMPILE A MEDIA LIST

The professional publicist seeks to compile as large a media list as possible. Your list should include every relevant name in local print, radio, and television journalism, who can possibly make a difference to your organization. You should also get data on anyone in the national media if your story has national import.

When you compile your list, strive to be as precise and complete as you can be. Get a full name, title, address, phone and fax numbers, and even an e-mail address for each person. Partial names or just phone numbers don't suffice anymore in today's age of high-speed communications. An e-mail address is particularly useful for sending quick messages and even documents to your contacts.

Be sure to keep your list up-to-date by verifying it at least every six months. Job turnover in the media is extensive, and you don't want to get stuck in the middle of a big campaign, discovering that your lead contact at a certain newspaper has left the company and now you don't who to call.

How and where does one go about compiling the media list? Here are some suggestions:

1. *Library*. Your first stop should be your local library, where you can look at every local newspaper and magazine in their stacks. Scan these for the names of every journalist who writes on your subject. Finding comprehensive listings of media outlets isn't simple, because journalists don't go out of their way to make it easy to get information on them. At the library, the *Reader's Guide* lists key periodicals. Reference librarians can help you find copies.

Another valuable resource that many libraries carry are directories such as *Bacon's Publicity Checker* and *Editor and Publisher Yearly*, both of which list thousands of names and addresses of people in the media. If your library doesn't carry these directories, inquire at a local public-relations firm; they may have a copy you can consult. (The appendix to this book also has some valuable lists of media outlets).

Don't stop your list at the obvious print media. Magazines and daily papers aren't the only print media out there. Consider newsletters and trade publications that deal with your issue. And don't forget local weekly newspapers. Small, community-oriented weeklies have a loyalty and intensity of readership, often in inverse proportion to their size. This is because they focus directly on what's happening to their readers and their neighborhoods: who's getting married, what the city council is debating. what's on the menu at the local schools. Local weeklies are often ideal forums for news about locally oriented charity projects.

2. *Newsstands*. Another vitally useful idea is to visit your local newsstand, with pen and paper in hand. Open magazines and

newspapers to the masthead pages—where the staffs are listed—and jot down key names, titles, addresses, phone and fax numbers.

3. *Wire services.* As to the national level, check to see if there are news-service offices in your community. The Associated Press (AP) is a member-owned nonprofit service with more than 1,700 print publications and 2,000 radio and television stations as subscribers. It offers its subscribers continual national and international news through its "A" circuit wire. Its "single-circuit" wire is used mainly by smaller papers. And its "broadcast wire" provides five- to ten-minute news and sports summaries, as well as immediate bulletins, financial and regional news, all through the day, in a format designed to be read over the air. Meanwhile, the United Press International (UPI) is a profit-making service that sells a similar range of news and features to the media.

You should find out where the closest offices of both services are, the names of its local bureau directors, and any reporters who specialize in your topic. Anything they write about you and your group truly has the potential to go over the wires across the nation, so this is a resource you can't afford to ignore.

4. *Radio.* The electronic media are a pervasive force in our lives today. Radio in particular reaches people everywhere—from the gridlocked freeway to the beach to the office to the secluded mountain cabin. Many nonprofits and leaders of causes believe strongly in the power of the radio, because it's a medium that really draws people in, creating a sense of intimacy between the people speaking over the airwaves and listeners. Also, radio can respond to breaking stories with breakneck speed. Radio reporters often are highly mobile because their equipment is compact and portable. They can come to where the story is breaking quickly if your organization has a story that needs to be heard.

As I said in the last chapter, the media need you, and this is very true for radio stations. They can't convey visual images, so word pictures become vitally important. That means someone with a real story to tell is a marketable commodity in their eyes.

So do your homework. Get familiar with all the radio stations in your area, not just the big ones. Use the publication *Talk Show Selects* to find a list of stations that host talk shows in your area.

Small stations sometimes have a listening audience that is more loyal, if not as numerous, as the larger ones. Successful radio personalities at stations large and small develop a rapport with their regular listeners that can translate into credibility for projects or causes that they give attention to.

"Learn who the personalities are on each local radio station, what their focus is, where they're coming from in terms of interests and outlook," says Gary F. Millspaugh, executive director of the Allentown Rescue Mission in Allentown, Pennsylvania. "Identify the names of on-air reporters and newscasters. Phone the stations to get names of news editors and the producers of any programs that you've determined might be appropriate for dealing with your issue."

5. *Television and cable.* Use the same process for television. You might normally think of the relationship between TV and non-profits as mainly confined to the airing of thirty- or sixty-second public service announcements (PSAs) on behalf of charities. While PSAs can indeed be an important part of a promotional strategy, even for a fledgling charity with minimal resources, the opportunities for television don't stop there. Many TV stations and cable operators offer locally oriented talk shows or public-affairs programs. News programs often include soft "feature" pieces, creating opportunities for the kind of human-interest stories about people in need, or people whose lives are being turned around, that your nonprofit may generate on a regular basis.

Familiarize yourself with the TV stations in your area, their local programs, personalities, and news directors, editors, and producers. You should be able to get names of the behind-the-scenes people through a phone call or two to each station. Note: you need more than just names and numbers for TV. For instance, you'll want to list the names, themes, and times of various programs, as well as hosts, producers, and deadlines.

PUBLICITY GOES HIGH-TECH

In recent years, a plethora of high-tech approaches to PR has started to facilitate the work for many nonprofessionals who need to do their own publicity. For example, you can now find special PR software, such as the Windows program called *PublicityBuilder* from Jian Software that contains templates for press releases, worksheets to help you refine your goals and product positioning, and many additional features to make working on press releases easier.

Scripps-Howard columnist Terry Mattingly urges one to become proficient at using the computer for communicating with people. "One of the banes of both the journalist's and the publicist's tasks these days is the answering machine," he notes. "People find themselves playing telephone tag over the course of hours, if not days—perhaps just to set up a time for a formal interview. By contrast, by using the computer, with the quick exchange of just a couple of electronic mail [e-mail] messages, two parties can make all the arrangements and have all the communications that eluded them as they kept getting each other's answering machines."

The Internet also offers a vast range of useful information for people promoting charities and nonprofits. For instance, there's *Mediasource* (www.mediasource.com), a site run by the New York-based public-relations firm, Middleberg and Associates. It includes a study of how journalists use the Internet, and links to sources journalists can contact. You might want to try to get your organization listed as a source on whatever your subject of expertise is. *Editpros Business News Media Directory* gives e-mail addresses of many business journalists (www.editpros.com/media.html). Newspaper, magazine, and broadcast station listings can be found on the *Gebbie Press All-In-One Media Directory* site (www.gebbieinc.com).

Building Your List One Name at a Time

Compiling a media list tailored to your needs is a major task, especially if you're going to do it right. There's no way to go about it effectively without a systematic effort. It simply takes time to complete. Think of your chore as building a wall, one brick at a time.

Eventually, you'll have a collection of many publications and names. For my own list, I use a large alphabetized wheel Rolodex. But do what is most comfortable for you. Some people use file folders, others put information on 3"x 5" index cards and put them in a shoebox; still others keep three-ring notebooks with multiple listings on a page.

Candy Lightner, founder of MADD, knows what putting together a media list is like. "It's a lot of work to compile," says Candy, "but it is essential to any serious promotional strategy. I look to see whose beat coincides with my area of concern. But I look as well for writers who appear to be sympathetic with my perspective. I put the names of all these people on my list. But I don't stop there. I also contact the paper or magazine to find out the names of editors in the sections that could deal with my issue. Also the name or names of any chief editors who supervise other editors. All these people go on the list. And often I will contact more than one of them when I'm promoting an event or topic concerning my organization. Don't just send your press release to an editor. Sometimes reporters have a more intimate knowledge of the issue, and might see a newsworthy angle where the editor would miss it. So contact both writers and their supervisors, and hopefully you'll get a conversation going between various people at the paper or magazine about your idea."

PLANNING YOUR YEAR

Once you've developed your media list, the next essential step is to work out a calendar for your activities. Calendaring requires planning every major aspect of your strategy. You must block out time for writing letters, preparing publicity packets, making follow-up phone calls. Every step along the way proceeds at a pace you have set out in advance.

A wall calendar is a good tool for making sure the task list is always visible. A large desk calendar can also work, provided it is open and in view, an ever-present-reminder of the required daily work toward your goals.

Here's a example of a what your tracking calendar might look like:

PUBLICATION	DATE CONTACTED	WHO CONTACTED	MATERIALS SENT	COMMENTS	RESULTS
Evening Post	2/14/98	Jason Smythe	press release	spoke first on phone	article printed 2/17/86
KCJT	3/19/98	Sarah William	media kit and video	she called to thank us	possible interview arranged

As you can see, on one axis, you list the names of publications and radio and TV outlets, while the other axis shows a series of columns for each data point you need to track: date contacted, who was contacted, materials sent, comments, results, et cetera. This type of tracking sheet is the best way to get a quick overview of your promotional campaign's success.

I also recommend that you write an inspirational phrase on your tracking calendar, to keep you going when you're asking yourself whether all this promotional effort is worth it. Up at the top of the sheet, put down a quote from someone whose words inspire you.

THE POWER OF PUBLICITY

"Publicity, publicity, PUBLICITY is the greatest moral factor and force in our public life." So said the great newspaperman Joseph Pulitzer. A strong statement, but not far from the mark, when you consider how publicity can change the course of human events. Here's one of my favorite examples.

In 1949, the Reverend Billy Graham was a little-known evangelist who had come to Los Angeles to conduct a series of evangelistic tent meetings. During the course of that "crusade," the famed newspaperman, William Randolph Hearst, demonstrated how promotion can dramatically transform the life of one individual—and by doing so, can touch the lives of millions. Here is the story, as recounted by Graham in his autobiography, *Just As I Am*.

"When I arrived at the tent for the next meeting, the scene startled me. For the first time, the place was crawling with reporters and photographers. They had taken almost no notice of the meetings up until now, and very little had appeared in the papers. I asked one of the journalists what was happening.

'You've just been kissed by William Randolph Hearst,' he responded.

"I had no idea what the reporter was talking about, although I knew the name. Hearst, of course, was the great newspaper owner. I had never met the man, but like most Americans I had read his papers. The next morning's headline story about the Campaign in the *Los Angeles Examiner*, followed by an evening story in the *Los Angeles Herald Express*—both owned by Hearst—stunned me. The story was picked up by the Hearst papers in New York, Chicago, Detroit, and San Francisco, and then by all their competitors. Until then, I doubt if any newspaper editor outside the area had heard of our Los Angeles Campaign.

"Supposedly, [Hearst] had sent a message to his editors, 'Puff Graham,' but there were so many stories about how we might have come to his notice and about why he might have been interested in promoting us that I did not know which, if any, was true....

"The newspaper coverage was just the beginning of a phenomenon. As more and more extraordinary conversion stories caught the public's attention, the meetings continued night after night, drawing overflow crowds.... God may have used Mr. Hearst to promote the meetings, as [my wife] Ruth said, but the credit belonged solely to God."

The moral: When you have a project of caring and sharing, attempting to make the world kinder and more humane, there is absolutely nothing wrong with "puffing" yourself and your good work.

WRITING THE PRESS RELEASE

The press release is the basic element of every promotional campaign. It is your organization's formal "calling card." Phone calls and even personal visits to newspapers and radio and television stations are useful, but a well-crafted press release establishes your organization's seriousness and professionalism.

The rules for a good press release are actually fairly standardized. This is one reason why you need to learn how they are done; a press release delivered in the wrong format or written poorly will tip off an editor immediately that you are unfamiliar with working with the media.

The key to writing press releases is to think like a reporter. Julia Duin, an editor at the *Washington Times*, clarifies this, saying, "That means you're conveying news. Apply the traditional elements of a news story: Who? What? When? Where? Why? How?"

It is best to follow the classic inverted-pyramid style of newspaper writing. This means that you should always start with the broadest statement of what it is you're trying to publicize. The incidental details come later, after the really large, important points.

The next most important rule is to be sure to *type* your press release double-spaced. Use one-inch margins on clean, white paper. Journalists get a blizzard of releases, and one that isn't clearly typed and easy to read is destined for the round file.

Other major pointers for writing professional press releases are

1. *Tell them who you are.* Journalists want to know who is contacting them, so put the name of your organization prominently at the top of your release. Any ambiguity on this point invites skepticism.

2. *Date and time the release.* It might say RELEASE IMMEDIATELY if you want the media to use the information right away. Or it might say RELEASE AT WILL if there is no time-sensitivity to the material you are providing. But if you have an event set for an appointed time, you might not want information published about it too far in advance. A specific release date can help ensure that media notice is close enough to the event so it will be fresh in the public's mind. A release date also lends an air of expectancy and importance to the information you're sharing.

3. *Use active language.* Stress that a person is doing something or that an event is happening. Example: "A thousand bicyclists will converge at the high school April 10 for a ride-athon for charity." The words "will converge" convey activism, dynamism.

4. *Get your facts right, and state them clearly with specificity.* If it's a bicycle ride for charity, don't leave out the word "bicycle." A mere "ride for charity" could mean a gaggle of Harleys.

5. *Place the crucial information at the beginning of the release.* This is because smaller newspapers actually print the press release verbatim, and some TV and radio announcers read it verbatim on the air, but to save space or time, they sometimes cut a few of the later paragraphs. This means that if you don't have the essential information up front, it may get lost.

6. *Quote someone from your organization.* Include in the body of the release a quote giving an opinion or expressing optimism about the event from a member of your group. Whenever you can include a name and a quoted statement, you add personality to your release. If the person involved is you, go ahead and quote yourself. Whoever you quote should be uttering concise, cogent remarks that would make nice copy in a news story that you hope will be built on your release.

7. Snap, crackle, pop—*especially in headlines.* Make your headlines lively if you can. Use alliteration, puns, a dash of humor. But even if you adopt a more straightforward style, be to the point. You shouldn't expect a newspaper to use your headline at the top of its story, but a sharply focused, catchy head can catch the eye and steer coverage of your event or issue.

8. *Be brief.* Brevity pays, in the body of your release as well in headlines. Journalists are busy, and their trade teaches them to lead with the basics of a story so they're going to look for your basic message in the first few sentences. If you haven't succinctly and concisely told the reader, at the top of your copy, why you want their attention, you won't get it. So make your sentences and paragraphs short, simple and declarative. Much closer to *Dick and Jane* than to Dickens.

9. *Add details.* Although brevity is important, so is emphasizing a few interesting details. These can bring your story alive.

10. *Don't overwrite.* Don't attempt to write the story for the journalist. Media people have pride just like the rest of us, and you might earn unnecessary demerits in someone's eyes if you give the impression that you're trying to tell the journalists their business.

11. *Write conversationally.* Don't use highfalutin writing. "This serves to inform you" is the kind of stilted phrase you should never use. Read your prose to yourself and ask whether those are the words you would use to convey the same message if you were speaking to someone.

12. *Have something to say.* What you have to say is as important as how you say it. There must be something there, i.e., some substance to your release. This is where your promotional creativity intersects with the demands of PR. The release will have much more impact if it's advertising something—an event, a campaign—that displays creative verve. Certainly, there are some cut-and-dried occasions, such as the naming of a new member to your organization's board of directors, that warrant a press release too. But see how much more pizzazz it would have if the new director, say, was a former down-on-his-luck recipient of your charity, who has turned his life around. In other words, there is a case for letting substance follow form—that is, for making substantive decisions with an eye not just to the intrinsic merits of the matter, but also to the publicity, the promotional potential of what you decide.

13. *Keep your audience in mind.* Tailor each release to the interests of that particular media outlet. Remember that the needs of TV will be different from those of radio, and also from those of newspaper journalists, so vary your release accordingly. For instance, in a release to television stations, you might emphasize the visual possibilities in the story you're promoting. For radio, you might stress that a brief interview—either in the field or over the phone—can be obtained with a principal figure in your organization. With newspapers, you might mention an opportunity for an interesting photo.

14. *Don't ignore geographical distinctions.* If you're sending releases to areas outside your own community, keep in mind that interests and concerns can differ from place to place. One angle of your story that might appeal to journalists and their audiences in San Francisco, while quite another angle might capture interest in Indianapolis. Tailor your promotional emphasis with location and local attitudes in mind.

15. *Include a contact person.* What good is one-way communication? You want journalists to be able to get back to you for more of your insights and golden words. So provide a name, telephone number, address, maybe an e-mail address and a fax number as well.

16. *At the end of the release, put the characters # # #,* which is the commonly used symbol to indicate that the reader has reached the end of the release.

Examples of Press Releases

Following are several examples of press releases.

Short and Sweet Release

Here is a good example of a succinct press release. Notice the first paragraph.

Make-A-Wish Foundation	12121 Wilshire Blvd. Suite 310
of Los Angeles	Los Angeles, California 90025
	(310) 207-3023
	FAX: (310) 207-6989

FOR IMMEADIATE RELEASE	FOR MORE INFORMATION
December 6, 1997	Ann Flower/Hollis Maiers
	(310) 275-0777

ANNOUNCING THE LOS ANGELES CHAPTER'S MAKE-A-WISH FOUNDATION
THIRD ANNUAL "LOVE OF FLYING" WINE AUCTION

Santa Monica, CA—The 1996 "Love of Flying... For the Love of Children" Wine and Lifestyle Auction is set to be held at the Museum of Flying, located at the Santa Monica Airport, on February 9. The Wine House will once again co-sponsor the event with the Los Angeles Chapter of the Make-A-Wish Foundation, to raise funds to grant the wishes of children with terminal and life-threatening illnesses.

Over forty wineries and eight top Los Angeles Restaurants are expected to participate, with over one hundred items alone in the silent auction, including rare wines, travel packages and unique Hollywood themed items. A five-night stay at the Ritz Carlton Mauna Lani Resort on the big island of Hawaii, including airfare, is one of the auction highlights.

The wine and food tasting and silent auction commences at 6:00 P.M., with live auction beginning at 8:00 P.M. Tickets are $50 per person in advance, $60 at the door.

For more information or to reserve tickets, please call Trish Cantillon, Make-A-Wish Foundation, at (800) 322-WISH.

# # #

Perhaps you noticed that all the basic information was is presented in the first paragraph.

- ✦ *Who?* The Make A Wish Foundation.
- ✦ *When?* February 9.
- ✦ *Where?* Museum of Flying.
- ✦ *What?* An auction.
- ✦ *Why?* To raise funds.

Long Press Release

This release was sent out by the Presidents' Summit for America's Future ("the Philadelphia Summit") which was held in 1997. The full release was actually three pages long, far longer than the accepted length of one page, but the writers were announcing such a powerfully newsworthy event that one might argue they had an obligation to go on for more than the recommended one page. This was not a release that was going to be ignored by the media, regardless of length. But, in general, for your own community charity efforts, the one-page rule applies.

FOR RELEASE:
January 24, 1997

CONTACT:
Jim Issokson
1-800-639-1288
or 202-371-8122

CLINTON, BUSH ANNOUNCE PRESIDENTS' SUMMIT ON SERVICE

Washington, D.C.—President Bill Clinton and former President George Bush, joined by Vice President Al Gore, today announced "The Presidents' Summit for America's Future," aimed at bringing America to a new level of commitment to volunteer service, especially targeting the nation's young people.

President Clinton, former President Bush and the other former Presidents will serve as honorary Co-Chairs of the Summit, which will be held April 27–29 in Philadelphia....

General Colin Powell will serve as General Chairman....

In announcing the Summit, President Clinton said, "Much of the work of America cannot be done by government, much other work cannot be done by government alone. The solution must be the American people through voluntary service to others."

In today's East Room announcement, former President Bush said, "The Philadelphia summit is about getting more people off the sidelines, It is about citizens pulling together, leading by example, and lifting lives."

Summit partners point to growing evidence that young people today face serious threats to their futures—and even their lives; thus, the urgency leading to the April Summit. Studies show, for instance, that:

- A child is abused every 13 seconds in America, with almost 3 million reports of such abuse filed each year.
- 1 in 9 African-Americans between the age of 12-15 are victims of violent crime.
- The number of children under age six living in poverty has increased 50% since 1979.
- Cigarette and marijuana use is increasing again among high school students.
- Suicide rates for children between 5-14 doubled between 1970-1988

The Summit is organized on the proposition that America's young people must have access to five fundamental resources that can help them lead healthy, fulfilling and productive lives:

- An ongoing relationship with a caring adult or mentor;
- Safe places to learn and grow;
- A healthy start;
- A marketable skill through effective education;
- An opportunity to give back through community service.

In the weeks leading up to the Summit, a national partnership engaging dozens of leaders and organizations from all sectors will develop targets for specific increases in volunteer service and put in place the framework for an extensive follow-up campaign.

Some of the substantial commitments that already have been made include the following:

- Columbia/HCA Healthcare Corporation has committed to immunize one million children by the year 2000....
- LensCrafters will provide one million needy people, especially children, with vision care by the year 2003.
- Communities in Schools will expand its programs [to serve] an additional 750,000 young people in need....
- The Greek Orthodox Church in America has committed to assist one needy child per every ten families in the more than 550 Greek Orthodox churches nationwide.
- Big Brothers/Big Sisters has committed to doubling their mentoring relationships, reaching 200,000 matches through the year 2000....
- Shell Oil has made a corporate wide commitment to support all five goals of the Summit at every level of the company through expanded employee volunteering, targeted corporate philanthropy, and promotional support.

# # #

As you can see, this release offered plenty of basic information, plus a variety of facts and statistics to support its position. You can do the same, although it is generally better to do so using one page, not three.

Humorous Press Release

Consider this example from the chemical company, Monsanto.

NATIONAL S.W.A.T. TEAM WAGES WAR ON WEEDS

St. Louis—In one of the most intense busts of the season, a S.W.A.T. Team descended upon Miami's Metrozoo this month. The Spontaneous Weed Attack Team sponsored by Roundup® grass and weed killer launched a full-scale attack on weeds in the Miami Metrozoo. More than 100 volunteers joined the S.W.A.T. Team to help eliminate weeds; volunteers covered over 500,000 square feet of the zoo and parking areas.

"With the aftermath of Hurricane Andrew, the Roundup S.W.A.T. Team couldn't have come at a better time," said Ron Magill, assistant curator of the zoo. "Roundup has been used by the zoo for many years. It's the one product we've found that won't harm the animals and still does a great job of removing unwanted vegetation." Since the hurricane, zoo staff has focused on restoring animal habitats and creating support systems for the thousands of trees that were uprooted by the hurricane winds.

The Spontaneous Weed Attack Team visit to Miami's Metrozoo was the final stop on a ten-city tour including San Antonio, Houston, Dallas, St. Louis, Salt Lake City, Chicago, New Orleans, Denver and Minneapolis. The S.W.A.T. Team descended on each of these cities between March and June.

The Spontaneous Weed Attack Team partnered with local community beautification groups in each of the above cities to maximize the local involvement in the project.

(Note: The release makes it clear that it can end here after one page, a helpful point of demarcation for busy journalists, but it also includes the following additional facts on subsequent pages)

S.W.A.T. leaders at each community organization identified a site in need of clean-up efforts, recruited local volunteers to join the S.W.A.T. Team and helped to organize the clean-up day. The list of community partners from 1997 is an impressive one. [A series of philanthropic city-beautification programs is mentioned here: this is a good plug for groups that have lent assistance to Monsanto's project.]

"The S.W.A.T. Team was designed to respond to specific needs of each community. Each S.W.A.T. event reflected the enthusiasm and dedication of a different group of people," said Danna McKay, Roundup brand manager for Monsanto. "Roundup is proud to have been a part of so many worthwhile projects."

# # #

In this release we see the same pattern, in which the essence of the message is painted in broad strokes in the first paragraph. The second, third, and fourth paragraphs provide support, with examples and quotes, which all to add the substance. Quotes are effective in personalizing the release, and in giving subjective interpretation in the guise of something resembling news reportage.

In these ways, the best press releases mimic newspaper writing. The opening paragraphs answer the classic questions—who, what, when, where, and why—and the successive paragraphs provide supporting information.

Timing Your Press Releases

A press release should be timed to hit the newsroom with maximum effect. When you're sending to TV and radio stations—and you have a breaking story about an event you're doing—it's best to get it in the journalists' hands by ten in the morning, so it can be used for the noon, afternoon, and nightly news.

Timing of the event itself is also important, if you want the event to generate publicity. Pay attention to news cycles: Do press conferences in the mornings, for instance, in order to get under the wire for those midday newscasts. And weekends are dicey for holding press conferences and other publicity-seeking functions. The competition for the public's attention is massive on the weekend, so even if you do get some media coverage, the impact is diluted.

As for how many releases to send out, follow the advice of PR consultant Jeff Davidson. "The media need grist for stories," he said. "The average person doesn't realize that the media need them. Most news releases get thrown away. But the number of column inches that even one can get, as opposed to paying for an ad, is really quite a bonanza."

Many publicity consultants suggest getting in the habit of sending out a release at least every thirty days or so. They add that you must find substantive reasons for doing so. "I had enough things going that I could send out at least one a month to various publications," he says. "I wrote a news release about my writing news releases. It was called 'Local consultant publishes two-hundreth article.' You, too, can do it for the three-hundreth, for the four-hundreth—it's like Hank Aaron hitting home runs. It's news."

Keep plugging, because the people and organizations who persist, have an automatic advantage over others—simply because most others don't. "The paradox of promotion is that the average person doesn't like to sell himself," says Davidson. Your challenge is to rise above such misconceptions and accept that it's a privilege to be able to tell the world about your good work.

Tips from Professional Publicists on Press Releases

Here are some tips from a variety of journalists on getting your release read and your information placed, as recounted in a newsletter published by New York publisher Jack O'Dwyer.

✦ PR veteran William Parkhurst, says, "People believe that TV producers and editors are too busy to take telephone calls—that their feature ideas spring exclusively from their staffs. But they're wrong." He adds, as the *Washington Post* puts it, that tens of millions of dollars' worth of media exposure is given away every day by 1,699 daily newspapers, more than 5,000 magazines, 4,857 commercial AM stations, 4,500 radio, television and cable talk shows, 3,421 commercial FM stations, and other media in the United States. The formula for getting some of that free coverage is simple, he says: "You have something to say, you're excited about it, you take it to the media and you benefit from the exposure."

✦ George Tabor, editor of *Business for Central New Jersey*, said the first question he wants answered is, "Where is the organization located?

✦ Chuck Lyon, publisher of a Forbes chain of seventeen suburban weeklies, emphasized that his newspapers "niche" in the community is important in determining what releases to pay attention to. This suggests that it is important that you be sure you understand the mission of a local newspaper before sending them your press releases and expecting them to publish your news.

✦ Hannelle Rubin, lifestyle editor for the *New Brunswick Home News*, prefers "little old lady" people stories. This human-interest angle ought to be easy for charity groups that work with people in need of help.

✦ Terry Mattingly, a columnist for the Scripps-

Howard News Service, says, "Call the reporters and editors to whom you've sent the release, telling them you wanted to make sure they got it. Tell them you would be glad to answer any questions. In fact, it can be effective to have another point concerning your issue—something held back from the release itself—to add when you reach them by phone, so you can strengthen the case for their running your story." Mattingly adds that if the journalist says it's unlikely your release will trigger an immediate story, you might suggest that they keep the information on hand, as material for a feature piece later dealing with the issue your nonprofit is all about. Remember: Reporters and editors are hungry consumers of good ideas for feature pieces. If you have genuine fodder for this need, they will welcome you as a water-bearer is welcomed across a desert plain.

✦ Mary Toothman of the *Tampa Tribune* expresses a gripe that "most news releases do not contain much news." Also, many of those seeking publicity don't know "what information they should send which reporter." A preparatory phone call to the news room can help on that score.

✦ Andrea Adelson, a writer for the *New York Times* business section, says the key is newsworthiness. "For a press release to grab my attention, it has to be genuinely newsworthy," she says. "The release has to be more than fancy writing—although, frankly, writing that has flair is a great help, too." Themes that provide some irony or juxtaposition are what catch Adelson's eye. "For instance, there was the small clothing company that described their battle to get farmers weaned off of pesticides and to grow organic cotton. I thought, that's fascinating, a credible manufacturer—but a small one—trying to change an entire manufacturing base; a small David taking on a Goliath of sorts." As for length of press releases, Adelson has "four pointers," she says: "One page, one page, one page, one page."

A TITLE SAYS A THOUSAND WORDS

A brochure lists the phone numbers and addresses of the many Jewish Federation Beneficiary Agencies, from the Bet Tzedek Legal Services, which offers counsel to the needy, to the Jewish Family Service of Los Angeles, which provides counseling and dozens of programs for people of all ages, to the Jewish Vocational Service, which provides job-search assistance. The brochure is entitled, creatively and accurately…

The Other 911

WRITING A PITCH LETTER

Writing press releases may not be your style. Entertainment-industry columnist Marilyn Beck says she prefers receiving a letter. "If it is personally addressed, and written to me individually, it has more impact than a formal press release," she says.

The same basics of structure and clarity apply with letters to the media as with press releases. "With a pitch letter, you're doing just that—pitching a news story idea," says Ken Grubbs, editor of *World Trade* magazine. "You want to tell the editor a little bit about your story, enough to spark some interest. You write it as a personal letter, then follow up with a phone call in which you flesh out the story and suggest interview subjects."

If you decide to write a letter rather than a press release, be sure to include your own name, address, and phone number, in case the recipients want to get in touch with you. Address the letter to the editor of the appropriate division of the news organization (Sports, Lifestyles, et cetera), by name. Then, in no more than three short paragraphs, tell the editor the basics of the story—who, what, when, where, why. "The letter should offer to help with arranging interviews and other fact finding, along with photography possibilities," says Grubbs. "And it should promise a follow-up call from the writer at a set time."

"Your pitch letter can only be as good as the newsworthiness of the story," says Jeff Nelligan, communications director for one of the major committees of the U.S. House of Representatives, and formerly an editorial-board member of the *San Diego Union*. This means that you need to develop the instincts of a journalist. Think of these questions:

◆ Is what your organization is doing really something that would interest the media's audience?

◆ Is it timely? If it happened last week, or even two days ago, you're no longer talking about hard, "breaking" news. It then has to be something that can be pitched as a softer feature or human-interest piece.

◆ Is the story something that you don't read about every day? If it isn't, if it's not unusual, you might want to rethink promoting it.

◆ Is it a subject that would have wide interest among the public? Ask some of your friends the question. If you have strong doubts, cast about for a livelier subject.

In addition, don't count on journalists reading everything in your letter, word for word. Most of them are too busy, too distracted to take much time with any particular pitch letter—or, indeed, any one news release. They want to see the basics of your story, which means you must crystallize the message as succinctly as possible, just as in a press release. On the other hand, don't assume an editor knows and understands everything about the subject that you do. While you shouldn't talk down to anyone in a letter, keeping your prose and message understandable for any level of education is a must. If you're writing about computers, write as if your reader thinks of sweaters and cotton pants when he hears the term "software."

And, just as with news releases, know what kind of publication you're writing to. This is a big point, and an area of big mistakes for too many charities and nonprofits seeking to promote themselves. Too many people simply don't read the newspapers or magazines to which they're sending material. The competent publicist never makes that mistake. In my office we receive the *New York Times*, the *Wall Street Journal*, *USA Today*, and the *Los Angeles Times* every day, and I read them, every day. I also read a significant number of periodicals weekly or monthly, along with trade and industry publications. Of course, I don't read everything from front to back, but I do read the vast majority of the stories. The fact is, every paper has an individual tone and texture. The *New York Times* is very different from *USA Today*; the *San Francisco Chronicle* has a feel and outlook quite distinct from, say, the *Orange County Register*. Someone who tries to pitch a story to a newspaper without knowing its individual focus risks throwing away time, stamps, and money for the phone call. It simply isn't smart—and it definitely isn't professional.

"This problem is especially acute, in my experience, in religious groups and the community of smaller nonprofit organizations," says Terry Mattingly, a columnist on religion and culture for the Scripps-Howard News Service and an assistant professor of communications at Milligan College in Tennessee. "Lots of people in nonprofits, I've found, seem to assume that, because they think it's a big story, the editor or reporter that they call up will have to see that it's printed. A lot of people don't bother to learn who the appropriate editor is for their topic. It's easy enough to get this information—in advance—by calling the paper, or the news service."

Indeed, Mattingly suggests that some charities and nonprofits see people in the media from a sense of entitlement, a belief that the media should be an automatic pass-through mechanism for their important story. "They have to learn that the media itself is an audience that they've got to sell," he says. "It's not a matter of a message being transmitted directly from nonprofit or church group to the general public. Rather, it's like the bumper shot in a game of pool—instead of the story moving directly from sender to receiver (through the passive hands of editors and reporters), the diagram is from sender to news personnel and then, possibly, to mass audience."

GOBBLE, GOBBLE FOR A GOOD CAUSE

"Radio station promoters have found creative uses for turkeys during the holiday season.

"Two stations raised 1,000 pounds of donated food for the Atlanta Community Food Bank with "turkey bowls." For a can of food, contestants got to roll frozen turkeys down bowling lanes for strikes and spares. There weren't any holes in the turkeys, so it was a two-handed task.

"Another station raised $1,200 selling three chances, for a dollar donation, to toss a ten-pound turkey through a basketball net. The food bank also got all the birds."

The Atlanta Journal and Constitution,
December 14, 1991

SPECIAL ISSUES FOR RELIGIOUS GROUPS

When she was a religion writer and editor in southern California, Roberta Green Ahmanson became accustomed to dealing with the sense of entitlement that Mattingly talks about. "People used to call me up at the newspaper and tell me God had told them I would write their story," says Ahmanson, who is now executive vice president and COO of Fieldstead and Company, Inc., a private philanthropy founded by her husband, Howard Ahmanson. "I told them that when God told me that, I would."

In his Scripps-Howard column, which reaches more than three hundred newspapers, Terry Mattingly has identified some key mistakes—and offered salient advice—to religious groups and charities seeking a better relationship with the media. Here is one such column.

"It never took long to learn if the angry caller on the other end of the news editor's line was from a church.

"This is a green frog," my boss would say, in a post-root-canal moan. "Would you please take care of this?" By definition, a "green frog" was an irrational, irritating reader and the quickest way to earn this label was to mention God. Back in the late 1970s, the *Champaign-Urbana News-Gazette's* editors knew that my goal was to become a religion writer. Thus, I handled all the religious "green frogs." These callers often had good reasons to be mad. Studies have shown that journalists commit sins of omission and commission when it comes to religion news. The media often ignore pivotal religious events and trends and mangle important stories.

However, irate callers can do more harm than good. I thought about these "green frogs" recently when a colleague, James Davis of the *Fort Lauderdale* (Fla.) *Sun-Sentinel*, posted a call for help on the Internet. He had agreed to speak in a church forum and was listing steps readers could take to improve religion coverage. So I sent him a list of my favorite ideas and he sent me his. Here's a sample.

✦ Most religious people, especially conservatives, assume that journalists detest them. This is wrong. Some journalists detest religious people, but research indicates that many more don't care about, or know much about, the lives of religious people.

✦ I've heard war stories about how coverage was improved through one step: clergy and lay leaders inviting journalists to lunch or to visit their churches…. Researcher Quentin Schultze suggests that church leaders seek out journalists as guest speakers.

✦ Church folks should volunteer names and telephone numbers for journalists' files of quotable experts and sources. The goal is to create channels of information. Journalists can't cover stories, or include viewpoints, if they don't know that they exist.

✦ Return telephone calls from journalists promptly and, during interviews, never assume that they understand your flock's divine dialect. Slow down and define your terms.

✦ Learn to call the right persons. Davis stressed that it doesn't help to whine to the religion reporter about a copy editor's mistake, or to a city editor about a wave of editorial-page columns. The same is true of calls praising stories.

✦ Luckily, newspeople are—in an age of declining readership—striving to improve public relations. The local newsroom may have a staffer in charge of public affairs who can provide names, telephone numbers and explanations of who handles what news chores.

✦ It helps to learn newsroom mechanics—such as deadlines and proper formats for press releases. Religious leaders who pay close attention to newspapers will do a better job of discerning what editors do, and do not, consider news.

✦ Callers must stress to editors—and mean it—that they are not interested in eliminating critical coverage. The goal is balanced coverage of controversial religious and social issues.

✦ Once a dialogue has begun, religious leaders can use rulers and scissors and do some hands-on research— such as measuring and counting quotations, stories, letters and editorial-page pieces.

A "green frog" who calls and says, "Why is your paper doing everything it can to destroy churches and send souls to hell," will accomplish very little. It's different to call and say, "Excuse me, I've been reading your paper closely for three months and, I know you're very busy, but are you aware that you've run twenty-five columns criticizing religious people and only two defending them? Did you know that you've printed one local religion story in three months in a city in which more people attend worship services in a month than attend sporting events in a year?"

In other words, the wise religious leader may, on occasion, need to inspire journalistic shame. Many editors could care less about theology, but might be shaken if chided—accurately—for committing journalistic heresies.

MAKING FOLLOW-UP PHONE CALLS

After a press release or pitch letter, a follow-up call can be useful, but only if you do it with grace and integrity. Show some consideration for the editor's schedule by asking if he or she is on deadline, can you speak now or can you call back later. The middle of the afternoon, from two-thirty or so to four P.M., usually offers a lull in many newsrooms, as reporters do research on the stories that have been mapped out in noon-hour editorial meetings. If you call before the deadline crunch approaches from four-thirty P.M. on, you're likely to get someone on the other end of the line who isn't too hurried. When you speak with an editor, be clear and accurate with your facts. And don't keep pushing if the journalist shows a lack of interest. You want to retain the editor's goodwill for when you're promoting a story in the future.

OTHER OPPORTUNITIES TO GET INTO THE PRINT MEDIA

There are three additional methods by which your organization can get your name into the mainstream print media:

✦ Writing op-ed articles.
✦ Writing letters to the editor.
✦ Appearing at an editorial board meeting.

Here are details on each method.

Writing Op-Ed Articles

In addition to press releases, many leaders of nonprofit groups try to have articles they write published in their local newspapers' opinion-editorial (op-ed) sections. This can be a very useful tool for a charity organization.

In fact, one of the earliest promotional campaigns in American history was conducted by means of newspaper opinion pieces. The Federalist Papers were a collection of op-ed pieces written to promote the proposed Constitution of the United States. The writing campaign to win the Constitution's adoption was conducted by Alexander Hamilton, John Jay, and James Madison. Political scientist David Truman has called it "one of the most skillful and important examples of pressure group activity in American history." Historian Allan Nevins called it "history's finest public-relations job." So the opinion piece as promotional tool has a glorious lineage.

Good op-ed writing is a basic but important element in the nonprofit's arsenal. It helps put your organization in the public's eye. Submitting opinion articles or letters to the local newspaper can be a valuable form of promotion in itself. For example, when Oliver Stone was finishing work on his film *JFK*, the movie was ferociously criticized in the *Washington Post* for taking liberties with historical truth. Not long afterward, the *New York Times* reported that Warner Brothers hired Frank Mankiewicz, the Washington press-relations executive and former campaign manager for Robert F. Kennedy, to promote the film and seek support in the news media for Mr. Stone. The article reported that Mankiewicz coached Stone in writing. A few weeks later, people began noticing thoughtful articles written by Oliver Stone in many of the nation's op-ed pages. This public-relations ploy helped muffle criticism of the film, which went on to box-office success. "Frank just knows how Washington works," Stone says. "He got us into the right audience, got the movie presented as a serious historical statement."

In addition, op-ed writing often hones your personal skills in public speaking. When you write editorially about a project that your group is undertaking, or a cause your group seeks to promote, you are forced to distill your thoughts and set them down in an orderly form. This pre-thinking makes you more lucid, more coherent about your ideas, so if the occasion arises for you to give a presentation about your organization before a group or even in one-on-one conversation, you are well prepared.

You may find it difficult to get an editor to commission an article by you, if you lack a track record. You'll probably have to submit your offering on a "for inspection" basis. However, Tom Gray, editorial-page editor of *Investor's Business Daily*, says, "Many editorial-section editors are more likely to consider a freelance opinion piece if the author has some special personal expertise, and brings that extra edge of authority. And it's good to look for a news hook, something in the headlines recently, that your article addresses or uses as a point of departure." Make sure your facts are all straight, he cautions: "Along with writers' special knowledge about a subject, their credibility is what you're valued for."

Here are some tips on writing op-ed articles.

✦ *Aim for clear, simple writing.* Choose short words over long ones, and familiar words over unfamiliar. Keep sentences brief and simple in structure. Write like you talk. Write to express, not impress. Avoid unneeded words. Use words that readers can picture.

✦ *Grab the reader's attention from the outset.* Although most opinion essays have three parts—a statement of the subject, a comment on it, and a conclusion or solution—these sections don't necessarily have to proceed in that order. "It is important, however, that the opening...be sufficiently provocative to attract the reader or listener," journalism professor Harry Stonecipher noted in his book, *Editorial and Persuasive Writing*. He cited a colorful opening passage from a *Gainesville Sun* editorial about the dangerous conditions in the local schools.

"Wanted: Young, skinny, wiry fellows not over 18. Must be expert riders, willing to risk death daily. Orphans preferred."

That's how the Pony Express advertised for mail carriers back in 1860. It was a cliff-hanging occupation defying Indians, weather and renegades.

But the advertisement also pretty much describes the hazards of the Alachua County school system....

This op-ed opening certainly makes you want to read on, as you think the piece has something to do with the Pony Express. However, the author used the difficulty of being a pony express rider as a metaphor for what it is like to be in the local school system.

✦ *Argue logically, in a straight line.* Try to have each of your points follow the previous one naturally, linked by a reference, implied or explicit, to the thought just finished.

✦ *Write at the level of your readers, and write to persuade, not to bludgeon.* Consider what your readers' perspectives are. If you know that many of them hold opinions different from yours, take those opinions as a starting point, acknowledging them respectfully. Then set forth your rational, calmly-expressed reasons as to why readers should consider a different outlook.

✦ *Provide plenty of factual references.* You'll be writing on behalf of a nonprofit cause, which probably means you'll be attempting to inform more than to argue. That makes it especially important that you provide concrete examples of the problems your group is tackling, and the success you've achieved. But even opinion articles require solid factual examples if they are not to be dismissed as "just" opinion.

✦ *Close by appealing to readers' aspirations, not their fears.* Don't end with a dispirited conclusion that suggests there are only problems, not solutions. After all, you, and your charity, are the solution you want readers to accept. Convey a sense of optimism about your work; it can be contagious.

✦ *Get to know the paper and what kinds of pieces they tend to use.* Whether they might be straight political opinion, or feature pieces that look at people and culture, or occasional humor essays. And when you're submitting to a local paper, get as much local angle into the piece as possible.

For op-ed pieces, keep your length to around 750 words. Fax it or mail it—or both—to the editorial-page editor, or opinion-page editor whose name appears in the opinion section. Follow up with a phone call.

Here is an example of an op-ed piece I wrote, expressing my opinion about the dire lack of heroes in our culture.

Current times do not produce many legendary heroes. Although we have an abundance of "celebrities," few seem to possess the eminence that leads to enduring fame. Vying for space in *People* and *US* magazines by posing for photos in bathtubs and telling often too much about their personal lives on numerous talk shows, today's celebrities, however talented, have devalued the currency of stardom. As Emerson suggested, "Every hero becomes a bore at last," and the process today is swift.

Curiously enough, we haven't really cherished heroes for a good twenty years. Though the assassination of President Kennedy, the Vietnam War and the Watergate affair are convenient and overused targets of blame for all sorts of national ailments and trends, these events did indeed reduce our want or need for heroes or, perhaps, the country's ability to embrace them.

A shift, however, may be under way, particularly among youth and adults under thirty. In a recent survey taken by the Roper Organization for a national news magazine, respondents clearly accepted the concept of heroes and noted a liking for the movie stars Clint Eastwood, Eddie Murphy, Jane Fonda and Sally Field; the movie director

Steven Spielberg; the pope; and former President Reagan. Interprets the George Washington University sociologist Amitai Etzioni: "We're back to yearning for leadership."

Yet a great difference lies between a widely admired personage and a legend. Within the last half-century or so America has had its share of heroes, including Charles Lindbergh, the generals Patton and MacArthur, and President Franklin D. Roosevelt. But precious few still captivate our collective imaginations. Among those who do, five names come to mind and stand out: Elvis Presley, James Dean, Babe Ruth, Marilyn Monroe and John Wayne.

What makes these five disparate personalities legends? What compels people to pay $6,500 for an 18-inch, porcelain model of Monroe or to dedicate rooms in their houses to Presley memorabilia? None of the five had any impact on politics, economics or the physical betterment of the nation. Ruth played baseball, and the others were entertainers. Why revere them, and not great physicians and scientists?

In sober analysis, actors aren't real-life "heroes." Although fans are aware that Clint "Make My Day" Eastwood doesn't really bend laws and bypass the bureaucracy to justly punish brutal criminals, it's what he represents on the screen that counts. Thus, the fantasy projections ultimately develop a kind of substance in the minds of viewers.

Values, then, are the key. Each of the five legends came to stand for something—common but unarticulated feelings or values—far greater than career success. Ruth embodied the rugged, individualistic, winning image America had of itself; Presley and Dean provided a voice for the disaffected and restless youth of the postwar generation; Monroe represented the vanguard of the sexual revolution; and "Duke" Wayne cannot be psychically separated from his patriotic political stance.

Other elements of their lives certainly contributed. An untimely death surely catalyzed the Dean legend; the relatively early passings of Presley and Monroe lent them a tragic aura. All but Wayne grew up poor, orphaned, or abandoned by their parents and started out against great odds. Each, despite glamour, also had a common touch. Yet all five projected an element of danger, a volatility that nonetheless was attractive.

As the historian Marshall Fishwick explains in his book, *American Heroes: Myth and Reality:* "Our legends [believe] they can do any damn thing they set their minds to." Our idols, he believes, "don't like fences." Presley, Dean, Ruth, Monroe, and Wayne were strong, willful, fence-busting personalities. Moreover, at a time when celebrity is precarious, when notable figures wear thin, these five transcend celebrity. It may be a long while before anyone else can speak for and capture the hearts of so many, like these legends that won't die.

Writing a Letter to the Editor

This is another opportunity to get your opinion in print, as most newspapers print several letters every day. For a letter to the editor, keep your submission under 200 words to maximize your chances of getting published. Make your point with pithiness and precision. Letters that wander without getting to any point are unlikely to run. Also, try to address an issue recently in the news—preferably a story that was generated by the paper you're writing to, as opposed to a wire story: This adds timeliness and immediacy. Although letters can be mailed to a newspaper, many papers now have fax numbers and e-mail address that they also list on their editorial pages. Surveys show that letters to the editor have a high readership, so this is definitely one avenue to consider.

Scan the news for items that can be tied, in a letter, to issues that your nonprofit works on, so you can bring your organization into the community's discussion of current events easily and naturally.

Editorial Board Meetings

There is one last form of newspaper-related work you can attempt to get your organization into the press: the editorial board session. This is a meeting that you and your organization can have with the editorial writers at the newspaper. Such a meeting holds the potential of triggering a mention of your group in one of the newspaper's official editorials, the unsigned essays that are meant to be statements of the newspaper's positions on issues of the day.

To set up an editorial board meeting, a phone call to the editorial-page editor is appropriate, followed, if the editor requests it, by printed information faxed or mailed to the paper. You are more likely to have your request for a board meeting granted if you have genuine, hard news to report about your organization, and if the news has an important impact on the community. Try to tie your news angles to issues of controversy that are in the press day-in-and-day-out. Relate your organization's issues to a matter that happens to be getting a lot of press today. Offer your own experience as a newsworthy perspective on that issue. Keep your presentation short—twenty minutes is ideal. And bring some coherent fact sheets to leave behind.

One more pointer: Avoid going to editorial board meetings in large groups. This can get unwieldy. One or two people from your group is sufficient.

BUILDING A FULL MEDIA KIT

If you're ambitious enough, and your organization has resources for the investment, you might consider going beyond the mere one-or two-page press release every so often by distributing full-fledged media kits to targeted producers, editors, and reporters. However, you should be aware that media kits can be very expensive to prepare and mail.

In the most common format, a media kit includes a number of items, including

✦ issue briefs, which are well-written essays or papers explaining your organizations mission or cause;
✦ reproduced news clippings from stories already printed about you;
✦ fact sheets about your cause or organization that succinctly present the data you want the media to know; and
✦ a current press release.

All of these items should be printed on 8½"x 11" paper and placed together in a glossy folder with pockets. Many organizations add some photographs as well. In addition, to distinguish your kit from others, you might want to have logo or some kind of identifying title or statement printed on the outside of the folder. While that feature can run up the cost, a "naked" folder with no logo is less likely to draw the journalist's attention and more likely to be misplaced or get thrown away.

How effective is a media kit? "It has physical bulk, and for that reason it probably stands a better chance than a press release of being kept and filed for reference in future stories," says Julia Duin. Andrea Adelson of the *New York Times* appreciates media kits—but only if all the handouts in them have hard information." Duin says that including photos increases the chance that a story will run. "A photo draws the journalist's eye, and can capture the imagination. At smaller papers, where the photography staff is slight, it also gives the editors a graphic to use without having to send someone out with a camera—and that might make them more inclined to do a story."

With larger newspapers especially, the hard truth is that even the best-written press release or meatiest media packet doesn't guarantee you immediate news coverage. How many nonprofit press releases trigger news stories? "Very few," longtime *San Francisco Chronicle* editor Jerry Burns told public-relations writer Dave Knesel.

"Most are of such narrow (albeit sincere) interest, we just toss them. There are some exceptions, of course, such as when the Salvation Army celebrates the one-hundreth anniversary of its Christmas kettles or something like that. We're not bad guys and we like to help when we can, but we've got only a finite amount of room in the paper and there is great competition among articles for space."

This is one of the reasons that a media kit, packed with useful information about a social issue and the nonprofit's response to it, can be especially valuable. As Julia Duin says, it is more likely to be kept around for future use than a mere press release. On the other hand, a *Wall Street Journal* report noted that 90 percent of its coverage originates with companies making their own announcements—which most of the time begin with a press release. For many smaller, lightly staffed newspapers—community weeklies in particular—a similar dynamic is at work. Certainly the prospects rise at such publications for a nonprofit getting a story in right away. But even with these journals, you have to present something that's truly "newsy," as Andrea Adelson puts it.

A BROCHURE WITH HEART AND SOUL

The eight-page, pocket-sized informational brochure put out by the Los Angeles Free Clinic skillfully describes some flesh-and-blood needy clients of the clinic, without intruding on their privacy. The effect of writing such personal stories is powerful, and worth emulating

"It's early morning at the Los Angeles Free Clinic Hollywood Center. A sixteen-year-old runaway is huddled by the door, determined to be first in line for one of Project STEP's day labor jobs. Soon she is joined by a brother and sister who ran away from an abusive stepfather, and an eighteen-year-old whose mother threw him out of the house, saying she couldn't support him any longer. A few miles west, at the Los Angeles Free Clinic on Beverly Boulevard, another line is forming. A homeless man pushes his cart up to the doors, seeking treatment for his blistered and bleeding feet. Soon he is joined by a woman who is taking the morning off work to see a doctor about her chronic cough. Next a young mother pushes her stroller. Her tooth has been aching for days and she can't stand the pain anymore.

"All of them will find the help they need at The Los Angeles Free Clinic. Whether it's finding a job, medical care, dental care, legal assistance, or a sympathic ear during a crisis, it's all there at The Los Angeles Free Clinic, and it's free."

Producing Photos for Your Media Kit

As indicated above, photos can be very useful in a media kit. If you include photos, make them black-and-white, proportioned so that they are readily adaptable to a newspaper's column dimensions. A "tight," close-in shot works better than a wide-angle view, which would require more space on the page, or come out so small as to obscure detail. "Show some kind of action," says Duin. "If you've got a day-care center, a good photo would show a teacher actively assisting a child in some activity, not a child or a teacher standing, inert, smiling at the camera."

Be sure to identify everyone in the picture, or at least everyone who is in the foreground. And interesting camera angles also help.

How can you gauge whether it would be appropriate to send a photo? Ask yourself a couple of questions. First, does your news angle include a central "object," such as a building or product, that is photographable and interesting to look at? Second, is your story about an individual—a volunteer at your organization, someone who's been helped by your group, a new officer or director, or a donor? If you can't answer yes to either of these questions, save your money and don't send a photo.

However, if you can answer yes, keep these strategies in mind when sending photos.

+ Consider offering your photo for a particular publication's exclusive use, marking it clearly—for example—"Exclusive to the *County News*." This can increase the chances it will be used.
+ Don't use a cheap camera to take your shots. No Polaroids or Instamatics. A 35-mm camera is the only kind that will do.
+ The best size for photos is 8"x 10", but 3"x 5"s are also acceptable.
+ Make sure the print is not too dark. Newspaper editors tell me this is a common problem with the photos they receive with press releases.
+ If a particular newspaper or magazine is interested in your story, you might ask about the possibility of their shooting a photo themselves.

Producing Videos or Audiotapes for Your Media Kit

Some groups prepare elaborate media kits with videos or audio-tapes. If you think a video would benefit your campaign, a relatively inexpensive way to produce one is to call a local college that teaches film. You are often able to find a talented and ambitious student who is eager to do just the kind of project you have in mind, for little or no cost.

Some video pointers to keep in mind:

+ Keep your footage fairly succinct, so the media recipients don't have to scan through a long video.
+ Put the chief spokesperson for your campaign—yourself, if you're the one—in the video. Keep the remarks to a few carefully chosen, important points about your organization.
+ Have some voice-over (offscreen) remarks as well as comments by the on-screen personality.
+ Vary between static head shots and shots showing movement.

Example of a Media Kit

The media kit sent out by the Presidents' Summit for America's Future ("the Philadelphia Summit") to promote volunteer work included eleven elements.

1. The white folder had the Summit's logo (an American flag whose "stars" were people outstretched arms.) The event's purpose was summarized in five words printed across the bottom of the folder: *Mentor Protect Nurture Teach Serve.*

2. The press release (which you read earlier in this chapter starting on page 93) was located on the left in the unfolded packet. As I pointed out, this release is much longer than the usual "ideal" length of one page that many journalists prefer, but the most crucial facts were summarized in the first paragraph. There were quotes from Presidents Clinton and Bush, adding a personal note to the document. Some of the social problems addressed by the event were neatly summarized, as were some of its goals. And major corporate commitments to the project were listed in bulleted format.

3. The media packet also included a three-page "Organizers' Mission Statement," which called the event "both a celebration of our nation's heritage of volunteer citizen service and a call to action."

4. There was a three-page handout covering "Key Questions and Answers." For instance, this document answered the question "How is the Summit being funded?" by informing readers that the funding was provided by the Amelior Foundation, the Annie E. Casey Foundation, the Robert Wood Johnson Foundation, the Ewing Marion Kauffman Foundation, the W.K. Kellogg Foundation, the David and Lucile Packard Foundation, and the Pew Charitable Trusts.

5. A one-page document headlined "Five Fundamental Resources for Children and Youth" gave details on such goals as "A

Healthy Start," "A Marketable Skill Through Effective Education," and "An Opportunity to Give Back Through Community Service."

6. A one-page document with the *Newsweek* masthead reproduced at the top showed an excerpt from a column by that magazine's writer Jonathan Alter. "This is hardly a minor story," Alter wrote. "In the centrist world of the late nineties, it's in the private sector, not in Washington, where children will be mentored, workers trained, social problems solved."

7. A fifteen-page handout detailed "Summit Commitments" made by corporations, nonprofits, and other entities, ranging from Pillsbury's contribution of $1.75 million in mentoring grants in 1997 alone, to the Jewish Social Justice Center which offered 100,000 volunteers and aides, to the city of Tucson, Arizona's offer of mentors for 2,000 youths in need.

8. A two-page sheet on "Summit Collaborators" listed allied organizations, such as the Corporation for National Service and the Points of Light Foundation.

9. A three-page handout called "Summit Sponsors" listed the various foundations providing funding.

10. A six-page release described the "Community Teams Participating in the Summit"—127 groups of ten citizens each, who were working to implement the Summit's programs.

11. Finally, a sheet listed "Communities Invited to Send Delegations" to the summit—including every state and major city in the country.

Technically speaking, these handouts contained overlapping information, but each had a unique angle and allowed to stand on its own by providing data that could assist a reporter in preparing a story on some aspect of the summit.

Your own organization's media kit could be broken down similarly, with handouts on the group's mission, history, major contributors, volunteers, number of people served, and success stories.

BUILDING BRIDGES WITH THE MEDIA

What gives some promotion people an edge in getting their projects into print? In my view, the best promoters are those who see themselves as building bridges to the media. These people take a long-term view of relationship-building. Even if one story does not run, they don't abandon hope, but rather recognize that they must maintain consistent, credible communication with the media.

Jack O'Dwyer, a New York–based publisher of publicists' newsletters, offers a number of tips, all based on the principle that you should create an ongoing relationship with journalists. Here are his musings about the characteristics of the best promoters.

+ They serve notice [to their staff] that the press is their number one priority. They always take press calls.... No assistants ever say they're "in a meeting" or are allowed to ask such questions as, "What is this in reference to?"
+ They are available at all times—because reporters sometimes write their stories at night, weekends, et cetera.
+ They spend lots of time outside their offices—breakfasts and lunches with editors, visiting editors at their workplaces on occasion, attending trade events and meetings where reporters gather.
+ They instantly produce needed documents that are "on the record," such as news clips, annual reports, speeches, lawsuits, et cetera....
+ They often send news clips on subjects being followed by reporters, displaying their knowledge of the reporters' areas of interest.
+ They never charge a reporter with being "inaccurate"—a wounding, insulting word that the reporter will surely not forget. Rather they praise the reporter for the many facts he or she got right and point out the problem.

In brief, the best promoters develop a "working friendship" with members of the media, and make themselves invaluable information resources on the issues the organization addresses (as well as any others the leadership knows about). Send news clips on those issues to selected journalists, even when the clips don't specifically mention your organization, and you'll gain credibility as someone who can offer real insight on a subject, not just a programmed plug for a particular group.

Summary: Goodness Guide

1. Start your publicity efforts by setting up a base camp—a site for storing files and conducting promotional business.

2. Develop files for your news clippings, broadcast logs, media list, promotional photos, cards and stationery, organizational brochures, letters to the media.

3. Your media list should include every publication, news service, and radio and TV station in your community, with appropriate contact people, and multiple means of getting in touch with them (phone, fax, address, e-mail). Update your list regularly.

4. Press releases should be clear and concise, and contain real news. Include all the classic journalism elements of who, what, when, where, and why. The lead paragraph should be strong and active in style, and contain all the essential information. Lesser details can follow in subsequent paragraphs. One-page is optimal length.

5. Pitch letters are more personalized than a press packet. Addressed directly to a targeted editor, a pitch letter briefly summarizes a story idea, and promises a phone call to follow. In the call, you expand on the story idea, offer help in setting up interviews, and try to establish a rapport that can continue regardless of whether the journalist picks up on this particular story.

6. Always follow up sending a press release or a pitch letter with a phone call. Emphasize graciousness and professionalism.

Don't push yourself on a journalist who is busy or obviously uninterested in the subject.

7. Opinion articles (op-ed pieces) offer a chance to raise your organization's community profile in a dignified context and build a reputation for expertise on selected issues. Submissions should be around 750 words.

8. Letters to the editor should not exceed 200 words, and should be crisply written. Your letter should take note of a recent news event which offers an opportunity to mention your organization's mission.

9. If you have the resources, make up a full media kit, including a glossy folder with your logo on the front. Inside, put your press release, and whatever informational handouts on various aspects of your organization and the social problems it addresses that you can. Add photos, if they're tightly-shot and action-oriented, and/or audio tapes and videotapes and if the investment is worthwhile for you.

10. In all your contacts with media people, attempt to build long-term relationships. Show yourself to be a reliable resource on the issues your nonprofit addresses. Volunteer names and telephone numbers of quotable experts and sources—and try to get yourself or your organization seen as a source for information relating to the social issues you address.

4

BE RADIO-ACTIVE
FOR YOUR NONPROFIT

If you haven't any charity in your heart,
you have the worst kind of heart trouble.

BOB HOPE

L ET'S face it: We are living in the age of electronics. Today, radio and television have become the primary forms of information transmittal in our era. While many people still subscribe to newspapers, no business or nonprofit group can afford to ignore the electronic media. Today, there are just two speeds for any business or nonprofit group: fast or dead. You can either learn to use the new media or you court death.

"We are in the communications business, the business of conveying messages to the human brain," said the late David Sarnoff, founder and president of RCA. "No man is wise enough to know which avenue to the brain is best. Therefore, the sensible idea is to make all avenues available for carrying the message."

In short, a sophisticated promotional effort, even for the most fledgling charity organization, must target the electronic media to effectively reach the audience you want as contributors and volunteers. This chapter will show you how to tap into the great world of radio.

RADIO STATISTICS

1. Half a dozen years ago there were only a few hundred talk radio stations in the country. Today, the number is around a thousand, and it is expected that this growth will continue to be phenomenal in the coming years.

2. Radio commands people's time. Whereas among avid newspaper readers, the time spent with a paper on any given day is generally only a few minutes, people tend to listen to radio for up to several hours per day. Here are some statistics from a 1995 study by Statistical Research, Inc., that show you how much time people spend with their trusty radios.

RADIO LISTENING TIME PER DAY		
AGE	MEN	WOMEN
18 and under	2 hrs. 58 mins.	2 hrs. 44 mins
25–34	3 hrs. 21 mins.	2 hrs. 46 mins
35–49	3 hrs. 10 mins.	2 hrs. 45 mins
50+	2 hrs. 36 mins.	2 hrs. 44mins.

3. Radio is omnipresent. Here are some figures from Statistical Research, Inc., indicating what percentage of people in different categories listen to the radio from three locations.

LOCATIONS FROM WHICH PEOPLE LISTEN TO RADIO			
	MEN 18+	**WOMEN 18+**	**TEENS 12–17**
At home	69%	76.3%	92.1%
In car	84.7	77.4	78.8
Other	46.7	38.2	50.2

UNDERSTANDING THE MEDIUM OF RADIO

Radio is the oldest of the electronic media, and it has a number of characteristics that are important to understand if you want to use radio properly in your promotional campaigns.

First, radio is the medium that brings you closest to your audience. Radio can make you feel like you're having a chat with millions of listeners, just as President Franklin Roosevelt had his famous "fireside chats" with the nation, via radio, during the Depression. For listeners, radio calls the senses into active involvement with the message to a degree that television doesn't. The mind's eye goes to work, creating images to go along with the inflection of the voice on the radio and the pictures painted by the words. Old-time radio dramas and comedies had that effect, conjuring up vivid pictures in the minds of families gathered around "the wireless." The possibilities for you and your charity to give mental pictures to your audience, and to capture their interest in deep and probing ways, is powerful.

I speak with experience on the ability of radio to link speaker and listener. I do a weekly radio commentary on KFWB, an all-news station in Los Angeles, and I am a frequent guest on talk-radio programs across the country. I am also frequently interviewed by national and local radio-news people for comments on Hollywood culture, the media, and marketing and publicity. The response I get from people who hear me over the radio airwaves is quite extraordinary. Invariably I find people grappling with the content of my comments far more when they've heard me over the radio than when they've seen me say something on television. A listener who has heard me on the radio will typically ask me to explain, elaborate, or provide justification for some point I made. In contrast, people who have seen me on TV are more likely to give me a simple comment, such as "I saw you on TV!" without pursuing any issue or stance I may have taken on the television show.

Second, radio is a fast medium, allowing you to get out a message quickly. While it took five months to get word back to Queen Isabella about the voyage of Columbus, and two weeks for Europe to hear about Lincoln's assassination, it took only 1.3 seconds to get the word from Neil Armstrong that a person could walk on the moon. Today, it takes less than thirty seconds to let the world know about anything, from the latest turn in Middle Eastern diplomacy, to a report that Madonna had her baby. The speed of radio is useful to keep in mind whenever you have a timely announcement that you believe you must get across quickly.

Third, radio is still largely unfiltered, allowing ideas to be tested and tossed around in robust debate. While some of the hosts and callers of talk radio sensationalize their messages, or are pure-and-simple wacky, radio at its best offers a modern-day equivalent of the old town-hall gatherings, where everyone is free to give vent to their opinions and complaints and the marketplace of ideas is at its most vibrant. This can be useful for charities and nonprofits who can benefit by tapping into the collective social conscience of a community through discussion and debate.

Finally, radio is still a regulated medium that is supposed to carry a modicum of public-interest fare. According to the Communications Act of 1934, the Federal Communications Commission (FCC) is empowered to issue radio broadcasting licenses "if public convenience, interest, or necessity will be served." Although these words are interpreted very broadly today, many radio stations see themselves as having a social responsibility to broadcast interviews, feature stories, and public-service announcements (PSAs) designed to promote local charitable ventures. This is obviously a significant advantage for charities and nonprofit groups.

DESIGNING YOUR RADIO STRATEGY

Tapping into your local radio network is actually not difficult. The first step is to become familiar with the radio stations in your area. Which ones have public-interest segments or programming themes that are compatible with the message you're trying to get out?

The only way to discover which stations are best for you is to systematically listen to every station in your community. To save time, a good approach is to apportion out the listening task among many members of your organization. Each person can be assigned a few stations to listen to and report on. I recommend that you listen to each station over the course of a week, studying and getting familiar with their announcers, their style and type of programming, and the audience they appeal to.

After listening to the stations, begin making contact with the program manager at each station. Begin by calling the stations and asking for the program manager's name. Then write a letter to the person, asking about the station's policies on feature programs, special interviews, and public-information spots to profile a charity such as yours.

In most cases, you will receive a reply letter spelling out the policies. Pay close attention to every point and nuance that the manager includes in the letter you get back, because if you submit material for use by the radio station, it must comply in form with any rules or parameters that the station has given you. For example, you can't expect station personnel to rewrite a press release or a public-service announcement that is longer than station rules dictate. You must take note of those rules from the outset, and make sure any announcement you send the station abides by them.

When checking out radio stations, don't be put off by a radio station's emphasis, whether it is an all-music or mostly-music format, or all-news. All of these formats potentially provide some opportunity for a charity to get its message broadcast. Even all-music or all-sports formats often make space for spot announcements during breaks for advertising.

To improve your chances of being of interest to a station, you must therefore be closely in tune with the station's audience. You need to figure out their interests, their age ranges and demographics, so you can make your pitch in language that they can relate to and with examples that draw them in. If it's a sports-oriented station, for example, sports analogies would make sense.

The following survey provides an idea as to what kind of people listen to different stations.

PROFILE OF DAILY LISTENERS OF RADIO STATIONS BY FORMAT				
FORMAT	MALE	FEMALE	MEDIAN AGE	MEDIAN INCOME
Adult Contemporary	44.02%	55.98%	35.84	$46,555
All News	54.91%	45.09%	46.8	$58,276
Album-Oriented Rock (AOR)	58.7%	41.3%	30.48	$47,662
Black/R&B	40.99%	59.01%	38.32	$34,633
Classic Rock	58.86%	41.14%	33.1	$47,373
Classical	55.96%	44.04%	44.0	$55,980
Country	47.84%	52.16%	38.97	$36,030
Easy Listening	48.01%	51.99%	47.69	$41,444
Golden Oldies	49.07%	50.93%	39.39	$45,899
Religious	45.09%	54.91%	40.49	$35,394

Five Ways to Get On the Radio

There are five basic methods of fitting your group into the programming at radio stations:

+ spot messages,
+ feature stories,
+ news,
+ interviews,
+ becoming a reporter.

Here are details on each method.

Spot Messages

Spot messages are short public-service announcements that most stations are required to carry as part of their license agreement. Getting a spot is not difficult; you must simply fulfill the program manager's criteria for the types of charitable organizations the station is willing to sponsor.

If you are approved, some radio stations will write the public-information spot for you. You need supply only the grist, the basics about your cause and your organization, and perhaps some flesh-and-blood examples of how you've helped.

But don't count on getting such assistance. In the majority of cases, the staff is too busy to do this work for you. And even at stations where they're prepared to help, supplying them with copy that requires minimal alteration makes it more likely your spot will eventually get made and aired.

If you need to write your own spots, here are basic tips for making your spot appealing.

1. First, remember that spots are typically only a minute long, so the message must be conveyed in a tightly-wrapped form, with the accent on getting the listener's attention from the very outset.

2. Spot messages can be *informational*, telling listeners about the problem your organization seeks to alleviate and how you go about doing it. In this case, you need to accent the human dimension of things: a story about someone you've helped, or an individual volunteer's experiences, for instance. Alternatively, a spot message can be *motivational*, urging listeners to get involved and help give the problem a cure. These kinds of spots demand a tone of enthusiasm and challenge. They're pitched directly at the listeners, summoning them to respond personally. The appeal should be frank, candid, direct—yet upbeat, not an exercise in guilt-tripping. "You have what it takes to help a child in need," is a good example of a positive way to appeal to someone's best instincts. In contrast, a downbeat tone, intended to shame people into helping your cause, doesn't conform well with the radio medium: People are listening for enjoyment and entertainment, and a public-information spot that hits a discordant tone is likely to cause irritation—or a switch of the radio dial.

3. No matter what station the promotional spot will run on, keep the language conversational. Don't write in long, run-on sentences. Use short, active phrasing. ("We want to hit a home run against hunger," for instance. Not: "The societal disorders evidenced by homelessness should give us all pause for concern.")

4. Write with directness to take advantage of the immediacy of radio. Speak to listeners as if they were your friends. Be personal and friendly, projecting a relationship between your organization and your listeners with liberal use of words like "you" and "yours."

5. Avoid jargon, slang, acronyms, or unfamiliar words that might cause people to scratch their heads instead of focusing on the important things you have to say.

6. If the radio station runs your spot, be sure to write a note of thanks. "Station personnel are like everyone else," says Pete Weitzner of Century Cable. "They like to feel appreciated, and organizations that show appreciation are more likely to be helped by people at the station again in the future."

Feature Pieces

Feature pieces are another form of programming that can provide you an opening to a station. Your feature piece could be an interview or a report on an event you are sponsoring in your community. Feature pieces are usually more analytical and in-depth than spots or news stories.

If you identify a local radio station that does occasional features, call to find the names of the producers who oversee them. Write to these people about your project, and the social problem you are covering. Give solid examples of people being assisted by your efforts. Say that you would be happy to help the station with your experience and expertise should they be interested in doing a feature dealing with your issue.

As with newspapers, I also recommend following up your letter with a phone call, telling the producer you "just wanted to make sure" the letter arrived, and you'd be happy to answer any questions he or she might have. Again, as with follow-ups for standard press releases, it's useful to have additional noteworthy facts to offer when you make phone contact, to spark more interest.

Feature stories are most interesting when they include real people. If there's someone whose life has been turned around by your charitable organization, that's the kind of story people like to hear—and radio can convey it effectively. So make sure the producer knows if there is such a potential story about your nonprofit.

News Stories

A charity can be proactive in its approach to radio news, attempting to generate news stories about itself with press releases. Those releases should be geared to the style of radio-news writing—which gets the basic point of the story across in the first sentence or two, adds some descriptive imagery, and ends fairly quickly.

There is also the possibility that your organization's work could be mentioned in the context of a "hard news" story. In fact, when you write to the radio-station producer for any reason, you might gain a special advantage by linking your organization's story with a topical story in the news that week or month. "If your message can be wrapped into a news story...that catches a programmer's eye, he or she is likely to add it to the end of an announcer's newscast," writes Marty Schwartz, vice president of sales at New USA, a public-relations firm in Virginia. "Of course, not every message can be...successful. There has to be some news value or public-service value inherent in the message. If it just a 'product' pitch, programmers will make their own pitch—into the circular file—and be sore that you wasted their time. So this is where some creative thinking about how it can be presented is really valuable."

Even if an expanded feature program doesn't fit into the station's schedule, a producer or news director who finds your story interesting might see the opportunity to broadcast an interview with you, or to let someone in your organization interview someone else involved with the charity.

Interviews

Radio interviews can be divided into three broad categories.

1. The first is akin to feature reporting—a longish interview, conducted by someone with the station, in which the subject matter and general questions are known in advance. Such exchanges can even be scripted. But authenticity is enhanced when there is some spontaneity, so it is better to request a format in which you don't stick to a text, but only to an overall framework of questions that have been agreed to in advance.

2. There is the interview conducted by the charity itself. While these can be effective, especially if done with leeway for ad-libbed conversation to boost credibility, there is something more authoritative for many listeners when a station employee conducts the interview.

3. There is the news interview conducted by a reporter. These can be the most intimidating exchanges for the interviewee, because the questions aren't reviewed in advance, so you have to be quick on your feet in answering.

If you have an opportunity to choose among these various formats, the one that usually offers the most potential to show you and your organization to best advantage is the first, because it is more relaxed and you're usually given a chance to know what you'll be asked about and to frame your responses in advance.

If you are interviewed, it is recommended that you try to get to know the interviewer before the tape actually starts rolling. This will help you relax during the interview itself. When it's under way, don't step on the interviewer's questions, and pace yourself in your answers.

And when it is over, make sure get a record of your appearance. Just as with any print stories that appear about your organization, you should collect your radio "clips"—i.e., record your appearances—and assemble a little cassette of your best sound bites. These can be used for an "audio press kit" to help line up future radio appearances.

Becoming a Reporter

A last way you can gain access to radio is to become something of a reporter or commentator for a station in your area. If you play your cards right, you can turn into a station's local expert, who is called on whenever news relating to a specific issue arises.

Gary Millspaugh, executive director of the Allentown Rescue Mission in Allentown, Pennsylvania, knows the value of becoming a resource to a radio station. "I attended the Presidents' Summit on volunteerism in Philadelphia," he says. "I thought hard in advance about how to turn that trip into publicity for our rescue mission, which serves up to eight hundred homeless men per year, and has a 70-percent success rate in getting people out of the debilitating problems that led them to the streets. Our graduates get into jobs and a responsible, self-sufficient life."

To turn his trip to the Summit into more than just a jaunt to Philadelphia, he called his contacts at major radio stations (he is meticulous, he says, in always nurturing relationships with key people in the local media) and he let them know that he would be attending the Summit and could offer first-person perspective. His efforts won him two rounds of publicity.

First, he got coverage prior to the Summit for being a local service-provider who would be going to the event. Second, he got publicity while he was in Philadelphia. After President Clinton's speech, for instance, Gary called one of the largest Allentown-area stations, and was put on the air during drive-time (the afternoon "rush hour," when listenership is highest). "I basically became their on-the-scene commentator on the president's speech and the Summit," he recalls.

This kind of vigorous courting of the media is "essential" for any charity that wants "to survive in the incredibly competitive world of nonprofits today," Gary argues. "The inescapable fact is that if you're a nonprofit or a charity, you're engaged in a competitive activity. You have to view it as competitive. As rough as it might sound, you're in a win/lose proposition. If you don't put your resources to a winning use, you'll lose—and be out of the business of helping others."

If you're as successful as he was in winning an opportunity to become sort of a freelance reporter on a social issue, keep in mind some basics of radio journalism. Facts should be conveyed clearly and accurately. Keep your sentences short. Use words that carry color and meaning. Make the chronological presentation orderly and understandable.

LEVINE'S LAW FOR PITCHING WITH PANACHE

Whenever you are making a pitch over the phone or in person, whether to a newspaper or magazine journalist or a reporter or producer in the electronic media, there are fundamental rules to follow. To some extent, they coincide with universal rules that you should apply to all human relations—courtesy, honesty, respect, integrity—but some of them are relatively unique to media relations, such as the advantage of having a topic that grabs by the collar and won't let go.

Here are my ten commandments for pitching the media:

1. Underlying everything should be the five F's: you must be fast, fair, factual, frank and friendly. These words spell credibility, a currency worth its weight in platinum.
2. Never be boring. Never.
3. Know the media you contact. Watch, listen, read.
4. Know your own subject thoroughly.
5. Don't just take "yes" for an answer. Follow up. Follow through.
6. Always keep your temper in check and your composure cool.
7. Don't be intimidated in designing your pitch. You have to make the first move, or no move will be made. The media won't come to you.
8. Turn any nervousness to your advantage by emphasizing your genuineness, the fact your aren't a slick, insincere salesperson.
9. Make yourself understood. Don't use jargon and technical language. You won't be making yourself seem less intelligent by doing so. Quite the contrary. Some of the most brilliant people I know speak with disarming simplicity.
10. Be prepared for dialogue once you've made your pitch. A simple "yes" or "no" is less likely than getting a series of follow-up questions from the journalist. This is an opportunity to expand on your case and build rapport with the person you're pitching to.

And the eleventh commandment: Keep a healthy, reasonable perspective. This isn't nuclear weaponry negotia-
tion. Keep cool and have fun.

Excerpted from Guerilla PR *by Michael Levine*
HarperCollins

THE GREAT WORLD OF TALK RADIO

In addition to the above methods of getting your message on the
radio, there is also an entire world of talk radio which offers you
instant access to the airwaves. In fact, talk radio offers excellent
possibilities for organizations with a socially significant message,
especially if you have someone in your organization who can be
seen as an expert in a field. (Ironically, the more you appear on talk
radio, the more you become an expert, as one's expertise usually
gains a heightened status from being on the radio.)

One advantage of some talk-radio shows is that their audiences
may be more affluent, with more money to invest. This observation
should perk up ears among charities and nonprofits looking for
donors. But while talk-radio provides fertile ground for publicity,
you should still remember that radio stations operate not to perform
charity but to generate ratings so they can make money. So they're
not going to invite a spokesman for a charitable group on who has
nothing interesting to talk about. They're not going to devote their
time to conversations about next weekend's fund-raising car wash.

This means that your creativity is highly tested if you seek to
get on talk radio, just as with all other aspects of promotional campaigns. When you contact a radio-station producer to suggest
focusing on something that has to do with your nonprofit cause,
the producer is going to ask what's unique and interesting about
your subject: What is it that will grab listeners and keep them from
pushing another button on the dial? That's the question you have
to ask yourself about every idea you consider pitching to any media
outlet. You have to be able to answer it again and again during your

marketing efforts. If you can't answer it, you have no business doing promotion in the first place.

One wonderful advantage of radio today is that you don't have to be in the studio to perform your part. You can be on the phone, calling from your office, car, or from across the country. You are simply "patched in" to the show, with the audience knowing nothing about where you are located.

Interviews on talk-radio programs can vary from fifteen minutes to an hour in length. On many shows, guests are also asked to take calls from listeners. If you have an opportunity to be on a talk show, it is useful to give your host a list of ten to fifteen questions that you would like to be asked. Although there is no guarantee your questions will be used, many hosts appreciate having your questions supplied because they interview such a wide variety of guests that they can't be well-versed on all the subjects under discussion. Your questions therefore act as pointers and cues that make them look intelligent and knowledgeable.

On the other hand, be careful about getting too scripted. When an organization seeks to get on talk shows, it is best to choose the person among its staff or officials who is most knowledgeable and articulate about the group and its work and can ad-lib. Many shows like to be flexible, taking a diversion from the announced subject. After all, nothing runs as smoothly when it's scripted. The worst shows are the ones where they just read off a list of questions. So be sure your spokesperson is comfortable talking on his or her feet.

Here are a few additional pointers for targeting talk radio.

✦ To increase your chances of being on radio stations around the country, submit your name and organization's project to *Newsmaker Interviews*, a publication to which dozens of radio stations across the country subscribe. It lists potential guests and their topics in detail. Another publication to consider is *The Yearbook of Experts, Authorities and Spokespersons*, which provides an "encyclopedia of sources" to subscribing hosts and producers from media outlets nationwide. It has a Web site: www.yearbooknews.com. Talk-radio producers are heavily worked, almost always busy lining up guests and arranging the logistics of each programs. You might not reach a producer the first time you try calling. Persistence is usually required.

✦ When you call a talk-radio producer, show that you know something about the program by mentioning a recent topic or guest.

✦ Try to link your idea with some issue or event that's in the news. Most producers look to the headlines first in trying to line up show topics.

✦ If you can inject controversy into your topic, you have an advantage in trying to get a guest spot. Talk radio generally thrives on dramatic issues and exchanges. It isn't supposed to be sleep-inducing.

HOW TO BE RELAXED AND EFFECTIVE ON-AIR

How does one stay calm, relaxed, and focused while being interviewed on the radio? I've been both a guest and a host, and I've heard the nervousness in the voices of many callers, and seen it in the eyes of some first-time guests. But I also know that it goes away with experience—even though that might be small comfort to newcomers who have the jitters. But until you have that experience, here are some tips for making the most of your time on the air.

Make the Media Your Friend

"One of the big problems is that people see the media as adversaries," says Joe Merica of the Merica Burch and Dickerson public-relations firm in Las Vegas. "We tell our clients that the media are their friends. An interview is an opportunity to share your company's views with the public." It is just as much an opportunity for the nonprofit service provider. Seize the opportunity. Prepare for it. Let it work for you.

Breathe Deeply

You have probably heard this advice a million times, but honestly, it works. Before going on the air, inhale a few times very deeply, close your eyes for a moment, roll your head slowly around and relax your muscles—let them fall limp for a moment. Then tell yourself that this is just a conversation with a host and perhaps a caller or two. Talk to them as friends, not as a demanding, judgmental audience. And keep the big picture in mind: If you are going on the air to talk about a worthwhile philanthropy, that powerful purpose should give you a special confidence and keep your thoughts focused on what it is you want to get across. When you're thinking about how important your message is, you don't have as much time and energy to spend thinking that ought to be nervous.

Media consultant Peggy Klaus uses an interesting metaphor. She counsels her clients to think of the microphone as a fan of theirs. "I tell them to imagine someone they love and who loves them is sitting there just dying to get the information," she says. "This helps elevate the enthusiasm in the voice."

Learn to Be Brief

"Radio obviously focuses very directly on what you say," says reporter Sharon Katchen with KFWB radio in Los Angeles. "Your words and the sound of your voice define you for the radio listener, whereas appearances can be more central to the impression left with people watching you on television."

For this reason, one of the central pointers for radio interviews is to learn to be brief and to the point. "Radio demands that you cut the fat out of your language," says Katchen. "Make it lean and lively—get in with a point quickly and get out, and on to the next point."

Learn to Use Sound Bites

Perhaps more difficult than simply being brief, the electronic media demand that be witty in what you say. There is a well-known phrase for this type of word-nimbleness: It's called talking in sound bites. These are phrases that encapsulate a big thought in a small, memorable kernel. A politician who wants his budget plan to make a lasting impression doesn't say, "We're going to survey the appropriations schedule with an eye to increasing efficiencies, maximizing economies, and identifying and hopefully reducing areas of redundancy and overspending." He says, "We're going to perform liposuction on the budget."

Susan J. Douglas is a Hampshire College professor, media critic for *The Progressive*, and author of *Where the Girls Are: Growing Up Female with the Mass Media.* She is also something of a master of sound-biting, an art that helps her promote her book and her feminist philosophy. Here are a few of her soundbites.

◆ Concerning the megahit book, *Men Are from Mars, Women Are from Venus:* "It sounds to me like a big apology for men not taking out the garbage—women have to try to understand men, they all came down from a spaceship."

◆ On the thin, waifish look that became popular for a time in modeling: "The image we're all supposed to conform to is that of a thirteen-year-old anorexic. I don't begrudge Kate Moss the chance to make some money, but go eat some pizzas. My God."

◆ Concerning her five-year-old daughter: "She's still angry that a girl didn't free Willy."

Learning to speak in this kind of colorful language is not easy for many people. The approach to take is to think how you can convey your message in shorthand, with a sassy zing. "You can be more discursive and detailed when you're doing a print interview," says Sharon Katchen, "Because there is room for more facts to be spread over the page, and the reader has time to ponder them. In contrast, quickness and brightness are the keys on radio."

Roger Ailes, chairman of Ailes Communications, Inc., and a

communications consultant to corporations and their CEOs, illustrates the point by setting side by side several thoughts expressed in two ways: one way is deadly boring—the other, filled with life. Which would you rather hear?

DULL

A. The two leading ways to achieve success are improving upon existing technology and finding a means of evading a larger obligation.

B. To construct an amalgam, you have to be willing to split open its component parts.

C. Capital will not produce great pleasure, but it will remunerate a large research staff to examine the questions proposed for a solution.

INTERESTING

A. "The two leading recipes for success are building a better mousetrap and finding a bigger loophole."   EDGAR A. SCHOAFF

B. "To make an omelet, you have to be willing to break a few eggs."   ROBERT PENN WARREN

C. "Money won't buy happiness but it will pay the salaries of a large research staff to study the problem."   BILL VAUGHN

Tell Stories

Another key to radio savvy is to be able to tell your message in the form of a story. We all love stories; we all urged our parents to tell us stories when we were little, and the human urge to hear a good story never goes away. Struggling smaller charities often have great stories to tell, but just as often aren't getting their stories out on the modern electronic media.

Whenever possible, you should therefore seek to find a personal story to relate in your radio time. Keep your story short, but make it as moving and emotional as possible.

Stay Focused on Your Message

Many newcomers to radio get stumped if their host strays from the topic or asks questions for which they were not prepared. When this happens, try to come back to your topic. If the radio interviewer continues to ask you questions that get away from your central theme, don't evade the questions, but be quick—and polite—in answering, and then switch back constantly to the major points you want to emphasize.

GETTING YOUR MESSAGE ACROSS

"It's your responsibility—not your listener's—to insure that your message gets through," says Roger Ailes, mentioned above. Although he is famous for his television productions (he was executive producer of the most widely syndicated talk show in America, *The Mike Douglas Show*, and NBC-TV's *Tomorrow Coast-to-Coast*, Ailes has also made radio commercials and TV campaign spots for several U.S. senators and three U.S. presidents.

Ailes tells of an encounter he had, at the outset of his career, with Bob Hope. The great comedian arrived on the set of the *Mike Douglas Show*, before the show had hit syndication. Hope's appearance was conceived of as a brief interview to promote a book. Ailes was a green, twenty-something assistant producer, but none of the first-line producers were around at the moment, so the burden of explaining the show's format to Hope fell on him.

And he basically fell silent—tongue-tied in the face of the great comedian. Hope had to take him aside, away from his entourage, and prod Ailes to spit some words out. As it happens, when Ailes was finally able to communicate, his request—that Hope stay for the entire show, not just a brief interview segment—must have had some effect, because that's exactly what the comic did, to the delight of the audience.

On departing, Hope turned and pointed at Ailes. "Next time, speak up," he said with a smile. Ailes says, "I never forgot that lesson—and I've never been afraid to speak to anyone since then." From that lesson he derives the point that you have a responsibility to get your words across—and to do so in a way that makes the statement "not only believable but also reassuring, strong and positive."

Getting Professional Media Training

If you expect to participate in many opportunities offered by radio and television, it may be useful to seek professional media training. Most cities have coaches for hire who can teach you how to appear relaxed and comfortable on the air. Many corporate executives obtain this training, which can be accomplished in anywhere from a few hourly sessions to a few weeks.

As Aaron Cohen of the Las Vegas Business Press points out, there is a vast difference between those professionals who can do this and those who cannot. Which one would you rather be?

Worst case: The evening news camera is on a business executive. He sweats and stammers. He looks intimidated. He doesn't answer the questions, rambling on without making much sense. He looks like a fool. His company looks like it's run by fools.

Best case: Another executive looks comfortable and confident in front of the cameras. She answers questions, even tough ones, directly and with authority. It seems she's taking over the interview, putting forth her company's agenda. Her interview is better public relations than a high-priced commercial.

As public-relations executive Tim Chanaud puts it, the goal of media education should be "to level the playing field," to teach "what the media is looking for in responses."

SWEET-TASTING CHARITY

Have you ever dreamed about dinner at David Letterman's? If you can get the lid off a jar of salsa and rip open a bag of chips, you've got the first course covered. Would the menu at Dave Barry's be any better? Substitute a jar of peanut butter for the salsa, grab a spoon, and lunch is served. If these low-maintenance munchies are ruining your fantasy life, then imagine grilled jumbo shrimp at Calvin Klein's Hamptons beach house. Or pasta puttanesca whipped up by Harrison Ford.

The favorite recipes of more than 100 celebrities from film, fashion, television, news, sports and politics are now available for public consumption in *Feast for Life*, a cookbook. Five years ago, Gretchen Sandin Jordan and Linda Provus Bartlett, two Chicago women who are interested in cooking and active in fund-raising, asked a "wish list" of well-known personalities to donate a recipe that had personal significance. They added photos of the contributors and amusing illustrations, spiced the mix with personal anecdotes, and gave the calories a cause: All proceeds from the book go to the Pediatric AIDS Foundation in Los Angeles, which funds AIDS research, and the Design Industries Foundation fighting AIDS/Chicago (DIFFA), which helps those living with the virus.

In Style, October 1996

ADDITIONAL RULES FOR DEALING WITH THE RADIO

Here are final pointers for dealing with radio stations, adapted from the National Association of Broadcasters and the Defense Information School, as reported by Kenneth Jarvis, executive director of West Virginia Public Broadcasting.

✦ Accept suggestions from any radio station people you deal with. Remember, they are experts in a field that is alien to you. Listen to what they say.

✦ Planning an appeal for funds or support? Check with the station first. Many have a policy against this type of program or broadcast. Also check your local statutes for the legal requirements for fund-raising. Many require that your organization be licensed before beginning a fund drive.

✦ Treat all stations fairly and equally. Do not favor one station, even if the others do not favor you.

✦ Respond cheerfully and completely to any station's request for information, advice, or assistance.

✦ Keep a file of the "hot line" number for each station—a number that is to be used for providing news and giving telephone "beeper" reports. A beeper is so-called because of the beep sound required on all recorded telephone messages, including recordings made over the telephone for later replay over the air.

✦ The best people for you to know at radio or television stations are the public-service director, the program director or manager, and the news director. Whether you are trying to get time on a program, spot announcement, or hard news or feature story, the backing and support of the station manager is invaluable. The program director (or public service director) in turn is ultimately responsible for finding a place in the broadcast day for such programs or announcements. Accept the fact that no matter how important your chairperson or board thinks a particular story is, it must stand on its own merits—being newsworthy to the audience the station serves—and that decision rests with the news director.

Summary: Goodness Guide

1. Get to know the format of each radio station in your community, the characteristics of its listeners, and the various on-air personalities.

2. Identify which stations run public-service announcements about charities and nonprofits; which run feature stories about social issues; which have news programs that might be appropriate for a mention of your organization.

3. Get the names and contact numbers of program directors and producers of any radio shows that offer promise for your group.

4. When writing a thirty- or sixty-second public-service spot announcement, keep the sentences brief, the structure simple. Follow any guidelines that the station issues to you to the letter.

5. In press releases or pitch letters to radio stations, try to wrap a story about your nonprofit into a larger, topical news story. The result could be that you'll get coverage on the news, or a feature piece might be developed.

6. There are several types of radio interviews, ranging from highly scripted exchanges for features programs, to spontaneous interviews for breaking-news programs. A more structured interview—with questions revealed in advanced—is preferable for charity workers inexperienced in media relations, although a fully-scripted exchange may not be as desirable, because it sounds stilted and insincere.

7. When being interviewed in a spontaneous format, remember to be brief and cool—don't step on the interviewer's comments. No matter where the questions lead, after answering them politely, always return to the main points you want to convey.

8. Just as with clippings of print articles about your charity, keep recordings of your radio appearances (many stations will provide an audiotape of the program on request). Build an "audio press kit" to use in seeking further radio guest spots.

5

GETTING TELEVISED

*Eloquence lies as much in the tone of the voice, in the eyes,
and in the speaker's manner, as in his choice of words.*
LA ROCHEFOUCAULD, *Maxims, 1665*

TELEVISION can inflate your nonprofit organization far beyond the level of notoriety it now has. As the famed media critic Marshall McLuhan pointed out decades ago, "the medium is the message." By this, he suggested that getting TV coverage gives a power and credibility to a message that no other medium can impart.

I know firsthand about the power of TV. I appear on CNN regularly, and I am interviewed by the other major networks frequently about communications issues and their effect on society. I have seen the value of the medium, which is its undeniable power to boost people into the limelight on a national scale and turn their names or causes into household words. I have also witnessed a serious drawback to the medium, which is that far too many viewers tend to focus more on appearances than on issues.

Nevertheless, as a potential source of promotion, I heartily recommend television as a medium that charities and nonprofit organizations should tap into. Pictures and images move people with a force that words, even the most eloquent, usually fail to do. Television is also dispatched across vast distances to millions of households where your organization can shape opinions and ideas in the way you need to do.

OUR LOVE/HATE RELATIONSHIP WITH TV

A 1997 column by Jeff Jacoby of the *Boston Globe* called for Americans to turn a blind eye to television for a week. "Mark next Thursday on your calendar," he urged readers. "National TV-Turnoff Week runs from April 24 through April 30.

"With luck and a little publicity, hundreds of thousands of idiot boxes from sea to shining sea will stay dark for seven days. Who knows? Americans may read a few more books than usual, have a few more conversations, do a little more homework, play a little more baseball, spend a bit more time on the crossword puzzle. If enough TV sets are kept unplugged—and in a nation where a majority of the public can name the Three Stooges but only 17 percent can name three Supreme Court justices, that's a big if—the national IQ ought to be up a point or two by May 1."

This was stinging rhetoric, although most of us would admit that there's some truth to the complaint that millions of Americans let TV intrude into their lives far too much.

However, you cannot afford to be among the complainers. You should be busy trying to find ways to publicize your charitable efforts and recruit more supporters. TV is your friend—if you approach it wisely. The next time you doubt the value of television for your organization, keep in mind the following statistics.

+ There are 220 million television sets in this country.
+ Ninety-eight percent of American homes have at least one television.
+ In the average American home with children, the TV is on almost sixty hours per week.

In short, the TV is something you must reckon with if you want to engage your community in your cause. You have to plug into the common carrier of our cultural conversation.

FINDING THE RIGHT TV FORUM FOR YOUR CAUSE

Just as with radio, you need to begin by becoming familiar with the television stations in your area. This includes both the national broadcast stations and the local cable stations. Note what kind of programming is offered on each channel. Are there any local morning talk shows or magazine shows which might be able to interview someone from your organization? Are there news programs that put an accent on stories about individuals doing unusual or heroic things, or other kinds of "soft news" feature fare?

In most communities, the local cable stations have public-access programming that allows anyone in the community to produce a show. This might be an opportunity for you to develop your own show, or you might be able to appear as a guest on an interview program hosted by a local newsmaker or community activist.

As you identify appropriate stations, call each one and get the name of the assignment editor. This editor supervises all producers and other members of the station's news staff. It is to this editor that you need to begin directing your press releases, story pitches, and other forms of media advisories.

If you find a story idea you can present to a station, you will need to write it up and send it to the editor as a query letter. When writing up story ideas, sum them up in one page or less, packing as much of the vital information (who, what, where, when, why) in the very first paragraph. Be sure to think in terms of television, not print or radio. As Jeff Rowe, an editor for *Century Cable* in southern California, reminds us: "In trying to come up with story ideas, think about what will provide interesting visuals for a TV camera and a TV audience."

Be sure to include your name, address, phone and fax number, and indicate that you will make a follow-up phone call. Then, as we pointed out earlier, when you make that call, you will have some additional information to add to your discussion, rather than simply waiting for a yes-or-no answer.

A DOLLAR GOES A MILE TO HELP TEENS

"THUMBS UP to the Tulare teens participating in the 'Mile to Klub Kaos' fund-raising event for the teen center. The innovative fund-raiser works this way: Teens stand along both sides of Tulare Avenue from K to Cherry Streets—a line a mile long—to raise money for Klub Kaos, the teen center. The idea is to have a dollar ready when you drive down Tulare. The dollar will be placed in line as they move bill by bill to Klub Kaos. This is part of a commitment to raise $7,700 each year to contribute toward the operation of the teen center."

The Fresno Bee, May 2, 1997

HOW TO DO TELEVISION INTERVIEWS

Television interviews are perhaps the most common format for nonprofit groups. When doing television interviews, the first rule is to make sure you can fulfill a specific goal with your appearance. I call this keeping the end in mind. You must know what your purpose is in appearing and what message you want to get across.

When I am considering going on the air, I try to ask myself what do I want viewers to think when I am done. On a few occasions, I have actually declined television interviews when I realized I didn't have an end—a message—that made the interview worthwhile. But when I do have something to say and it has value, I prepare for the entire enterprise using the message as my guide. Having an end in mind means more than harboring some vague, warm fuzzy goals or a belief in one's head. It means writing out the end, and writing out the plan to make that end a reality. In my opinion, you don't have a plan for anything unless it's written. You're unprepared, and cruising for failure.

I kept the end in mind recently when I was called by an editor at a prominent magazine and asked if I wouldn't mind being featured among those men the magazine designated "the Most Eligible Bachelors of Los Angeles." I thought for a second, then while flattered, answered no. I am single (divorced), and the end that is in my mind is marriage and a family. Somehow, I suspected that gaining a reputation as being contented as a frequent dater would not help me make the kind of impression I'd like to make on women in search of a family life. So the end that is important to me governed my response, and you won't be seeing me in that magazine.

In addition, it is very useful to assist your interviewer by providing background information about your organization before the show. In considering what points to stress during the interview, be aware of the kind of audience—in terms of age and interests—that the program draws. If it's mainly homemakers, and your nonprofit works with poor people, you might stress the mothers and children whom you serve. When you've determined what themes are most appropriate to stress, work on getting them down into bite-sized morsels of comment. And then tell your interviewer, in advance, the areas you hope to stress.

Television Dos and Don'ts

Here are several additional tips for appearing on television interviews.

1. *TV is a "cool" medium.* That means you should work at being cool, relaxed, and intimate with your interviewer and with the

camera. Don't speak as if you were booming at a hall full or people. Rather, talk in a conversational way. The microphone is only inches away, so there is no need to project your voice. As *Century Cable* anchor Pete Weitzner counsels interviewees: "You're coming into people's homes on a one-on-one basis and you want to address them with all the easy assurance of a valued friend."

2. *Vary your pitch and tone, to avoid sounding monotonous.* It's okay to add some degree of passion to your voice, because the camera has a moderating effect, diluting some of the emotion that a speaker expresses.

3. *Be prepared.* That means thinking about your points in advance. Know the two or three points you intend to drive home, and make sure you always get back to them during the interview. Remember the parable of the wise and foolish virgins that I expounded on in chapter 1. "Preparation means anticipating the interviewer's probable questions, and coming up with answers in advance," says Jeff Rowe. "It means getting to the station perhaps as much as thirty minutes before you're scheduled to go on. If you have a chance to talk to the interviewer beforehand, do so. Try to establish a rapport. And ask about the boundaries of the interview; good journalists will tell you."

4. *If necessary, go ahead and bring notes with you.* But as veteran anchor Pete Weitzner says, "Refer to them only occasionally and casually. You won't look relaxed or sincere if you end up reading them."

5. *Visual aids such as large charts or photographs, can help an interview sometimes.* If you decide you need such aids, let the station know in advance and get their approval.

6. *Be sure to find out how long the interview will last and who else will be involved.* Is another person going to be interviewed along with you? Will the format be a debatelike exchange, or mere questions and answers?

7. *Find out also if the interview be broadcast live.* If not, be sure to learn if anything will be added after taping. If something is going

to be added, you should consider requesting to see this footage. A responsible station will grant your request. (Note: See the section below for more on what to do if you are involved in an interview that will be edited.)

8. *Choose your dress carefully.* Dark colors, blues, and charcoals come across well on TV. Whites do not look so well; they tend to look too bright. A blue shirt is preferable to a white one. Narrow stripes or checks are not advisable—they tend to dance around on the screen.

9. *Your body language should project relaxation and confidence.* To nurture this effect, focus on the interviewer, not on the camera or the many viewers in their homes. You're having a conversation with someone who is sitting or standing with you—don't let your mind carry you beyond the immediate setting.

10. *Be ready to keep moving.* Your host's job depends on providing a very quick pace. In general, tailor your answers to ten- to thirty-second responses. Keep them snappy and brief. However, prepare to be interrupted a lot. Remember that television differs dramatically from radio in the pace and momentum of its interviews.

11. *When the program is concluded, express gratitude to the interviewer and depart.* Station personnel are busy and it's possible that the set will soon be used for another taping; a non-employee who tries to hang around quickly can become a nuisance. If you want further contact with the interviewer, follow up with a friendly note or phone call a day or so later.

Additional Advice from Professionals

James Todhunter, a California video consultant, offers a number of additional tips for people who'll be doing television interviews.

> *Lighting.* Try to get there early to work with the technicians to get the lighting right. When you're in front of the camera and looking at it, the light to the camera's left is called the Key Light. It can be maneuvered in ways that

can do remarkable things for one's appearance. For instance, if it is moved so that it is just over the camera itself, it can dissolve crow's feet and any other facial lines that run at a somewhat diagonal angle. The light behind you, as you stand in front of the camera and face the camera, is the Back Light. If placed directly over one's head it can create a halo-like effect. If the light in the studio is particularly harsh, you might ask to have the atmosphere warmed up, figuratively, by the addition of a rose-colored light. This gives skin, as it's picked up on camera, a healthy, glowing appearance.

If you have heavy glasses, you can ask technicians to spray them with a faint mist that lightly mats the glass, reducing glare, without hindering vision. Also, people with glasses should remember to tilt their heads slightly down so as not to catch the studio lights too directly.

Clothing. Look at your eyes, your teeth, and the colors in your inside lower lip, for blues and reds. It's in these places that you will find your own personal primary and ancillary colors that your clothing should match and complement.

Not appearing shifty-eyed. Put your arms straight out in front of you, and take note of the boundaries thus created. During the interview, don't let your eyes move beyond those boundaries either to the left or to the right. If you must move further in either direction to look at someone, move your head, not your eyes.

Gesturing. Generally keep your hands quietly folded in your lap. Do not point at anything or anyone using a single finger. If you're going to gesture with a hand to emphasize a point, keep your hand open and your fingers together, and slice the air downward with an ax-like effect—but do it in a restrained fashion, with the hand moving right in front of your heart. That comes across on television as a relatively refined movement, unlike finger-pointing, which can appear crude and threatening.

Making your point. Return again and again to the central point of your presentation. Over the course of a program, viewers will be tuning in and out, as they graze across the dial with their remote controls. Your message should be repeated—in different ways, if possible, so that the program's various audiences during its time span all get a chance to hear it.

Tracy D. Connors, executive director of West Virginia Public Broadcasting, offers a few additional points of advice.

Looking poised. Assume that the camera is on you and "live" every moment; although it may not be at that instant, it is far better to assume this and be poised and in control all the time rather than to be caught off guard "picking your nails" on occasion.

Understanding the process. Pay attention to and work closely with the stage manager—the director's representative—in the studio. Ask the stage manager to demonstrate the signals to be used and explain the meaning of each so that you will have no trouble recognizing and understanding them while on camera. When you move, move slowly and in the ways planned with or by the director.

A Note on Edited Interviews

The interview techniques discussed here assume you are doing a live interview, or one taped to be broadcast in its entirety later. Many people will only do this type of interview, as there is a strong argument that getting involved in an edited interview (i.e., one that allows cutting and pasting by TV editors after the interview itself concludes) is risky. One person who vigorously declines to participate under such conditions is *New York Times* columnist William Safire. He points out, "Anyone who submits to a television interview in which a producer can select portions, picking and choosing the most damning things, has got to be crazy. The assumption in print is that the words are being filtered by the writer, whereas when you sit in front of your television set and look at a person speaking, the natural assumption is that you're watching a verbatim interview, that you're getting reality, which is not the case."

As sensible as Mr. Safire's objection might sound, however, it might not be a practical one for a representative of a small local nonprofit to abide by unconditionally. It all depends on the nature of the program: Does it have a track record of dirt-digging investigative reporting—or is it a community forum with an uplifting emphasis, which simply happens to broadcast edited interviews? These are questions that you must find out when doing the due diligence that should precede all your efforts to promote your cause to the media. Knowing everything you can about a media outlet is simply common-sense communications strategy.

PRACTICE MAKES PERFECT

I recommend to my clients that they practice for being on television by sitting in front of the mirror. The mirror can actually be a very good listener and critic. Practice getting your points across, and answering the questions you anticipate getting. And practice a warm, confident smile. After practicing in front of a mirror, try yourself out in front of friends and family members. Sit with them and rehearse answers to hypothetical questions.

Be aware, though, that even intense practice sessions don't give you all the psychological preparation you'll need. This is because the TV studio is a world that's hard to replicate. There are many people floating about: producers and set crew moving around to their own rhythm, cables crisscrossing all over the floor, and hot lights everywhere. Most people new to television complain about the lights, because they can make you feel baked if the air-conditioning is not strong enough to cool down the studio to a comfortable temperature.

Once you go on-air, you will likely feel a jolt of energy. This is an amazing feeling, as you will suddenly feel invigorated and excited. Remember to sit up straight but don't be rigid, and look only toward your interviewer. Don't get ahead of yourself and start to hurry if you think your time is running short and you still feel you have a lot to say. There will be another day to say more. Focus on this interview and get as much of your verbal message across as you can. Leave viewers with the visual message that says this is someone who believes in a good cause.

The surprising thing about television is that you often feel you were worse than you really were. As a medium, television usually makes people *look* very good, and it often obscures the quality of their message. You may think you were inarticulate or stupid, but most people don't pay as much attention to what you say word for word. Even after some of what I thought were my most eloquent and witty appearances on TV interview programs, I've had people come up and compliment me not on my words, but on how great I looked.

For many viewers, what they see on the tube transcends what they hear. Ideally, though, you should strive for the perfect match of cool comments and a style that speaks sincerity.

PUBLIC-SERVICE ANNOUNCEMENTS

In addition to interviews, another opportunity for charities and nonprofits is, like radio, through the public-service announcements that many stations agree to do.

To arrange a PSA, begin by making contact with a station's public-service director. If you do not know who this is, ask the assignment editor with whom you may have spoken when you called about interviews. In some stations, the assignment editor is the same person you need to speak to about public-service announcements.

If the station offers PSAs, get their guideline sheet with their rules as to length, style, and what kinds of visuals can accompany the text. Some stations that air PSAs produce them entirely in-house, with even the copy written by staff members. In this case, your responsibility is to provide neat, accurate information about your organization.

If, on the other hand, the station considers PSA scripts submitted by charities and nonprofits, make sure you abide by the rules on length and format. Your prose should consist of short sentences, and the basic facts (who, what, when, where, and why) concerning the subject. Typically, PSAs run either ten, thirty, or sixty seconds. You must time your copy accordingly, generally allowing twenty words for each ten seconds of air time.

If the announcement is keyed to a specific event that your nonprofit is putting on, note that on the text you're submitting, and indicate the time period during which you'd like the PSA to run. Submit your copy at least ten days prior to when you'd like it to begin airing. Triple-space all copy on 8"x 11"-inch paper, leaving ample margins all round. If you're submitting visuals to accompany your PSA, slides are as preferable as photographs. If you choose photos, use matte (dull-surfaced) ones, because studio lights reflect off glossy pictures.

THE SON OF ONE PRESIDENT APPLAUDS THE CHARITY OF ANOTHER

One of the participants in the Presidents' Summit for America's Future was Jimmy Carter, who has set an excellent example of volunteerism, donating countless hours to Habitat for Humanity, building houses for low-income people. While I have my political differences with Jimmy Carter, I applaud him in this: His volunteerism is not "photo-op compassion."

MICHAEL REAGAN,
son of President Ronald Reagan

PRODUCING EVENT VIDEOS

Another idea that charities and nonprofits can use to tap into television is to produce a video of a fund-raising event you sponsor. New York video producer Margie Goldsmith points out, "Nonprofit groups are stepping up their use of 'event videos' in order to pack more punch into fund-raising drives. An event video can illustrate your cause and position your group as part of the solution in a way that gets results because it 'tugs at the heartstrings' of the audience. It can graphically display horrors, such as a child with an incurable disease or a homeless family, that even the most eloquent speaker could only hint at. Using video is also a way for charities and nonprofits to extend the shelf-life of a black tie affair (and recoup the cost). You can play the video at cocktail parties to raise donations, or send copies to prospective large donors."

Today, the cost of producing and mailing such a video is cheaper than sending a hefty media-kit package that often includes four-color brochures and the like. There are also many ways you can keep the cost of making a video down: You can use stock background footage to fill in gaps in your own footage; you can hire college or graduate students willing to work at a low rate; you can edit at night when hourly costs are cheapest; among others.

TESTIMONIAL FROM A SUCCESSFUL SELF-PROMOTER

When Marcus Meleton was laid off from his job with a southern California engineering firm in the early nineties, he didn't let frustration or self-pity take over. He put his well-developed sense of humor to work and self-published a couple of lighthearted books, one on male-female relations (*Nice Guys Don't Get Laid*) and one spoofing a profession that is the butt of nearly everyone's jokes (*Hunting for Lawyers*).

Meleton also set about employing just the kind of creative promotional strategies that I advocate for charities and nonprofits. He touted his books to newspaper journalists and producers in radio and TV, making a special point to send pitch letters and phone calls that tied the themes of his books in with big news stories of the day. (A California ballot initiative that would have limited lawyers' fees, for instance, gave him an opportunity to promote his book with a number of media outlets.)

Meleton got himself into some of the publications that radio and television producers use to find prospective guests, such as *Radio/TV Interview Report*. And he's been vigorous and persistent in doing his own pitching. It's paid off: He's been on more than five hundred talk-radio shows and such major TV talk shows as *Montel, Geraldo*, and *Rolanda*. Some of his advice from the trenches demonstrates the power of the strategies this book has outlined for you.

> First, with radio, if you get asked on as a guest, it's helpful to mail or fax a few questions you'd like to be asked. Also, get permission in advance to mention, at least once, any 800 number that you or your organization might have.
>
> Most of the interviews are done by phone, and after a few of them, you become quite confident, because the question from hosts and callers tend to be similar over time. The trick in radio is landing your first few interviews through creative, well-thought-out pitches. Once you've got a few shows under your belt, you have an audio sample you can send to other producers. And they share information among themselves, too, so you'll hear from producers who heard about you from a friend at a station in another town.
>
> Also, radio stations tend to eat their young; people are hired and fired on a pretty regular basis, and they move from one station to another. So someone who had you on in Duluth might ask you on when he takes a job in Des Moines.
>
> Because talk-show producers have such a busy job— they have to prepare sometimes six shows a week, with one on tape, in the can, for Saturday—you can earn their favor,

and further your reputation, by suggesting other people, ideas, and topics that they could use.

How to break into television talk shows? Of course, you have to have something interesting to talk about. Watch shows that you might think would be appropriate for your subject. Learn about the host, what he likes. And one way to find the names of producers in any shows, national or local, is simply to watch the credits at the end of the program. You'll find that in TV as in radio, the producers bounce around a lot, so if you get on one program, you might end up later on another that's now staffed by the people who invited you on the earlier one.

So as you can see, it is quite possible to go from being, as Bob Dylan phrases it, "a complete unknown" to a well-known and savvy self-promoter, regardless what cause you are promoting.

TV AS A METAPHOR FOR LIFE

Let me make one last point about television to end this chapter. Even if your group does not appear on television, there is another way you can make use of this powerful medium: through analogies and references to television shows and characters. This is especially useful when you give speeches or talks about your cause.

Here is a story to illustrate why I suggest this. I once knew a ministry student who was attempting to write stirring, moving sermons for his congregation, often using literary metaphors and characters to make his points. Unfortunately, he ran into a dilemma, discovering that his audience did not fully appreciate his musings because they did not know his references to literature. With his busy life and his love of reading, he wasn't a TV-watcher, but it suddenly dawned on him that this was what he had to do to make his sermons and counseling resonate with his flock. "I was trying to make points about faith and life by drawing analogies to literary figures I was familiar with—from Dickens or Hemingway or Philip Roth," he told me. "But for many in my congregation, all this served only to make me sound obscure and aloof. I found I couldn't connect unless I used icons from television or the movies. When you're talking about duplicity, for example, it's easier to relate the point, for many people, if you use the example of the two-faced Eddie Haskell [from *Leave It to Beaver*] rather than some equally dishonest character in a Shakespeare play."

So, if you're going to attempt public speaking on behalf of your charity, this is an observation you shouldn't ignore. Whether or not you use television references to help make your points in public, it's valuable to be able to draw on your audience's shared familiarity with popular culture. TV and film are the common carriers of our cultural dreams, and communicators benefit by being familiar with them.

So while it may be chic to look down one's nose at "the boob tube," that "vast wasteland" of TV has proved its potential and its worth over the years, as an instrument capable of entertaining in the best sense, educating and even imparting moral uplift. Amid all the more conventional offerings, we have seen plenty of high-quality programming such as *Roots*, *Ken Burns's Civil War*, and the living-room broadcast of *Schindler's List*.

It is this potential—to edify and inform—that you can take advantage of.

SUMMARY: GOODNESS GUIDE

1. To launch a publicity campaign aimed at television, start by getting familiar with your local stations and the type of programming each offers.

2. In developing story ideas to pitch to a station assignment editor, be aware of the audience makeup for the shows you are targeting, and think about the potential for visuals to accompany your story.

3. Preparation is key for the television interview. Hone your message, anticipate questions, make sure you know the length and format of the program.

4. Talk in cool, conversational tones. Keep your body language relaxed. In dress, favor solids and avoid whites.

5. Arrive at the station early. Chat with the interviewer beforehand if possible. After the interview, express thanks and leave.

6. Contact public-affairs directors at local stations. Ask whether they run public service announcements (PSAs). Get a list of guidelines from those that do.

7. In writing your own PSA, use no more than twenty words for every ten seconds it will run. Be precise in defining the who, what, when, where, and why of your subject or event.

8. Type neatly, triple-spaced. Get the copy to the station well in advance of preferred running time.

9. For visuals, submit slides or matte photos. *Not glossy photos.*

10. In any other promotion you do, it's useful to become conversant in the fare that's currently popular on TV and in the movies, as a jumping-off point for metaphors and analogies between your cause and popular culture in today's media

6

Speaking Up for Goodness

Good communication is as stimulating as black coffee,
and just as hard to sleep after.

ANN MORROW LINDBERGH

THE *Los Angeles Times* recently surveyed a range of experts for their tips for promotion. Not surprisingly, they all suggested that a focused, well-thought-out strategy is essential. "Decide what you want to achieve, and then plan your campaign toward that end," said Jeff Davidson, author of *Marketing Your Consulting and Professional Services*. Effective marketing requires restructuring plans, thoughts, even patterns of behavior, he told the Times. "You've got to develop an effective publicity plan."

They also agreed that sales knowledge and ability are important, even for charity providers because, although you aren't "selling" a product in the traditional sense, you are selling your project, and that's just as important. "Everyone should read what salesmanship is all about," Davidson says. For instance, he points out that everyone needs to understand that "the average sale is made after the prospect says 'no' six times."

Davidson also stresses what is called "leveraging," that is, making the most of the fewest resources. "In marketing your career, your practice, or yourself, you don't have to appeal to a thousand people. There are fifteen, at most twenty, people you need to know: the director of the association representing your field and its publications director; a mentor or two; the local editor of your newspaper; leaders of voluntary and community associations."

I generally agree with Davidson, but I would add very quickly that, for charities and nonprofits, getting widely known is never a bad thing. And one of the best ways to become widely known is do public speaking as much as you can in your community. Speech-giving is actually a very important strategy in the charity promoter's arsenal of PR tools to generate donations, volunteers, and goodwill. For that reason, this chapter explores the nature of public speaking and provides advice and encouagement to help you get on the speaking circuit and get your organization some publicity.

THE VALUE OF PUBLIC SPEAKING

You have probably heard the joke that the top two things people fear the most in life are death and public speaking. Nevertheless, public speaking is an essential tool of promotion, for a variety of reasons.

First, public speaking is an extremely valuable skill to have for one simple reason: the need for public speakers is enormous. Many service clubs or business organizations meet weekly, or even more frequently than that, and finding speakers for all those gatherings is usually quite difficult. If you can give a good speech, you will be in demand. I can guarantee that.

To find out how true this is, make a list of service organizations in your area—the Rotary Club, the Optimists, the Lions, the Chamber of Commerce, Realtors' associations, trade groups, et cetera. Start phoning them and you will be amazed at the interest you will generate as soon as you give them a good account of the aims and importance of your project.

Second, public speaking forces you to think thoroughly about your project. When you know you have to get up and speak before others about your cause, you invariably end up asking yourself deep questions about your purpose and your clientele. The pressure to be articulate and thoughtful helps you learn how to explain your cause to others in succinct, effective language.

Public speaking also brings you into contact with real people—in the flesh. That is, your contact is more intimate, and potentially more meaningful, than the contacts you have with the public through the print media or over the airwaves. People can take their measure of you and your words with an immediacy that isn't available any other way. You get to learn firsthand what's on their minds about your organization, and you get insights that you can use to fine-tune your project to better serve your community's needs. "Exposure to other groups and organizations enhances your own perspective and gives your message a broader sounding board," says Art Stevens, author of *The Persuasion Explosion*.

Finally, public speaking can be a significant catalyst to generate other PR opportunities for your group. In fact, I believe that any public-relations campaign should take into account the "synergy" that multiple PR techniques used simultaneously can achieve, as opposed to relying on only one technique such as press releases. I therefore recommend to my clients that they intentionally try to support, reinforce, or play off each PR effort with another effort.

For example, here's how PR synergy works. Imagine that you get a story in the newspaper about your organization. To create synergy, you then approach radio or TV producers with a pitch that they do something that uses the newspaper story as a hook. Then if you get a TV or radio show, you turn around and send the tape or audio of the program you were on to another newspaper reporter in an effort to pitch another story.

Public speaking can be used the same way. Whenever you are called for a possible speaking engagement for a civic, service, or trade organization, send your press clips or tapes of prior appearances on other media so the organization can learn about you and see your capabilities. If they then schedule you to deliver a speech, send a press release of this fact to news editors or reporters whom you are cultivating. As you can see, each event builds upon the last, so that all your efforts combine into a powerful engine of promotion.

Here is an interesting—and very moving—example of synergy in action, courtesy of Glenn Cashmore of San Diego, a journalist who wrote to commend me on the publication of one of my previous books, *Guerrilla PR*, which has become a widely used introduction to public relations in the nation's universities, as well as a popular tutor for laypeople. Glenn wrote me:

> Dear Michael,
> While working the assignment desk at KGTV, I dispatched a crew to a stabbing incident with two men down. It was just a typical night of violence in a big city except that this time it was three blocks from my house. Not a neighborhood known for violence. When the story came back, the injured were two teenage boys stabbed by gay bashers out for a night of fun. After the newscast, the mother of one of the boys called me from Intensive Care regarding my story. I left the newsroom and headed for the hospital. When I arrived, one of the boys was dead.
>
> Your new book teaches people to take action and that's exactly what this situation called for. I employed your techniques and quickly transformed myself from an unknown assignment editor into a civil-rights activist. Starting with the front page of the *San Diego Union*, I used guerilla tactics to get myself featured on talk shows, CNN, *60 Minutes*, *The Advocate*, the *L.A. Times*, *The New Republic* and dozens of gay newspapers and magazines. I was elected to the board of a national journalists' association, I guest-lectured on college campuses, and I was keynote speaker at conventions and

rallies. I was also appointed to the San Diego Hate Crime Commission and worked with the lieutenant governor on the California Hate Crime Commission. I helped form a unique Citizens' Patrol and was elected to be a media organizer for the 1993 March on Washington. All of this happened in six months from the time I started being a guerrilla.

Although this book doesn't delve into the same guerrilla tactics that I taught in my other book, you can see how effective the synergy concept worked for this one individual. This is a PR secret that should not be forgotten.

DEVELOPING YOUR MESSAGE

Just as in the other forms of PR that we've reviewed so far, having a meaningful message is a necessary first step to meaningful public speaking. However, this is usually the least of the challenges for people involved with charities and nonprofits. In my experience, philanthropic organizations all have meaningful messages and stories to tell about the people they serve, the social issues they address, the changes that they've helped effect, and the vision of the future they'd like others to see.

However, to prevent your speeches from becoming preachy lectures that you repeat over and over again, it is worthwhile to spend some time thinking creatively about new ways to explain your charity's purpose with authority and conviction that will keep your audiences coming back for more. Here are two ideas that can help.

1. *Make use of surveys.* Surveys are a great way to generate interesting facts and statistics to use in speeches. You can often produce results that shock people and get the media to notice your cause. For example, many large, wealthy charities commission surveys by professional polling organizations to obtain statistics that back up their cause or to assess the public's opinion on a topic related to their purpose.

Of course, a small nonprofit organization does not usually have the funds for such surveys, but there are inexpensive options that can bring intriguing results. For example, if your organization serves the homeless or the hungry, you might do your own survey of restaurants in your community to see how many of them have leftover food at the end of any given day or week, and how many of them find ways to give it away. A few hours on the phone by staffers at your group, targeting a randomly selected group of restaurateurs, could produce an informal survey that packs a lot of publicity punch. At the very least, such a survey would be an interesting point of reference for speeches by members of your organization.

Another reason to brainstorm for new speech ideas is that having a good, substantial, interesting message makes the delivery of a speech that much easier. When you feel passionate about your subject, and you sense that what you have to say is new and different, you will find that the words tend to flow more readily and your audience will listen more attentively.

2. *Make use of parables.* Parables are stories with an implicit moral message that makes people think. In an interview with Leigh Behrens of the *Chicago Tribune*, businessman David Armstrong suggests that companies use stories to motivate employees and establish an identifiable corporate culture that everyone respects. Armstrong urges businesspeople to visualize their companies not as a business bound together by financial considerations, but as a "tribe" with common values, and with "stories" that illustrate those ideals. He urges managers to make a list of the company's important values—such as service or innovation—and to find examples of when an employee memorably lived up to one of them. He suggests turning those examples into illustrative stories, heroic tales that can inspire other employees to follow suit. Armstrong asserts,

> Go beyond dry, forgettable abstractions—like policy statements, organizational flow charts, and rules manuals. Teach and motivate your employees in the single most memo-

rable, time-honored, and effective way—by telling them stories with morals. Which makes a deeper impression—a set of rules or a story? Think of the Bible. The Pentateuch has 613 rules for living—how many of them can you remember? Compare those 613 rules to the impact of a single parable—the story of the Good Samaritan.

The same technique is very appropriate for speech-making. If you're giving a talk on behalf of your charity, find a parable that illustrates your organization's values and use it as a means to capture your audience's attention. "I tell stories about homeless families we have housed and fed and helped find work, and about the tears of joy that flow," says Mary Jo Copeland, of the Sharing and Caring Hands shelter for the poor in Minneapolis. Mary Jo is a frequent public speaker, and her parable-telling must have some effect: She has raised more than $7 million in private funds for her organization.

"The human-interest parable is really what we're all about," says Bill Grubman, an official with the Dream Street Foundation, based in Los Angeles. His nonprofit group provides camping programs for children with cancers, blood disorders, and other life-threatening diseases. "There are so many charities out there, such a pool for donors to choose from, that you have an obligation to tell people what you're doing, what sets your organization apart, with the most vivid, down-to-earth stories that you can derive from your nonprofit work." He tells audiences about tragically ill children breaking into smiles. And about the satisfactions—along with frustrations—of managing a charity while keeping overhead amazingly low. His parables apparently have power. Dream Street's supporters have included Disney, HBO, CNN, Whoopi Goldberg, and Larry King.

THE MAJOR STYLES OF SPEECHES

Once you have developed your message, the next task you face is deciding what style of speech you should give. Lance Izumi has been a speechwriter in the United States Justice Department and was director of speechwriting and research for former California governor George Deukmejian. He says that in planning a speech, "you first have to select the general subject and purpose. There are several broad categories from which to choose: A speech can be meant either to inform, to persuade, or to entertain."

While a speech can have elements of all of these styles, an effective speech should have only one of them as its general purpose. "For instance," says Izumi, "suppose the subject matter is education. An informational speech might tell people about the structure of school finance in your community. A persuasive speech might try to convince listeners that more money needs to be spent, or some other policy changed. And an entertaining speech might offer a lighthearted look at the life of a student."

In addition to these three styles, I would also add a fourth style: motivational. Similar in genre to the persuasive speech, in that you want your audience to do something after hearing you, the motivational speech differs from the persuasive in that it appeals to emotion rather than to reason. The arguments in a motivational speech don't usually follow a logical pattern, as they are aimed at making the listener *feel* something rather than think a certain way. In fact, many motivational speeches ask listeners to defy logic to overcome a problem or barrier to the group's cause.

Here are some examples of some of these great speech styles:

1. A classic *motivational* speech was Winston Churchill's first address to Parliament after being appointed prime minister, on May 13, 1940.

> I have nothing to offer but blood, toil, tears and sweat....You ask, what is our policy. I say it is to wage war by land, sea, and air. War with all our might and with all the strength God has given us, and to wage war against a monstrous tyranny never surpassed in the dark and lamentable catalogue of human crime.

You ask, what is our aim. I can answer in one word. It is victory. Victory at all costs—victory in spite of all terrors....

2. A classic *persuasive* speech was Minnesota Democratic senator Eugene McCarthy's denunciation of America's involvement in the Vietnam War, on December 2, 1967.

The scriptural promise of the good life is one in which the old men see visions and the young men dream dreams. In the context of this war and all its implications, the young men of America do not dream dreams, but many live in the nightmare of moral anxiety, of concern and great apprehension; and the old men, instead of visions which they can offer to the young, are projecting, in the language of the Secretary of State, a specter of one billion Chinese threatening the peace and safety of the world—a frightening and intimidating future.

The message from the administration today is a message of apprehension, a message of fear, yes—even a message of fear of fear. This is not the real spirit of America. I do not believe that it is. This is a time to test the mood and spirit. To offer in place of doubt—trust. In place of expediency— right judgment. In place of ghettos, let us have neighborhoods and communities. In place of incredibility—integrity.... In place of near despair, let us have hope.... Let us sort out the music from the sounds and again respond to the trumpet and the steady drum.

3. Another persuasive speech that offers a model for a charity advocate is the speech given by Bob Keeshan, "Captain Kangaroo," to the City Club of Seattle, April 13, 1988.

I speak to you because small children need big friends. Young children need older advocates who will plead in favor of meeting their needs, speak up for them because they cannot speak for themselves. They have not lived long enough to be politically sophisticated, only long enough to be abused and neglected.

The Bard on the Power of Persuasion

Marc Antony, the Roman politician, general and trusted friend of emperor Julius Caesar, appears in two of Shakespeare's plays. In *Julius Caesar*, he is called upon by Caesar's assassins to speak at Caesar's funeral. Their hope: that Marc Antony will drive home the point that Caesar was a tyrant who deserved his fate, something the angry crowd already believes. Instead, Marc Antony cleverly turns the anti-Caesar crowd against Caesar's murderers.

When Shakespeare wrote Marc Antony's speech, he created a blueprint for winning over any audience. Here are some lessons in persuasion from Marc Antony's speech:

✦ Speak briefly. Always keep important presentations concise—and effective. Work hard in advance to keep them short.

✦ Begin on common ground. Start by stressing the beliefs and desires you share with your audience. Without being condescending, indicate that you understand and sympathize with their needs.

✦ State your purpose often. Marc Antony persuaded the people that Caesar loved them by emphasizing that Caesar was not power-hungry and that those who slew him were murderers, not heroes.

✦ Keep your demands to a minimum. Make only one or two points in any presentation. Most people's attention spans are too short to absorb more.

✦ Imply that you have more information than you have

been able to tell your audience. Your goal here is merely to spark your audience's imagination, not to satisfy it.

from *Bottom Line/Personal* newsletter,
Sept. 15, 1996, interview with
George Weinberg, author of *Will Power!* . . .

OUTLINING AND WRITING YOUR SPEECH

The next step in preparing a speech is obvious: to write it.
However, rather than sitting down at your computer and banging
out your talk willy-nilly, it is best to begin by listing the main
points you want to make about your subject and then sequencing
them in a meaningful way. In a persuasive speech, for instance, the
main points will answer the question: Why is the change you propose needed? The main points of an informational speech will provide a description of the subject you are talking about. For
instance, if your speech is on school funding, you would detail the
sources of money for the school district. In a motivational speech,
your main points will answer the question, What do you want the
audience to do and why?

You then must decide what to say about each point, so that
your speech is not just a list of ideas. In a sense, each of your main
points needs to be expanded upon in some fashion so that you can
talk about the point for at least a few minutes. In a persuasive
speech, for example, you need to find at least one "proof," or piece
of supportive evidence. for each of your points. Proofs can include
statistics, anecdotes, comparisons, testimony, and quotations. If
your topic is complex, it also helps to use visual aids such as slides,
maps, diagrams, and motion pictures to give the audience something to engage with. Visuals increase the chance your listeners
will remember some of what they hear.

Motivational speeches often use stories strung together, one
after another, with each story reinforcing the message of the speech
and building a case for the audience to take action.

After expanding your points, effectively you have now built the body of your speech, the heart of what you want to say. All you need to do next is to plan an introduction and a conclusion. As you probably know, it is best to have a catchy opening, either a joke or funny story, or an arresting bit of information to open a talk. Once you get past that, you next tell the audience what it is you're going to tell them: the purpose of your speech, and why it's important for them. You can then launch into the main body. Finally, in the conclusion you simply summarize your points—unless it's a speech given for entertainment, in which case you end with a final humorous statement. If your speech was to persuade, you should give one last pitch for your position.

Once you have planned your speech, it is usually recommended that you put the main points from your outline onto note cards, one point per card. You can then refer to these cards as you talk extemporaneously, gently shuffling the cards as you go from point to point without having the audience notice that you are doing so. Most speech-givers swear that this is a much better method of public speaking than writing out the full text of a talk and reading it verbatim to the audience. In reading, speakers tend to lose eye contact with the audience and thus seem stilted and dull. In contrast, speaking in what appears to be off the top of your head (although you have rehearsed it) gives audiences a feeling that you are there with them and that you know your cause very well.

Podium Dos And Don'ts

After finding a subject you consider important, and outlining it, the hard part is clearly giving your talk. Here are some practical rules about speech delivery that you should take to heart.

✦ Find out, as much as possible, what the makeup of the audience will be in terms of age, gender, background. This can help you tailor what you need to say and how to say it.

✦ Develop a friendly intimacy with your listeners. Look out into the audience and find some friendly faces nodding and smiling at you. Use these people for reassurance when you need it. Try to avoid staring at an audience member who just sits there with arms crossed, not smiling. That type of person will only add to your nervousness.

✦ Beforehand, practice, practice, practice—preferably in front of a mirror. Practice with a tape recorder, too. It's one of the best ways of banishing "uhs", and "you knows" from your vocabulary.

✦ Use personal anecdotes to make your audience get the point. If you are talking about conflict resolution, for instance, you could tell how your spouse asserted herself gently but firmly at a restaurant to stop a large man from sticking his dirty hands into the salad bar. What listener is going to forget that disturbingly vivid message?

✦ Challenge the audience by starting with a who, what, when, or why question, or a quote or jarring statistic, or some kind of controversial statement. If the organization you represent serves the needy, for instance, you can draw on statistics or examples that illustrate the need your group is responding to.

✦ Don't use humor that someone might find offensive. The best jokes are self-deprecatory ones. In the same vein, never use ethnically demeaning or sexist language.

✦ Keep your language simple, using words with as few syllables as possible.

✦ Use props, such as articles, books, and studies to add impact.

✦ If appropriate, seek audience participation by asking for opinions or even taking a poll.

✦ Keep your message tight and focused: Tell them what you're going to tell them; tell them; and tell them what you told them—and end with as much of a challenge to the audience as you began with.

THE THREE MOST ANNOYING PUBLIC-SPEAKING MISTAKES

There are three common mistakes that people make when speaking publicly.

1. *Speaking too long.* This ends up boring the audience, so that even if your speech was good at the outset, they will leave feeling unsatisfied and disappointed. You must learn to tailor the length of your speech to the needs of the topic and the amount of time the audience is prepared to listen. Find out before speaking how long you should speak for, and stick to that time period.

2. *Using stories or anecdotes that don't relate to the subject.* People like stories, but if they can't understand why you told them a story, or what point, if any, it is tied to, they will think your speech wanders and you will lose their attention. Make sure every story relates to a point you want to make. If necessary, be explicit by saying, "I told you that story because...."

3. *Continually apologizing for being nervous.* When you talk about your own nervousness, it makes the audience focus on the problem and wonder if you're going to make it through the speech. Although you think it may help make the audience relate to you, it actually undermines your ability to keep them focused on your topic.

ENGAGE YOUR AUDIENCE

If you want to engage your audience the way the great TV commentators do, keep the following tips in mind:

◆ Tell a story rather than merely transmitting a list of facts. Give your story a clear point of view. Be sure it has a beginning and an end, plus interesting characters, a plot, good dialogue, humor, and illustration. Tell your story well by rehearsing first.

✦ Remember that even when you're not talking, you're communicating in the way you listen. Most of us look very grim instead of animated and pleasant when we're listening. To be like the TV-trained executive, animate your face to appear interested.

✦ Try to use some visual elements to make your presentation more interesting. Hold up charts, visuals, graphs, or objects from the topic you are discussing.

✦ Even though you may have prepared your speech, look spontaneous. The best television commentators can make themselves appear confident, knowledgeable, and powerful.

THE POWER OF CLARITY

In his *Speaker's Sourcebook II*, Glenn Van Ekeren, a seminar leader for business and nonprofit organizations, stresses the importance of clarity in speech-giving. He points out that "communication" comes from the Latin word *commune*, which means "held in common." He recites a humorous example of how clarity can be elusive, when your audience understands something completely different from what you intended.

Consider this scenario: A construction worker approached the reception desk in a doctor's office. The receptionist asked him why he was there. "I have shingles," he responded. She took down his name, address, medical insurance number, and told him to have a seat. Over the next hour he had his height, weight, blood, and urine checked and was asked to take off his clothes and wait for the doctor. When the physician came in the examining room, he asked what the man had. "Shingles," came the reply.

"Where?" asked the doctor.

"Outside in the truck," the construction worker said. "Where do you want them?"

The point is obvious, but too often not taken to heart. "Communication is not simply sending a message," as Glenn Van Ekeren puts it. "It is creating shared meaning and understanding— swiftly, clearly, and precisely."

SUMMONING YOUR COURAGE

Admittedly, reading about good speech-giving techniques in a book doesn't overcome what for many people is the most daunting thing about standing in front of an audience —the sheer nervousness it can cause. As I mentioned earlier, public speaking is a very basic fear for most people.

Nevertheless, I encourage you to recognize that public speaking is worth your time and energy to master. Public-speaking skills are crucial to your career. Fortunately, it is a skill that can be taught, and is taught in nearly every community in the country. You can easily find courses in public speaking at adult education centers, colleges, universities, and in many private executive-training schools such as the Dale Carnegie classes.

In the meantime, here are some pointers about how to overcome fear and summon courage:

1. Think positively. You are the expert and would not have been invited to speak if your ideas were not of value.
2. Recognize that your nervousness will be more obvious to you than to your audience.
3. Use breathing exercises and relaxation techniques to calm yourself down before speaking.
4. Arrive early and get to know the people in the first few rows. This will give you some friendly faces to focus on during the speech, allowing you to assess the audience's reactions to your talk.
5. Visualize yourself giving your speech. Imagine yourself speaking, your voice loud, clear, and assured. When you visualize yourself as successful, you will be successful.

6. Realize that people want you to succeed. Audiences want you to be interesting, stimulating, informative, and entertaining. They don't want you to fail.
7. Turn nervousness into positive energy. Harness your nervous energy and transform it into vitality and enthusiasm.
8. Gain experience. Experience builds confidence, which is the key to effective speaking.

NETWORKING YOUR WAY TO SUCCESS

In addition to public speaking, there is another highly socially-oriented communication skill that anyone working in a nonprofit organization must develop: the ability to network smoothly and extensively with many types of people. Networking is essentially defined as the skill to meet people and talk with them to build both friendships and contacts. Some business consultants also use the term "shmoozing," which is a Yiddish word that's been defined as "making light, friendly, gossipy conversation to meet someone."

Marketing consultant Terri Mandell, author of *Power Shmoozing—The New Rules for Business and Social Success*, says the art of shmoozing is a requirement for people who want to succeed at love, friendship, business—or a nonprofit venture. Mandell likes to juxtapose the old Miss Manners attitudes with the new business reality today in which everyone and anyone you meet may prove useful to your life:

> Miss Manners is the definitive expert on how things used to be. She's firmly against networking. She doubts its effectiveness and considers it contrary to genuine leisure, personal ties and friendship. I believe, in contrast, that networking is the only way to find friends—business or otherwise. Miss Manners also finds parties held for business purposes to be "cruel, cynical and inefficient exploiters of time and money," and believes that business cards should never be handed

out at social events. I feel that your private life and your work life are equal expressions of who you are, and the more the two blend, the more your world is expanded. And expansion is what it's all about.

My personal commitment to the idea and practice of networking is a passionate one because I believe that all new relationships with others have the potential to be life-changing, or even world-changing. One of the ways networking can literally change the world is described by a concept I've been credited with developing: the idea of the thought virus. It's a notion modeled on the computer virus. Someone has an idea, and shares it with someone else, who also shares it, so that eventually a network of people have been introduced to it. The idea continues to spread, mutating and perhaps flowering into something far more valuable and brilliant than in its first incarnation.

Another valuable thing about networking—beyond the potential for getting new friends, new supporters for your charity, new perspectives from people of diverse backgrounds about how your organization can succeed—is that networking requires exercise in building traits that make you a better and more creative person. Ultimately, this translates into also making you someone better at marketing—i.e., selling goodness—which is why I am all in favor of good networking skills.

Are You Shy?

Oddly enough, many people are afraid of networking, largely out of shyness. In fact, studies at Stanford and several eastern universities suggest that 40 percent or more of Americans feel they are shy. Unfortunately, this tendency is usually a hindrance to the development of your nonprofit, altruistic project through networking.

Where does shyness come from? Most psychologists think shyness is learned, rather than genetically programmed into us. Susan RoAne, author of the best-selling networking book *How to Work a*

Room, points out that most of us were taught as children, "Don't talk to strangers," but that this childhood conditioning often continues to instill dread in us as adults when we meet new people.

The good news is that many psychologists today believe that shyness can be unlearned. According to Lynne Henderson, a psychologist and director of the Palo Alto Shyness Clinic, formerly affiliated with Stanford, points to what she calls her "social fitness model," which likens learning to be at ease with other people with getting in shape physically. Both skills require "working out" and doing so regularly. She warns us that it's not going to feel good at the beginning to get out there socially, but if you have no pain, you also have no gain.

At her shyness clinic, clients are slowly forced to participate in activities they fear, like going to parties. They also work to erase negative patterns of thinking such as, "I'm going to say the wrong thing and look stupid," and they practice skills in listening, assertiveness, self-disclosure, and handling criticism.

If shyness is a serious dilemma for you, it might be worth your while to read some of the many self-help books available on overcoming shyness and/or seeking professional help. Living with this limitation in your life can be a serious detriment to full enjoyment and success in anything you do, but especially in allowing you to sell goodness for your organization.

Even lawyers can have a problem talking to people at parties, to judge from the fact that thirty-five attorneys attended a party/seminar given by the Barristers Club of San Francisco, with the theme, "How to Work a Room Without Being Unctuous."

"How many of you went to law school so you could sell something?" asked the seminar leader. No hands went up. The speaker took note, and went on to explain—as reported by *The Recorder,* a legal newspaper—that lawyers, just as other people with projects or visions to promote, must overcome the "inner dragons" that make them uncomfortable turning social occasions into opportunities to make new business relationships.

If you have a nonprofit project to promote, you have every bit as much reason to learn the networking art as any attorney. Don't let yourself be found guilty of ignoring opportunities for getting your good word out.

Where to Network and How

A savvy charity promoter will systematically plan opportunities to attend parties, mixers, and many other social events as they arise, deploying the tactic of networking or shmoozing with verve and grace. The standard social and business events offer the classic venues for networking opportunities, but they're by no means the only opportunities. To broaden your networking ability, consider all of the following as opportunities to meet others and talk about your charity work:

+ seminars,
+ alumni organizations,
+ church or synagogue,
+ school and college acquaintances,
+ business groups like the Better Business Bureau, Rotary, Chamber of Commerce,
+ recovery groups,
+ family,
+ hobby clubs,
+ political parties and organizations.

In general, the best networking is when you can be yourself and meet people without pressure or discomfort. However, many social events are initially "stiff" when people first congregate and size each other up. In those situations, here are some useful ground rules for smoothing out your networking efforts:

✦ Do it with a good attitude. Be positive and upbeat.

✦ Know why you are networking. Ask yourself what is your purpose for attending this event?

✦ Bring plenty of business cards, but pass them out in a discriminating way so that you do not appear to be solely interested in business.

✦ Be ready to talk about interesting things. Gather tidbits of information by reading the newspapers and magazines before you go so that you can have some news or interesting ideas to discuss. (Of course, also have your message about your own organization honed and ready to tell anyone who asks.)

✦ Introduce yourself, but keep your introduction to a pithy, interesting fifteen seconds and accompany it with a firm handshake and eye contact. And put a smile into your voice and eyes.

✦ If you are feeling uptight about approaching strangers, it is often suggested that you pretend to be the host of the event, who is looking for other white-knuckled guests. Look for someone with a tight grip on their drinking glasses, as this person will likely welcome your conversation.

✦ Read name tags, and wear your own on your right shoulder, in the line of sight of anyone you talk to. As you extend your hand, read the other person's tag and call him or her by name.

✦ Avoid hanging out by the walls of the room. Move toward the room's center, where the people are—and don't dwell on your feeling of awkwardness; remember the whole room is in this together.

✦ Don't get trapped in long conversations. Keep moving. If necessary, excuse yourself from someone with whom you've already spent time so you can find another person. Simply tell the first person, "It was interesting to talk with you."

✦ Smile and make eye contact with people. If you walk into a room and stand there looking forlorn, no one will want to talk with you. However, if you make yourself the most approachable person in the room, others will feel at ease talking with you.

Susan RoAne suggests a three-step process for starting conversation. First, make an observation: "It's cold in here." Second, ask an open-ended question. "Are you cold?" or "How does it feel to you?" Finally, say something revealing about yourself to ease tension: "I'm usually suffering from hot flashes."

Pauline Shirley, president of Toastmasters International, admits that breaking the ice may be the most difficult part of maneuvering at a party of strangers. "The most difficult thing is that first approach," she told *Investor's Business Daily*. "I introduce myself and describe where I work. The second step is to show interest in them by asking a question."

Posing a question allows the other person to do some talking right off, so you don't come across as too talkative and so that a speak-listen rhythm is established that leads to a mutually satisfying exchange.

As for appropriate opening questions, Shirley says, at a convention, you might ask, "What brought you here?" or "What do you think so far? Do you plan to attend the next session?" For a company event: "What department do you work in?" or, "How long have you worked here? Do you know a lot of people here?"

Another approach is to walk over to a group that is already talking. Listen for a while, and you can eventually join in with an observation or question. "It's easier to become part of a conversation if you walk over to a group," says Arthur Reel, a New York-based communications expert who teaches courses in conversational skills. "If you go up to just one person, then open with a comment that involves the environment around you, such as a smell coming from the kitchen or asking about what someone is wearing," Reel told *Investor's Business Daily*. "Just avoid money, age and weight."

"Most people are in the same position you're in: They don't know anybody either," said Jody Powell, chairman of Powell Tate, a public-relations firm in Washington, D.C. "They're also trying to strike up conversations in an appropriate way. So if you take the direct approach, you solve the problem for them, too."

Roger Ailes, chairman of Ailes Communications, argues eloquently for developing one particular skill if you are seeking to improve your networking: the power to listen. He writes that "human communication goes through three phases: reception (listening), information processing (analyzing), and transmission (speaking). When you overlap any of those, you may short-circuit the reception (listening) process. As a result, you should try to listen without overanalyzing. [On the other hand] the flip side of listening too little is talking too much. Most of us tell people more than they need to know. We ramble. We concentrate more on ourselves than on what other people are telling us. In sales, you can't go wrong if you listen too carefully; but you can really blow it if you talk too much. As the Greek philosopher Epictetus said, 'Nature has given us one tongue, but two ears, that we may hear from others twice as much as we speak.' "

Ailes also makes a powerful case for "lightening up." "A sense of humor measures our ability to see things through someone else's eyes—to recognize that others are like us," he writes. He urges people to ask themselves a series of questions designed to gauge their degree of self-focus—such as, "Do I take a lot of satisfaction in lecturing people or being tough with them?... Do I feel cheated by fate—in my career or in life? Do I think others around me have gotten ahead largely through luck? Do I still blame my parents for my problems? How often do I use the word 'I'?"

Says Ailes: "If you came out on the 'self-absorbed' side of even one of these questions, you need to lighten up. You're probably wearing out your friends, family and co-workers. The most important question you face in your career and in life may be this: Do you bring other people up or down?"

All in all, it is useful to take the view that networking is no different than making friends. Seen this way, networking simply requires curiosity and respect for others, and a sense that every relationship can build your character or even change your soul.

Summary: Goodness Guide

1. Identify local service clubs, trade groups, and community groups that use guest speakers. Call them, tell about your nonprofit and the social issues it addresses, and offer to give a presentation on it.

2. Speeches are classified, in general, as *persuasive*, *informative*, *motivational*, or *entertaining*. Plan which approach you will take.

3. Know what kind of audience you'll be addressing.

4. Preparing a speech requires identifying the principle ideas, some evidence for each point, a brief attention-getting introduction, and a conclusion that draws the main themes together.

5. Outline your remarks and try to deliver your talks from note cards. Avoid reading a speech. Strive for eye contact and a conversational style of delivery.

6. Arrive early and talk casually with members of the audience. Use them as "supports"—friendly faces to whom you can look—during the talk, to overcome fear.

7. Use visual aids—slides, charts, photos—if possible.

8. Use anecdotes more than dry statistics. Develop parables, human-interest stories, about how your organization has helped specific individuals—stories that illustrate your group's defining values.

9. Seek clarity in your speaking. Be sure your audience doesn't take what you say in a way you didn't intend.

10. Other than public speaking, networking is another invaluable means of expanding your organization's contacts and supporters. Develop strategies for overcoming shyness and approaching strangers at business and social functions. As a nonprofit worker, you're someone interested in other people. Act on that instinct when you're in the company of strangers, and sincerely seek to meet new people and learn about them.

FUND-RAISING WITH FLAIR

Goodness is the only investment that never fails.
THOREAU, *Walden*, 1854

POVERTY. Homelessness. Crime. Broken homes. America faces daunting problems in all of these areas, says Russ Reid, chairman and CEO of the Russ Reid Company, which specializes in fund-raising and PR for a number of major charities and nonprofits. In an address to the National Catholic Development Conference, Reid pointed out that government hasn't been able to fix things alone. In his view, the solution involves "a spiritual dimension. We must become one at the bottom level of society—with love and service. But with some nine hundred thousand charities and non-profits, the people and programs are already in place to begin to solve these problems."

Nevertheless, Reid believes there is a major obstacle in the path for most charities and nonprofits: the lack of a marketing perspective. He rightly points out: "Nothing happens until somebody sells something. Unfortunately, marketing is suspect because of inappropriate advertising claims. What is needed [by nonprofits] is the professional discipline of marketing." He cites Mothers Against Drunk Driving and Habitat for Humanity as examples of organizations that have used marketing know-how to build their programs and change society.

Reid is absolutely, 100 percent correct. There is a empirical link between marketing and fund-raising that cannot be denied. It's all well and good to talk about love and service, but if the dollars are not available to implement the love, and there isn't the publicity to draw volunteers for service, your organization is left only with happy talk at the end of the day.

This chapter therefore deals with the means and method of fund-raising, which is the lifeblood of any nonprofit. We will examine how to seek outright donations from the various market segments, how to partner with businesses in joint alliances, how plan a capital campaign, and how to host large events that raise cash and attract publicity.

New Options for Giving: Charitable Remainder Trusts

The suggestion that charities encourage planned giving on a larger scale from prosperous donors, rather than continually hitting them up year in and year out for relatively small contributions, leads charities and nonprofits to look in several potentially fruitful new directions.

One vehicle that has gained popularity as the stock market has increased substantially in value over the past decade is the "charitable remainder trust," which allows the giver a form of relief from capital-gains taxes on appreciation in stock values. Here's how this vehicle for giving works.

An investor creates a charitable remainder trust and then donates his or her stocks or other assets to the trust. The trust pays the individual, or some other designated beneficiary, a specified percentage—at least 5 percent—of the trust's annual fair market value. These distributions run either for a fixed term of up to twenty years, or for the life of the beneficiaries. When the term has elapsed, the trust's assets are distributed to charities that the donor had selected.

Charitable remainder trusts offer a number of tax benefits for donors. First, when the trust sells the appreciated property, no capital-gains tax is imposed, so it can grow and reinvest proceeds from asset sales on a tax-deferred basis. And the annual payout is figured as a percentage of the trust's entire value, not its value less the capital-gains assessment. If the owner had sold the assets on his or her own, she would have had to pay taxes on the assets' appreciated value, and thus would have had less money.

A detailed discussion of this and other planned-giving vehicles is beyond the scope of this book. But it is important that charities and nonprofits know they exist and investigate their potential, both for donors and for the charities to which the donations ultimately go.

MARKETING STRATEGIES FOR FUND-RAISING SUCCESS

How do energetic, innovative charities and nonprofits revitalize their publicity and fund-raising efforts in an era when the public sector is cutting back and private individuals find themselves overwhelmed by requests for donations? The first task is to understand the potential target audience from which money can come.

Consider some of the characteristics of current charitable contributors. "About two-thirds of U.S. adults donated to a nonprofit in the past year," reported *American Demographics* in 1995. "Yet they differ in several ways from the average American. More than six in ten are married, compared with 54 percent of all adults.

Donors have a median household income of $39,100, compared with the overall median of $31,200. They are more likely than average to be women (61 percent versus 51 percent), white (89 percent versus 75 percent), college graduates (47 percent versus 20 percent), and older (a median of 43 versus 38)."

Such general statistics are useful, of course, but the savvy nonprofit fund-raiser needs to dig deeper and understand the specific markets for money.

The Largest Market: Baby Boomers

Without a doubt, the largest and most intriguing market for fund-raising is the baby-boomer generation, the huge army of Americans born between 1946 and 1964. America now boasts 81 million boomers, a number that dwarfs the older, fifty-five-plus population of 48 million, and the 33 million "Gen Xers" born between 1965 and 1980.

"Soon the only donors and prospects will be baby boomers and younger adults," writes nonprofit consultant Judith E. Nichols in the July 1996 issue of *Fund Raising Management*. "It makes sense to use the balance of this century to plan a transition from the traditional donor to the very different boomer audience," she argues. "As we move through the 1990s and into the twenty-first century, most not-for-profits will need to target baby boomers as new and renewing donors. The reason: The bulk of our population growth will occur because people are living longer rather than because more people are being born. Your contributors tomorrow will be those individuals you attract today!"

Fortunately, large numbers of boomers have the wherewithal to assist charities and nonprofits. Half of all boomers reported incomes of between $30,000 and $75,000 in a recent analysis, according to *The Boomer Report*. Eleven percent had incomes of $75,000 to $100,000, and 8 percent took in more than $100,000. Moreover, an estimated $10.4 trillion will be bequeathed to boomers over the next half century, the largest intergenerational transfer of funds ever. On average, each baby boomer family will receive $50,000.

But targeting this massive, affluent audience for donations of time and money requires more than operating a program worthy of contributions. It is necessary to understand the unique perspective of the baby-boom generation, very different from individuals born before the Second World War.

"Raised as 'idealists,' boomers have been taught to put others ahead of themselves," says Judith Nichols. "They see themselves as 'changing the world,' not fitting in with it like their 'civic' and 'silent' parents and grandparents." But their loyalty to any one charity over time cannot be won as easily as was the case with their parents. Perhaps because boomers—who have been catered to as a generation ever since their *Romper Room* days—see themselves as special, they have some exacting expectations of charities and nonprofits. For instance, according to Nichols, "they expect organizations seeking their patronage to cultivate them extensively even when they are contributing at modest levels. They also prefer to make contributions on a major scale yet won't or can't commit to the cost up front."

To create donor loyalty in baby boomers, Nichols suggests that charities and nonprofits concentrate on getting ongoing pledges rather than a single, large gift. She recommends that you seek a monthly payment because it helps boomers buy into your organization and helps you to identify them for recognition and extra cultivation. In her view, these monthly payments also break the psychological barrier; they enable the baby boomer to make a gift at an enhanced level that reflects his/her "apartness" from the crowd.

Fortunately, there is an inevitable demographic trend that should make the boomer obstacle a bit less daunting for charities and nonprofits. Russ Reid's opinion surveys suggest that the inexorable march of time can change outlooks and patterns of behavior among boomers. "As people get older they tend to have a greater religious connection because they are wondering what comes next," he reports. "Also the older generations are more community-focused than younger people."

Nevertheless, while these observations about boomers are

interesting and informative, the savvy nonprofit would be wise to be open to prospecting among many nontraditional groups as well, including the following groups.

The Black Market

One of the fastest growing and most intriguing markets today for charities and nonprofits is the new contributor base of black Americans. Giving among African-Americans throughout the United States is on the rise, suggesting that here is indeed a population offering fruitful potential for charities in search of new donors. Sixty-four percent of black families contributed to charities in a typical year in the 1990s, according to the report "Giving and Volunteering in the United States," published by *Independent Sector*. That is more than double the percentage of previous years, when 26 percent of African-American families were charitable donors. What's more, African-Americans in the early 1990s donated a larger percentage of household income to charities than the U.S. norm—2.7 percent compared to 2.2 percent. Black families with household incomes of $40,000 or above gave an average of $1,616 to charity, *Independent Sector* reports.

USA Today recognized a major news angle in this trend in a story by reporter Lori Sharn.

> William Mays gives away $250,000 a year. Mays, an African-American businessman from Indianapolis, donates to his church and to the NAACP. But he also gives outside the black community, to cultural institutions such as the children's museum and the symphony.
>
> "I want the quality of life in Indianapolis to be very positive." says Mays, head of Mays Chemical Co., one of the nation's largest black-owned businesses. "I believe in sharing success."
>
> His attitude reflects the "absolutely growing" phenomenon of wealthy African-American philanthropists who include nonblack institutions in their giving, says Emmett

Carson, author of books on black philanthropy. Carson says this reflects the integration of blacks into mainstream society.

There are large numbers of black professionals and athletes who are taking a broad public view of the impact their money can have, as opposed to an earlier generation who thought you support [only] the church and the NAACP," says Robert Franklin, a former Ford Foundation official. "It's an exciting period."

+ Atlanta Hawks guard Steve Smith says he's giving $2.5 million to Michigan State University for a student-athlete center....
+ Chicago Bulls star Michael Jordan gave $1 million to the University of North Carolina's new institute for families.
+ The late businessman and lawyer Reginald Lewis gave $3 million to Harvard University for an international law center.
+ Sheila and Robert Johnson of Black Entertainment Television have pledged $250,000 to Carnegie Hall in New York City for children's outreach programs....

The phenomenon of wealthy black philanthropists is so new that there is little research.

"It's not a big movement, but it's beginning to happen," says Charles Stephens of the Center on Philanthropy, at Indiana University. "There is a significant increase in giving by folks who are newly rich."

What is measurable is that black professionals are reaching the higher income brackets. In 1995, there were 259,000 black households with income of $100,000 or more. Adjusted for inflation, that's more than twenty times the number of households in 1966.

But this wealth is largely untapped. Most wealthy African-Americans are in their prime earning years. Philanthropists, black or white, usually wait until they're old or dead to give away most of their money.

Mays, at fifty-one, is an exception. He gives away about $50,000 of his own income and an additional $200,000 of his company's pretax profits every year. He estimates 40 percent of his giving is directed toward African-American groups....

But Mays also gives to the opera, even though "I really have no interest in opera. I don't even understand it. But I contribute to the opera because there are people who understand it and like it."

Sheila Johnson, forty-eight, is a former music educator who gives mainly to arts and children's organizations. She is executive vice president of corporate affairs for Black Entertainment Television and wife of founder Robert Johnson.

She says they give away $600,000 to $800,000 of their own money each year. She also distributes $1.5 million of corporate money.

The Johnsons also support programs that benefit all children.

"I don't like to set up a color quota for anything," Johnson says. "I tend to give from my heart and where the programs are needed."

The Growing Gen Xers

The so-called Generation Xers are not necessarily the self-absorbed and selfish population that some popular lore paints them, according to a Direct Marketing Association study. The 1996 report, "Lifestage Analysis," found "baby busters" (aged eighteen to thirty) giving to educational, environmental, religious, and political organizations, among others—"and they weren't all nickel-and-dime gifts," the study says.

Here are some points to ponder in crafting a marketing strategy aimed at these baby busters:

+ Half of them consider it important to have a "meaningful" relationship with a nonprofit group, yet only 37 percent of them feel they currently have such a relationship.
+ Busters are more interested than any other age group in getting regular communications from charities and nonprofits in the form of financial reports, videos, newsletters, even birthday cards.
+ Younger donors place less importance on a general perception of a charity's good work than on hard evidence of quality and effectiveness.
+ Nearly one-third of the Gen-Xers who link up with charities and nonprofits get their initial information about these charities through on-line computer services.

The study, which happened to be published by Russ Reid's company, also called into question the stereotype that busters lack religious commitment. It found that fully six of every ten Gen-Xers donate money to a church, synagogue, or other place of worship.

And one-third of busters describe themselves as conservative—a percentage that is about the same as in older age groupings. So don't be deceived by stereotypes.

Yes, Teenagers Have Money, Too

Finally, teenagers are perhaps that newest group that holds promising prospects for charities and nonprofits. An *Independent Sector* study reports that the number of Americans aged twelve to seventeen who are engaged in volunteer activities increased 7 percent, from 12.4 million to 13.4 million, between 1992 and 1997. Their motivations for volunteering are worth noting. Eighty-four percent do so out of a feeling of "compassion for the needy," according to *Independent Sector*. Eighty-four percent also said it's because the

"cause is important to them. To "get a new perspective on life" was
listed by 74 percent, while 73 percent said that "if you help others,
others help you." Seventy-three percent said volunteering "is
important to people they respect." And 63 percent suggested that
volunteering "looks good on a résumé"—which, of course, often is
true, and is another argument you can use legitimately in trying to
recruit young people for your organization.

The Ups and Downs of Volunteerism

Organizations that depend heavily on volunteers have
their work cut out for them in recruiting boomers. One
main reason is that boomers' involvement in women's and
men's groups, religious organizations, and political groups
has declined markedly since their parents' prime. Whereas
Americans born in the first four decades of the century
continue to display remarkably high levels of civic engagement and social trust, their children and grandchildren
raised in the 1950s, '60s, and '70s, appear to have been
struck by an "anti-civic" virus.

One strategy for attracting boomers to volunteerism is
to highlight in your marketing the number of boomers who
are already volunteering for you. The power of example is
more forceful than a sermon. Big Brothers/Big Sisters, for
instance, reports success with the publicity given to baby-
boomer producer John Wells's involvement in the program. Wells, executive producer of ER, was featured on
the Today Show with his little brother, and he was awarded a national honor by the Big Brothers organization.

Attracting Donors

Whichever audience you go for, attracting donors is not easy.
Nonprofit World, a publication of the Society for Nonprofit Organ-

izations, reports on a study by the Russ Reid Company that offers clues on how to find and keep donors. The survey, released in 1995, reveals three main reasons people give.

+ They believe in the cause.
+ They believe the charity spends its dollars wisely.
+ They believe in the organization's effectiveness.

The survey also found that a relationship between the non-profit and donor may not be as important as previously thought. Only 52 percent of the 1,164 donors surveyed felt that a relation-ship with the organization was desirable or necessary. Many were cynical about the very idea of a relationship. Those who do want a relationship are high-end donors, while those who don't care about a relationship are low-end donors.

Other key results of the survey:

+ The average U.S. donor is a religious, middle-aged, college-educated married woman.
+ Over 80 percent of those who give to nonprofit organizations also give to churches or other places of worship.
+ The most generous donors are people who have named charities and nonprofits as beneficiaries in their wills.
+ Two-thirds of donors would like to be given a regular chance to express their concerns and views to executives of nonprofit organizations.
+ Almost one-fourth of donors say that an 800 number would improve their relationship with a nonprofit. In contrast, only 14 percent said personalized letters improve their relationships with organizations, and just 18 percent said the same about thank-you notes.

The study held helpful clues about how you can find new donors and keep current donors:

1. Target people who give to churches, synagogues, and other houses of worship, whether or not your organization is religious.
2. Target middle-aged donors. Most donors are in their forties, with thirty-somethings not far behind.
3. Concentrate on planned giving, and target planned-giving donors for other forms of fund-raising.
4. Be sure people know that your organization is effective and efficient. Tell them where their money will be spent and what percentage of donations go directly toward your cause.
5. Identify donors' motivations, and use this knowledge to create new segmentation by message elements.
6. Support message segmentation with selective media or lists that are outside your current prospects.
7. Build relationships with donors who give over $500 a year. Do so by sending them relevant information and making sure they have access to the organization's leaders.

INSPIRING IDEAS TO IMPROVE FUND-RAISING

+ Create a logo.
+ Ask celebrities to donate items for a silent auction.
+ Consider getting donors' and volunteers' names included in the Congressional Record, having a flag flown over the Capitol, or getting a letter written from a member of Congress to your organization's supporters.
+ Ask the White House to produce letters congratulating your organization on the national week or month dealing with your cause, or other national special events that you are involved with.
+ Have your governor or mayor sign a proclamation declaring a certain day of the year as your organization's day, or as a day dealing with your cause.
+ Recycle good ideas. A speech or presentation can turn into an op-ed piece; a visit from out-of-town

people who deal with your issue can prompt a photo in the newspaper.

+ Develop a quarterly newsletter that you can mail to the media with your organization's news and upcoming events.

+ Send thank-you notes to reporters after they've published stories about your organization. And when you see interesting articles you think might be useful to reporters you work with, send them as an FYI.

+ Alternate your press releases with media alerts (who, what, where, when, why).

+ Remember to promote your program through volunteer leaders. Local stories with human-interest angle often get more coverage.

+ Fax your newsletter. This gives it a newsy, urgent appeal and will save your organization money on paper and printing costs.

Adapted from *Association Management*,
December 1995, published by the
American Society of Association Executives

PARTNERING WITH BUSINESSES

One of the top strategies for revitalizing fund-raising today is creating innovative sponsorship and partnership arrangements with businesses. "More than ever, nonprofits need what many companies can offer: crucial new sources of revenue," writes Alan R. Andreasen, professor of marketing at Georgetown University, in the *Harvard Business Review*. "But nonprofits offer corporate partners a great deal in return: opportunity to enhance their image—and increase the bottom line—by supporting a worthy cause."

Indeed, market and public-opinion pressures as much as anything else are motivating more and more businesses to search out opportunities to be seen as patrons of worthy community causes. A

1995 article in *Industry Week* magazine reported on this heightened business-sector commitment to social responsibility as follows:

> Walk into almost any company lobby today and among the first things likely to catch your eye, right there along with the ficus tree and the coffee table laden with business magazines, is a tasteful plaque tacked to the wall. It's the corporate "mission statement," earnestly proclaiming the firm's commitment to the highest ethical practices, community service, environmental stewardship, and other praiseworthy values. That's something you probably wouldn't have seen twenty-five years ago. Few, if any, mission statements existed. Not that companies were unethical, bad citizens, or wanton polluters. But basically they had a single mission that was well-understood: to make money for their shareholders.... Today, as the proliferation of mission statements incessantly reminds, a corporation's role is considerably expanded. A company's basic purpose, to be sure, is still to make a profit. Beyond that, though, it is expected to respond to a variety of other demands. As Craig Smith, president of Corporate Citizen, a Seattle-based think tank that performs research on corporate social-responsibility issues, declares: "A company now is responsible to its stakeholders rather than just its shareholders. And, increasingly, its competitiveness depends upon its ability to be part of the solution to societal needs."
>
> In all likelihood, the trend will continue. The public's demand for such goals as a clean environment, better public education, safer workplaces, equal opportunity, retirement security, and guaranteed health care hasn't waned. At the same time, however, the public also is demanding a smaller, cheaper government. Even more than in the last twenty-five years, the temptation will be to look to corporations to bridge the gap between the competing demands.

Underlying the broadened mission of corporations, though, is the public's expectation that they behave ethically.

Examples of how major charities partner with large-scale businesses abound if you are seeking a model for how to structure your program. American Express, for instance, developed a creative partnership with the hunger-relief organization, Share Our Strength. Through the "Charge Against Hunger" program, American Express donated more than $16 million to SOS, and in return has seen the use of its card, and the number of merchants accepting it, rise considerably.

"Since American Express's pioneering ventures," Professor Andreasen notes, "the number of alliances between nonprofit and for-profit organizations has skyrocketed. Avon, American Airlines, Ocean Spray, Polaroid, Ramada International Hotels and Resorts, Arm and Hammer, Wal-Mart Stores, and many other corporations have joined forces with national nonprofit institutions, such as the American Red Cross, the YMCA, the American Heart Association, and the Nature Conservancy, as well as local agencies tackling problems in their communities."

He cites three basic types of alliances:

1. *Transaction-based promotions*. Under this format, a corporation donates a specific amount of food, equipment, or cash in proportion to sales revenue. The American Express–SOS alliance falls in this category. Every time someone uses an American Express card between the beginning of November and the end of December, the company contributes 3 cents to SOS, up to a total of $5 million per year.

2. *Joint issue promotions*. In this type of program, a business and a nonprofit address a social problem through advertising or distributing products and promotional material. An outstanding example is Hand in Hand, a program promoting breast health. *Glamour* magazine and Hanes Hosiery have joined forces with the National Cancer Institute, the American College of Obstetricians and

Gynecologists, and the American Health Foundation to disseminate information to women between the ages of eighteen and thir-
ty-nine, through magazine articles in *Glamour*, in-store promotions
sponsored by Hanes, and a range of educational materials.

3. *Licensing.* In this third kind of marketing alliance, charities
and nonprofits license their names and logos to corporations in return
for a percentage or revenue or a flat fee. The American Association
of Retired Persons, for instance, announced in 1996 that it would
begin licensing its name to health maintenance organizations.

"How can nonprofit managers build a successful partnership?"
asks Professor Andreasen. "They can assess their organization to
see how it can add value to a corporate partner. They can identify
those companies that stand to gain the most from a cause-related
marketing alliance. And they can take an active role in shaping
the partnership and monitoring its progress."

If this type of "teaming up" interests you, remember that you
don't have to go fishing only for large corporate support. The United
Way of Massachusetts Bay, for instance, is explicitly emphasizing
connections with small businesses. "The base of brand-name companies is shrinking," says Marion Heard, president and CEO of the
Boston-based organization. "The new growth is at small, entrepreneurial companies. So we're creating lists and targeting franchises,
travel agencies, and cleaning companies, and other mom-and-pop
type operations with 25 to 100 employees, or sometimes 100 to 500."

When you identify one or more businesses in your community
that would be appropriate for a partnership with your nonprofit,
here are some examples of strategies that you could propose.

1. *Get donations of a company's product.* The selling points for
the business donor: It's a relatively easy approach, and does not
require the company to come up with new material or messages.
And it directly links the company's product or service with good
works. Longfellow Clubs, a health and recreation company in

Wayland, Massachusetts, donates use of its health-club facilities to children with physical challenges. Under the Handi-Racket Tennis Program, about twenty-five disabled children learn to play tennis weekly. Tennis-court fees are waived for the agency that runs the program and for the kids involved, and most of the tennis pros volunteer their time. The foregone fees come to less than $3,000 per year. The owner admits that the program sometimes can get in the way of the schedules of club members—but the up side is that even these occasionally inconveniences reinforce the club's image with the public as a business with a heart.

2. *Get employees involved.* This is another option to propose to a business when you're suggesting a partnership. the Santa Monica-based company Rhino Records gives additional days of paid vacation to workers who contribute sixteen hours of personal time per year to community service. This particular program leaves the choice of pursuits up to employees, but you could propose an arrangement under which your participating business recommended your nonprofit, perhaps along with some others, to its employees for volunteer participation.

Employees often find a spirit of fun and camaraderie in promotional projects. If you found an especially enthusiastic business patron, you might challenge the owners to get employees involved in marketing your charity with the kind of zany creativity that a California developer fostered for its own corporate promotion. As reported in the *Wall Street Journal:* November 20, 1995:

> At Kaufman and Broad Home Corporation, employees have leapt out of airplanes, stopped rush-hour traffic and clothed an elephant. The silliness started…when the California home builder handed each of its 1,200 employees a company T-shirt and challenged them to get the most exposure possible—legally—for it. The winner of the "short-sleeved ad campaign" would get an expense-paid weekend for two in Manhattan. Among the more than two hundred entries

in the six-week contest: an employee who wore the shirt skydiving and another who persuaded a gondolier in Venice, Italy, to wear it. Yet another wore the shirt while posing as a mannequin in a Beverly Hills, California, department-store window.

Doug Jones, a contract manager in the company's Modesto, California, office, asked a floor-joists supplier that uses an elephant in its advertising to bring one to a weekend promotion at a Stockton home development. Other suppliers paid most of the $1,200 cost for a super-size T-shirt for the animal....

"The South Bay division took the top division prize for slowing five P.M. traffic when all one hundred employees paraded in their T-shirts over a freeway overpass in San Francisco. The group was about to adjourn for happy hour, and "we told them they were going to have to earn those drinks," says Kim Chairez, the division's escrow coordinator. The crew spent twenty minutes on the ledge of the overpass waiting for a photographer to navigate the crawling traffic so he could record the moment. As an estimated 30,000 people drove by, Ms. Chairez says, "some people honked and waved, and others gave us that other sign."

Grand-prize winner Kristen Engle, a computer programmer, spent an estimated sixty hours putting together her entry: a mock forty-page magazine featuring articles, ads and Michelle Pfeiffer in computer-generated Kaufman and Broad attire. She then printed copies and distributed them. Though she found the project "fun," the effort didn't permanently bond Ms. Engle to the company. The twenty-five-year-old is applying to business school for next fall."

3. *Get a business's suppliers and customers involved.* Beyond trying to get the business's employees involved, you can also leverage the resources of your partnering company by asking that business to encourage its suppliers and customers to join in the contribution efforts. For instance, Music for Little People (MFLP), a Redway, California-based mail-order and record company, lets all possible suppliers know of its commitment to helping charities. "One of the questions we ask a new or potential supplier is, 'Do you make donations or support any charitable activities that we can mention in our catalog?' says executive vice president Jimmy Durschslag. "We have limited space in the catalog. So if we have a number of suppliers who can supply the same product and one is more socially conscious than the others, it could tip the balance in its favor." The company occasionally also prevails on suppliers to join it in donating a percentage of profits to a specific nonprofit.

Another strategy to suggest to a business ally is to enlist its own customers on behalf of your nonprofit. For instance, Sebastian International, a maker of skin, hair, and makeup products, based in Woodland Hills, California, established Club UNITE (for Unity Now Is a Tomorrow for Everyone) to make philanthropists out of salon customers. Participants write a check for $10 to one of seven foundations that Sebastian has screened; the customer then receives $15 in Sebastian products. As club members, they also get a passport of coupons for products and services worth up to $65. Since 1991 the company, which has some $100 million in revenues, has channeled more than $4 million to the foundations through Club UNITE and outright donations.

If you're trying to persuade a business of the value of assisting your nonprofit, you might want to share the story of Direct Tire Sales in Watertown, Massachussetts The firm pledged to give the Jimmy Fund/Dana-Farber Cancer Institute 3 percent of every purchase by customers who mentioned the business's radio ad campaign from August to December. The firm found itself flooded with customers, and raised $14,800 the first year and $21,060 the second. Barry Steinberg, the company's president, tells of a customer who didn't need tires but came in to buy a $300 gift certificate so that 3 percent would go to the cancer fund.

The benefits of such partnering programs between charities and nonprofits and businesses are numerous. Companies are able to attract and retain employees longer. They believe that what they put out in the world will come back to them. The firm's customers also feel a more intense bond with them. In fact, many companies don't even consider the publicity that often arises from such programs. In the end, the real value is that you can help a business inject humanity into the process of commerce. With business defined for so long as soulless, partnering programs give people a chance to express their caring through their company.

However, warm fuzzy feelings won't always be enough to sell most businesses on your proposal for a partnership. Maybe even the examples of other corporate/charity alliances won't work, either. In the end, you have to make the case that the work that your charity is doing fits well with the marketing needs of the business you're approaching for help. In the words of Professor Alan Andreasen, the marketing guru mentioned earlier: "A nonprofit can offer a corporation more than its image. When a corporation allies itself with a nonprofit, the corporation often saves on advertising and promotional costs because the alliance usually brings free publicity and many public-relations opportunities. The corporation also gains access to the nonprofit's clientele, staff, trustees, and donors, all of whom are potential customers. Such access makes nonprofits with large memberships especially attractive to many companies."

Partnering with the Big Boy

Burbank, CA, May 22, 1996—Philip MacDonald, of Bob's Big Boy Restaurant, announced today the introduction of the "Charity of the Month" program. Beginning in June of 1996, the owners Phil MacDonald, Mark McCabe, and Steve Funkhouser will donate 1 percent of all dining room sales to local charities. The estimated contributions could total more than $25,000 annually. Under the new program,

four local charities will be chosen each month, and customers will vote for the one charity to receive the proceeds.

PR Newswire

Taking Stock of Your Organization

To partner with a business, begin by taking stock of your organization. Ask yourselves what can you offer a business that might ally
with it? Here are several specific questions you should try to answer.

1. Does your charity have a positive image that would bring
favorable attention to a donor business?

2. Does your work have an emphasis that makes it especially
compatible with a certain kind of business (say, the way, a food
bank and a grocery store might complement each other)?

3. Does your group have clout or access with people that a particular business would like to reach out to?

4. What is your geographical focus? If your organization is local
in its service area, an alliance with a local company makes more
sense than with a national firm.

5. Does your charity have an experienced and stable staff and
leadership? Corporations seeking long-term alliances will usually
look for a group that has a long track record, good finances, a sizable
staff, and preferably experience as a marketing partner. If you do not
have those credentials, you may have to settle for a short-term
alliance, or for alliances with smaller, mom-and-pop organizations.

Such questions allow you to take an inventory of the vital signs
of your organization—a checklist that should be reviewed even if
you're not pursuing a business alliance. Strong, stable leadership,
for instance, is essential for a vital organization in any case.

Selecting Companies to Work With

On the other hand, you should also ask yourself what kind of company you want to look for in a partner. Your organization should be at

least somewhat critical about those businesses with which you decide to affiliate. Here is a checklist of questions to ask in this regard.

1. Does the corporation clearly recognize the potential value of a cause-related campaign, which makes marketing the idea of the partnership to the corporation relatively easy?

2. Will the promotion will be a logical or even essential component of the company's long-term marketing strategy? Partnerships that do not fit a company's strategy and are peripheral to its core interests will ultimately prove superficial to both parties—and perhaps to the public.

3. Does the company engage in any business practices that are antithetical to your mission?

4. Will the company devote funds and people to your alliance?

5. Does the corporation appear eager to involve its employees as well as its suppliers, dealers, and franchisees in the cause-related marketing program?

6. Does the corporation appear likely to place undue restrictions on your activities or otherwise interfere with its operations?

These questions are as valid to a community homeless shelter seeking assistance from a local hardware store, as they are to a national charity seeking an alliance with a Fortune 500 commercial giant. So be sure to spend time asking them and perusing the companies who express interest in your cause. Never jump into a joint program with a company until you have tried with "due diligence" to find out as much as you can about the company's reputation and character. You never know what skeletons might sleep quietly in a business's closet.

Winning Over Companies

Many charities and nonprofits make a pitch to local businesses, feeling their cause is just and the chances of getting the partnership are good. A few weeks later, though, they find out that the business has rejected them. Why?

One reason is that many businesses want to be involved in the development of fund-raising programs right from the start. For example, one California group, the Business Volunteers for the Arts of Sacramento, conducted a survey of local business leaders to determine how they could increase interest in funding nonprofit community arts programs. "Respondents said they would be more willing (and even eager) to support artistic causes if they could be partners in the project, not just a funder," the alliance reported. "This should not imply that CEOs are asking to shape the artist product per se (most believed the artist should have total 'freedom of expression'). Rather, they are suggesting that groups present their art within the parameters of the sponsor's agenda. Giving something back to their customers, instilling a positive image, children's education, and cultural diversity are all part of the Sacramento business community's agenda. It is up to the individual groups to work with sponsors to determine how they can fill these needs. It's a win-win situation."

"What all this means," says Gerry Ansel, who conducted the survey, "is that business donors want to be consulted as programs are developed, not presented with a finished product and asked to contribute." This principle applies to any nonprofit organization, whether it's involved in the arts or not.

Ansel is currently spokesman for AIDS Project L.A., which provides free support services for more than 5,200 people in Los Angeles with HIV/AIDS. He says his organization makes a point of keeping major donors abreast of program planning and soliciting suggestions. "A real, vital partnership does exist," he says, between the charity and its contributors, who include such major entertainment-industry executives as David Geffen, Barry Diller, Jeffrey Katzenberg, and Ron Meyer.

Another lesson from the Sacramento study concerns timing and preparation. "More than one respondent advised the arts community to be better prepared when asking for assistance," said the report. "Arts managers need to plan further in advance when asking for contributions: 'Nothing can kill a grant faster than "rushing" the donor to meet your deadline,' says the public-affairs director of a major electronics manufacturer. 'Play by the donor's rules and according to their time frame, and your chances of success will improve. Sometimes that's very difficult, but the fact is that's how business works.'"

CREATIVITY IN FUND-RAISING: THE PINK FLAMINGO CAPER

A church in a southern state gained considerable press attention, and raised a godly amount of money for its budget by conducting a wonderfully humorous fund-raising campaign. Called the "Pink Flamingo ransom," it worked as follows. Each night, a member of the congregation would put a plastic Pink Flamingo in another member's front yard. In the morning, the "recipient" of this gift would wake to discover the tacky bird in his or her yard. To get rid of it, he or she had to make a contribution to the church, but the person could then designate another friend to whose front lawn the bird would be transferred. This was done, of course, all in good fun—and good fund-raising.

DEVELOPING AN EFFECTIVE CAPITAL CAMPAIGN

Planning your capital campaign should begin several years before anyone does any fund-raising. Most campaigns include the following, overlapping steps, especially if they are complex and target getting money personally from large donors.

1. Develop your campaign budget, i.e., how much you want to bring in. This requires long-range planning by the board of directors and, for larger campaigns, a feasibility study by outside consultants to assess the likelihood of success.

2. Write a case statement. This is similar to a business plan for the campaign that explains why you need the money, why your

institution deserves it, who your leadership is, and what the timing for your fund-raising will be.

3. Develop donor lists. Rate prospects by their estimated ability to give. This helps you avoid the mistake of asking people for too little.

4. Make sure you have adequate resources to conduct your campaign, including enough people and computer power to handle your donor database and records. Included here is also your estimate of your volunteer force.

5. Develop a strategy and timetable for the campaign. This is the thinking part of the task, in which you determine how you appeal to the public, including fund-raisers, direct mail, events, promotions, et cetera. For large promotions, it is useful to get an outside consultant to work with you on this, to be sure that you keep things moving and don't get bogged down.

6. Prepare your printed materials. You'll likely need brochures, a manual, and pledge cards for volunteers who will meet with donors, as well as literature for direct mail.

7. Recruit and train your volunteers. Assign each person to prospects from whom he or she will solicit.

8. Promote the campaign. Make initial contacts with potential donors. In these information sessions, don't ask for money.

9. Solicit donations. Look for the largest gifts first. Having these monies can act as a catalyst to getting other donations.

10. Publically thank people who were involved. As indicated in chapter 1, lead by example. Recognize those who gave and those who worked on the campaign.

BUILDING YOUR BOARD

A nonprofit's board of directors is an extremely important tool for attracting funds. It is therefore vital to choose board members who represent a wide spectrum of community interests and perspectives, and bring probity, experience, and professional and practical skills to the table. You should be sure to seek out at least some people with financial backgrounds, and people with ties to the business community. Leo Latz, a consultant for nonprofits, argues for a pre-recruitment interview and a reference check in selecting board members. "Call other boards they're on," he says. "It's harder to join a country club than a board."

Latz adds that when you consider a candidate for membership on your board, speak glowingly about your function. "Elevate the importance of what you're asking the person. The worst thing you can say is, 'You don't have to give and it won't take much time.' "

The key position on your board is, of course, the chairperson, who must be a strong person. The chairperson provides leadership, vision, and serves as a facilitator at board meetings. In most cases, a nonprofit's board will meet every other month for two hours, and allow subcommittees to meet in the intervening months. Most consultants also recommend that you limit board members to specific term limits, in the event a person does not work out.

ENVISIONING SUCCESS WITH A MISSION STATEMENT

Beyond an active, strong leadership, another characteristic that marks a successful nonprofit—and which makes a nonprofit more attractive to potential business donors—is a clear, agreed-upon and well-understood mission. "You can't raise money in a vacuum," says Anita Joseph, director of financial development for the YMCA of the USA, headquartered in Chicago. "Sometimes that means going back to your organization's vision."

Earlier in the chapter, I noted the steep rise of mission statements among businesses and the fact that many statements now contain strong language expressing their commitment to community affairs. Charities and nonprofits can benefit from coming up with similar defining statements for themselves. Developing a concise mission statement helps the leaders and volunteers in your nonprofit clarity what they're doing and why. Posting it prominently at the organization's worksite(s) provides a continuing reminder and inspiration to everyone. Sharing it with potential donors also underscores the organization's seriousness of purpose.

A strong civic-minded mission statement can also lead to word-of-mouth publicity for your organization. For instance, one famous business case of a mission statement that has appealed to the masses is that of the Body Shop, founded by Anita Roddick. The company's statement makes a commitment to reject products that aren't deemed environment-friendly. Everyone who works for the Body Shop knows the mission statement, and is willing to educate customers about it. "We prefer to give staff information about the product, anecdotes about the history and derivation of the ingredients, and any funny stories about how they came on Body Shop shelves," Roddick says. "We want to spark conversations with our customers, not browbeat them to buy." As a result of the firm's commitment, the Body Shop has been able to succeed without any advertising (other than Roddick herself appearing on an ad for American Express), largely from the word-of-mouth marketing that has occurred around their products.

Here are some examples of mission statements.

Food Distribution Center (FDC),
of Orange County, California

FOOD DISTRIBUTION CENTER MISSION STATEMENT
To alleviate hunger in Orange County, the Food Distribution Center (FDC), Orange County's private non-profit food-bank, develops programs to increase awareness of the hunger problem and provides an opportunity for volunteerism and community involvement. To serve as a foodbank, FDC solicits and collects commodities and then distributes them to non-profit agencies which feed the needy.

The Food Distribution Center is a certified member of the Second Harvest National Foodbank Network. Second Harvest gives FDC access to surplus food supplies all over the nation and provides links with other foodbanks around the country to share food, information and ideas.

To back up its misson statement, this charity sends out a one-page fact sheet to current and prospective donors, with a brief and easy-to-read summary of the hunger problem and how the organization helps. Under the headline, "Did You Know?", the fact sheet lists eleven bullet-point items of information, including

+ Nearly 400,000 people in Orange County risk going to bed hungry sometime each month. That is 16 percent of the county's population and would fill Disneyland to capacity six times.
+ Over 2.5 million pounds of food are wasted each month in Orange County alone. Much of it because of appearance, damaged packaging, or manufacturing mistakes.
+ Each year, FDC's efforts prevent millions of pounds of healthy food from reaching our landfills.
+ The Food Distribution Center collects food for distribution to more than 280 local member charities that feed the hungry.
+ Over 180,000 people in Orange County receive FDC food each month. Nearly 60 percent of these are children and seniors.
+ A donation of 25 cents can provide a loaf of bread, a jar of peanut butter, a can of tuna, and a can of vegetables for a family in need.
+ Volunteers provide over 54 percent of the labor that keeps the Food Distribution Center operating. That is the equivalent of thirty full-time employees.
+ Since 1983, FDC has distributed over 100 million pounds of food to people in need in Orange County.

Aids Project Los Angeles (APLA)
Here's another example of a pointed and concise mission statement.

AIDS Project Los Angeles is a nonprofit, community-based organization which is a direct provider of, and resource for, HIV/AIDS services and information; and an advocate at all levels of government for people with HIV/AIDS.

AIDS Project Los Angeles is committed to serving all people infected by, affected by, and at risk for HIV/AIDS in Los Angeles County.

AIDS Project Los Angeles provides quality services with sensitivity to its diverse client base and will work in collaboration with other organizations to reduce the incidence of HIV/AIDS infection and to support people living with HIV/AIDS.

CORE VALUES

1. APLA is a resource for persons falling within the full spectrum of HIV.
2. APLA adapts as necessary to the changing course of the pandemic.
3. APLA aims for sensitivity and competence in providing services to its diverse client base.
4. APLA's programs and services are driven by client need. APLA primarily addresses the common needs of HIV seropositive clients and the needs of persons at risk for HIV disease.
5. APLA's services are determined by the degree to which APLA can make a critical impact.
6. APLA is a part of a broader, comprehensive system of HIV prevention, medical care and support services.
7. APLA is committed to working in collaboration and partnership with other organizations for the benefit of people with HIV and those at risk for HIV.
8. APLA seeks to establish a partnership with clients to help empower people with HIV to manage their illness to the maximum extent possible.

MISSION STATEMENTS THAT DEFINE, MOTIVATE, AND INSPIRE

Here are mission statements from several noted businesses around the country. See if, in your experience, the company's mission statement has translated itself into a reputation and level of service that you have personally experienced from that company.

✦ Quality Inns seek to "pursue excellence and become the most recognized, respected, and admired lodging chain in the world."

✦ Levi Strauss and Company's employees have this vision: "Above all we want satisfaction from accomplishments and friendships, balanced personal and professional lives, and to have fun in our endeavors."

✦ Hewlett-Packard aspires to "Performance. Not promises." Its mission statement also includes this objective: "To honor our obligations to society by being an economic, intellectual, and social asset to each nation and each community in which we operate."

✦ Federal Express's mission statement encapsulates the reasons for the company's phenomenal success: "We will produce outstanding financial returns by providing totally reliable, competitively superior global air-ground transportation of high-priority goods and documents that require rapid, time-certain delivery. Equally important, positive control of each package will be maintained utilizing real-time electronic tracking and tracing systems. A complete record of each shipment and delivery will be presented with our request for payment. We will be helpful, courteous, and professional to each other and the public. We will strive to have a satisfied customer at the end of each transaction."

LEADING BY EXAMPLE WITH GRATITUDE

As you recall, one of the ten maxims in my PR moral manifesto was to lead by example, by announcing to the world how various businesses and individuals have helped you.

One of the best methods of doing this is an awards presentation, during which you cite the individuals and businesses who have done significant work for your cause. The advantage of a well-advertised awards event is that you can often generate extra publicity from it, especially if the people receiving the awards are prominent in the community. (Note: If you know you will plan an awards event at the end of your campaign, it is well worth it to target affluent and successful prospective donors and announce their awards for their services to the community at large. This can increase your chances of getting that extra publicity.)

Awards events are also useful in two other ways. They can be a way to cultivate new patrons who are eager to imitate the people receiving awards. They also help establish your organization as an expert source of information about the issues or problems it specializes in, which can eventually turn into more media attention if a reporter needs a comment or news story that your group can supply.

Another way to show your gratitude is to feature those businesses who sponsor your group prominently in your organization's newsletters. This should be done as extensively and formally as possible, such as including photos and profiles of the various executives from your partnering businesses. Once again, this tactic can prove fruitful in getting additional media attention if you send your newsletters to your local press.

You could also take a cue from the Orlando law firm that celebrated its tenth anniversary by commissioning art that "coincidentally" celebrated some of the firm's best business clients. The firm got respected local photographers to take artistic photos of buildings or people associated with twenty local companies, half of which were clients. The firm held a reception and presented the companies with signed copies of the photos, and then arranged for them to travel as an exhibit to local schools. "We did it for name recognition," said a partner in the law firm. And to recognize—and help cement a relationship with—some of its key clients.

A New Outlet for Thanks— Online Web Pages

A great new outlet where you can display photos of donors and business sponsors, along with officers and staff of your nonprofit, is your website. What? You don't have a website yet? That's a deficiency that can be rectified cheaply, as many Internet access services provide help and sometimes discounted fees in setting up website for nonprofits. As I wrote in an earlier chapter, today there are two speeds for businesses and even nonprofits: fast and dead. Getting familiar with computer technology and using Internet opportunities to their fullest is part of being in the fast lane.

What should you put on your website? In the words of Scripps-Howard columnist Terry Mattingly, "Nothing less than everything meaningful about your nonprofit organization. That means your mission statement, any policy statements, memos on newsworthy issues, reports on your group's activities and achievements, human-interest stories, along with access numbers for staffers. You can then refer reporters to this information on your website when you call, write or fax them. If there are quotable statements or significant data on your site, journalists will appreciate this easy means of accessing it, without the hassle of having to call around and do interviews."

CREATIVE EVENT PLANNING FOR FUN AND PROFIT

A tuned-up and revitalized strategy for marketing and fund-raising should also include some creative thinking about special events. Today, many charities and nonprofits are going beyond the traditional awards banquets, golf tournaments, and silent auctions to sponsor extremely unique, themed events that attract a paying clientele. In most cases, such events are intended to be fun and enjoyable, with the fund-raising element left to implicit understanding.

For example, Dimock Community Health Center's "Steppin' Out" party, which in five years became one of Boston's premier multicultural events. This is a black-tie musical extravaganza that recreates seven jazz clubs of the 1930s and 1940s. Each club, sponsored by a local corporation, features a different type of music, from jazz and calypso, to reggae, fusion, and big bands. In one recent year, the event netted $135,000 and attracted three thousand people in a multiracial and predominantly senior audience.

The same organization also did another interesting fundraiser that tapped into the public's spiritual interests. Based on the Japanese tradition of making a paper prayer for those who are ill and hanging it on a tree so the wind will carry the get-well wishes, Dimock sponsored a three-week event called Paper Prayers. The "prayers" were works of art created by area artists to support the Boston Pediatric AIDS Project based at Dimock. In 1992, fourteen area galleries displayed two thousand works of art for three weeks in December. The way it worked was that people went to the galleries, picked out a prayer, and made a donation.

Another unusual technique employed by Dimock were house parties. One year, the organization hosted five parties, which eventually brought in nearly $60,000 to the organization. "House parties go back to the political tradition of inviting candidates to your house to meet the neighbors," said Dimock's president Jackie Jenkins-Scott. "We're an inner-city organization. A lot of people in the suburbs don't know about us. Such parties don't necessarily bring in a lot of money, but they generate interest and don't really cost much to put on."

Indeed, parties are one of the best ways to spread good cheer, goodwill, and good PR. They provide a wonderful means of reaching out in the community, and of making people feel special when they get a special invitation. It can be viewed as the quintessential membership card. Here are a few pointers for doing a party right.

✦ Don't use it as a place to overtly conduct business. Sure, business cards can and should be exchanged, along with promises, but the conversation should be kept on spirited note. While you should make a toast or otherwise formally thank people for attending, and briefly mention your project, don't divert them from their pleasure.

✦ Don't provide too many chairs and tables. People are more likely to mingle if there are fewer places to sit down.

✦ Don't go understaffed. You must have enough people helping you to ensure a smoothly running function.

✦ Novelties and surprises keep the atmosphere alive. Midway through, stage a novel event that relates to your organization, but don't let it go on so long that it causes people's attention to wander.

✦ Pick the day and date carefully, checking to make sure your party won't conflict with an event that might take precedence for many of the people you hope will come.

✦ Keep a happy, upbeat attitude. Parties tend to take on a life and rhythm of their own: If you've planned right, you can stop worrying and enjoy yourself.

PUT YOUR HANDS TOGETHER FOR A WINNING PROMOTIONAL IDEA

Hands Across America—in which people linked together nationwide to show concern for the less fortunate—was a promotional coup because it got people involved on a mass

scale, says Richard O'Connor, who has been a consultant
for the American Red Cross and Big Brothers. "It called for
personal involvement—and it got it," he recounts. "When
this stunt was pulled, it was during the American
Booksellers Association meeting, in Chicago, I think. By
God, the good-hearted, sophisticated and unsophisticated,
caring publishing folks formed a huge chain across the
convention hall at noon that day to demonstrate support.
I've no idea how many were involved, but is was a show-
stopper. Goes to show that when a cause touches a nerve-
ending, and you have a credible statement of concern
about a real problem, people of all stripes will respond."

HOW TO PLAY THE CELEBRITY GAME

Don't ignore the value of inviting celebrities to your functions. A
celebrity's name might not sell huge numbers of tickets, says Rita
Tateel, a Hollywood consultant who runs Celebrity Source, which
matches major celebrities with large charities and nonprofits. "But
it might help push someone who had been leaning in the direction
of going into making a decision to go. It also adds some glamour
and brightness to the occasion, and helps garner publicity."

Smaller charities can try inviting big celebrity names to star at
their functions, but the chances of succeeding are on par with winning a big lottery take. However, remember that the term "celebrity" must be understood in the context of where you are, and what
the perspective of your audience is. In some communities, a local
on-air television personality is a significant enough celebrity to
attract attention and attendance at your function. Other choices
include soap-opera stars, new TV actors who aren't as well known
yet, and people from your local artistic community.

The biggest mistake that many charities make is sending a poorly worded or insulting invitation to a celebrity. I've seen cases where
the celebrity receives a form letter, addressed "Dear Celebrity,"

without even writing the person's name. As you can imagine, letters like that hit the wastebasket immediately. Similarly, I've seen letters that ramble on for pages, never getting to the point that this is an invitation.

If you write a letter to a celebrity, keep it to one page. State clearly why you're writing, that you are requesting a charity appearance, and, hopefully, express some admiration for the person. Then thank them for their consideration, and sign off quickly, concisely, and   neatly. If you follow this format, you will find that your chances of a positive response increase immeasurably.

(Note: If you can afford it, mention also in your letter that you have arranged a limousine to transport the person and a hotel room, if needed. "When celebrities have little time for philanthropy, and when they are bombarded with requests for guest appearances, they'll look to see, first, how they can make the most impact with their limited time, and second, which of the prospects will be the easiest and offers the most perks and goodies," says Tateel. "You must stand out in those departments to get selected.")

As for costs, the general rule of thumb is as follows: If a celebrity must do something other than just show up and sign autographs, there is likely an argument for paying him or her. If you ask the person to perform, you're asking them to engage in their business. If this is the case, the celebrity must definitely receive compensation. Note that if you're able to arrange a celebrity to appear free of charge, you should *not* expect any supporting performers, backup singers, or instrumentalists also to perform for free. You will need to pay those people.

Los Angeles publicist Dale Olsen offers his own advice on celebrity-hunting for smaller charities and nonprofits. "Most of the charities around the country may not have the money or the clout to land a name star on their own. But they can go their local film chain, legitimate theater, concert promoter—anyone who might be bringing a celebrity or show to town—and make a deal with them to publicize their attraction in return for an appearance by the star at a charity event. This can work even when the entertainer is coming to town for just a one-day show. The association with the charity is announced in advance, in a way that also plugs the entertainer's paid show, and he or she makes an appearance with the charity a day before the performance for an additional photo-op to help the show."

ONE GOOD DEED DESERVES ANOTHER

Mitzvah means "good works" in Hebrew. When a group of congregations in L.A.'s San Fernando Valley announced a "Mitvah-thon" for a midwinter weekend, the local media gave it maximum exposure. After all, conventional distance-running events are a dime a dozen around L.A.—but an event in which people would try to test their endurance by performing a marathon of good works? Now that's innovative.

Participants engaged in all manner of charitable activities, from writing cards to shut-ins to collecting cans of food for the poor. Organizers weren't shy about trying to get some high-profile people to stop by—and Los Angeles mayor Richard Riordan answered the call.

The lesson here: Don't think it's impossible to get community notables and other celebrities to your event. Send them neat, respectful letters, and follow up with phone calls. You might well succeed. In any case, the Mitzvah-thon got plenty of press, and good times—and good works—were had by all.

THANKS (FOR) A MILLION

Although we cited one survey above that suggested baby boomers don't value individual thank-you notes as much as the opportunity for direct, continuing communication with the officials of a nonprofit, I cannot in good conscience suggest that you skip or skimp on formal expressions of thanks to donors of any age. Thanking people privately for their generosity is just common courtesy. No matter what the surveys indicate, it's also a means of building long-term relationships. "With competition for contributions so heavy, you have to do your homework, be clear about what you're asking for, and deliver," says Dimock's Jackie Jenkins-Scott. "Once you get the money, say thanks and follow up. Tell people how successful the project was. Ask them to come out for a visit. Even if they are too busy to come, they'll remember that you asked." And being remembered is 75 percent of what a relationship is about.

Summary: Goodness Guide

1. Baby boomers, ages thirty to forty-nine, comprise 47 percent of donors to charities and nonprofits. Woo them seriously, but be aware that their long-term loyalty to any one nonprofit is harder to achieve than was the case with their parents.

2. Try to involve boomers in long-term giving arrangements (monthly payment programs, for instance) to build a stable connection over time.

3. Boomers don't engage in volunteerism nearly to the degree of their parents' generation. Market volunteerism to them by promoting examples of those boomers who are already engaged in it.

4. Create novel communications links between donors and your organization, such as 800 numbers, and regular question-and-answer sessions with officials of your group. Surveys suggest baby boomers want such ready access.

5. Identify untapped donor bases, such as ethnic or racial communities you haven't marketed to before, and age groups too. Don't overlook "baby busters," the "Generation X" population between the ages of eighteen and thirty, as well as our current teenagers.

6. Build innovative relationships with businesses. Partnership models include the *transactional* approach, in which a business donates a fixed proportion of sales revenue; the *joint-issue* strategy,

where a business and a charity work in tandem to promote awareness of a social problem; and *licensing*, where a charity licenses its
name or logo to a business, and gets a percentage of the profits on
items sold bearing that logo.

7. In considering what businesses to propose a partnership
with, ask whether they would be willing to involve customers, suppliers, and employees in the program.

8. In selecting partners, look first at your own organization and
determine what kind of business might have a thematic connection with what your nonprofit does. A food bank and a grocery are
natural allies, for instance.

9. Before making a pitch to a business, examine the strengths
and weaknesses of your organization. Do you have an image that
will bring honor on a business partner? Does your board of directors include representation from a broad sector of the community,
and are there members with strong financial skills? Are your board
and your operating management functioning efficiently? Do you
have a clear mission—and a mission statement? Do you have concrete success stories to point to in your charity work? Do you have
a local presence in the community that the business's customers
and employees can identify with, so that the business will benefit
from being associated with you?

10. Make your link with a business a real partnership. Consult
your business donor when you are planning programs; don't just
present the business with a fait accompli and expect some sort of
underwriting. Don't expect rush decisions by donors. Respect their
timetables, and submit requests well in advance of when the support will be needed.

11. Get an online presence for your organization via a website.
List your members, executives, contributors, mission statement—
anything that can make a difference to the visitor in understanding how important your organization is.

12. Put a priority on devising innovative special events. Don't
think it is hopeless to try to get a major celebrity to an event. But

be realistic: the chances of getting a big name are not great, so look for alternatives as well. "Celebrities" from local TV, radio, and newspapers can also bring excitement to an event. In making a pitch to a celebrity, whether local or national, send a courteous, neat, personalized one-page letter. Expect to pay something if you're asking for a performance. The more goodies—such as transportation, presents, side trips, deluxe accommodations—that you can offer the celebrity, the greater the chance you'll get chosen out of the many requests he or she receives.

13. Always formally thank donors in writing. Report to them on the success of the project, and offer to give them a firsthand tour. Building long-term relationships is essential.

THE CHALLENGES OF THE FUTURE

Not what we give, but what we share—
For the gift without the giver is bare;
Who gives himself with his alms feeds three—
Himself, his hungering neighbor, and me.

JAMES RUSSELL LOWELL,
Vision of Sir Launfal, 1848

STRICTLY speaking, charity and philanthropy are not the same thing. Charity is traditionally seen as rising from a religious impulse and focusing on the poor and sick. Philanthropy, in contrast, is secular in origin, and involves a broader variety of projects, from educational and cultural institutions to wildlife protection to social work programs.

But I don't care much for such semantic debate. Philanthropy and charity are both about giving. And in the United States, nonprofits are the principal vehicles for both charity and philanthropy. Whether a nonprofit calls itself a charity or a philanthropy, it ought to be in the business of marketing itself—selling goodness with flair and energy.

I've said earlier that you should be proud to be involved in altruism, and your pride should manifest itself in promotion at every chance that comes your way. Just as an aristocrat takes pride in an ancient bloodline, charity providers can point to the venerable lineage of the practice of giving.

A History Lesson in Charity

If you work a nonprofit to make the world a bit brighter, you are part of a tradition that stretches back thousands of years. "The nonprofit sector originated in the compassionate practices of ancient religions and classical civilizations," notes Julie Vallone of the Nonprofit Policy Council, a project of the California Association of Nonprofits. "Guided by values of charity, neighborliness, and philanthropy, early charitable activities fell into two broad categories: assistance to the frail and indigent, and civic advancement."

In ancient Greece, the practice of charity for strangers was encouraged because of the possibility that the wayfarer could be a sacred being. To the Greeks, the gods were known to disguise themselves in human form, so beggars were not to be shooed away from one's door.

In ancient Rome, wealthy people commonly gave money to construct baths and other public facilities. Julius Caesar won renown for his generous funding of public structures in Rome. In Shakespeare's play about that ancient monarch, Marc Antony tells the crowd gathered after Caesar's murder how "he hath left you all his walks, his private arbors and new-planted orchards on this side Tiber; he hath left them to you and to your heirs forever; common pleasure, to walk abroad in and recreate yourselves."

Providing help and hospitality to travelers was widely regarded as a virtue by the ancients. The Roman statesman Cicero penned an essay, titled *On Moral Obligations*. In it, he quoted the poet Ennius's statement that "the man who kindly guides a stranger on his way, lights as it were another's lantern from his own nor is his light the less for kindling the other." Cicero drew this lesson from the poet: "[W]hatever kindness can be done without personal loss should be done, even for a stranger."

Cicero also hailed volunteerism. According to Robert H. Bremmer, a scholar of the history of philanthropy, "Because helping others by one's own effort and influence involved work and courage, Cicero deemed it morally superior to gifts of money. Whereas kindness that depended on the size of one's purse limited the number of people who can be helped and may dry up, those who help others in nonmonetary ways gain a double advantage in Cicero's eyes. The more they help, the more allies they will have in their good works, argued Cicero, and the better prepared and fit they will become for broader service."

BABYFACED ALTRUISTS

The Katahdin Area Women's Association (KAWA) is sponsoring a contest in which everyone wins. It's the Baby Photo Contest. The entry deadline is Wednesday June 15.... Mail a 5"x 7" photograph of a child, age three or younger, to Baby Photo Contest.... With your $5 entry fee, include a self-addressed stamped envelope for photo returns. Public voting is 8 A.M. to 5 P.M. June 19 to July 3 at the *Katahdin Times* office in Millinocket. All money raised from the entry fees and the votes—which are actually quarters—stays in the area served by KAWA.

The Bangor Daily News, June 8, 1995

THE JUDEO-CHRISTIAN VIEW

Charity is of course a valued mandate of the Judeo-Christian religious tradition. Care for the poor and sick is decreed in the Jewish testament, as a sign of obedience to God. In Deuteronomy, there is the command, "If in any of the towns in the land that the Lord your God is giving you, there is a fellow Israelite in need, then do not be selfish and refuse to help him. Instead, be generous and lend him as much as he needs.... Give to him freely and unselfishly, and the Lord will bless you in everything you do."

The prophet Isaiah conveyed to Jews both a command and a promise: "The kind of fasting I want is this: Remove the chains of oppression and the yoke of injustice, and let the oppressed go free. Share your food with the hungry and open your homes to the home-less poor. Give clothes to those who have nothing to wear, and do not refuse to help your own relatives. Then my favor will shine on you like the morning sun, and your wounds will be quickly healed. I will always be with you to save you; my presence will protect you on every side."

Maimonides, or Moses ben Maimon, the twelfth-century rabbi, philosopher, physician, and Hebrew scholar, authored a famous guide to the teachings of Judaism from the time of Moses to his own day. In Chapter Ten of Book VII of his Mishneh Torah, he took an unusual approach to describe generosity, inventing what he called the "eight degrees" of charity. Perhaps to embarrass the reluctant, he sequenced these from least admirable to the most worthy of praise:

1. Give grudgingly.
2. Give cheerfully, but less than you should.
3. Give after being solicited.
4. Give without being solicited.
5. Give to a recipient unknown to you who knows you.
   ("The great sages used to tie money in sheets which they threw behind their backs, and the poor would come and get it without being embarrassed.")
6. Give to a recipient you know but who does not know you.
   ("The great sages used to go secretly and cast the money into the doorway of the poor.")
7. Give to an unknown recipient who does not know your identity.
   (An example would be giving to a charity fund. "One should not contribute to a [such a] fund unless he knows that the man

in charge of the collection is trustworthy and intelligent and knows how to manage properly," Maimonides cautions.)

8. Help a needy person become self-supporting by a gift, loan, or entering into partnership with or providing work for him or her.

In the development of Christianity, too, charity became a paramount virtue. "Faith, hope, and charity," St. Paul commended in the First Letter to the Corinthians. "And the greatest of these is charity."

While Plato had listed the cardinal virtues as prudence, courage or fortitude, temperance, and justice, in the Middle Ages these virtues became central to moral philosophy with the addition of the Christian virtues of faith, hope, and charity. The Latin word *caritas*, from which our word "charity" is derived, meant for the medieval scholastics a high form of loving self-sacrifice for others.

OTHER RELIGIOUS TRADITIONS

Almsgiving to the poor is declared an important virtue in other religions as well. To this day, many poor people in Buddhist countries are supported by the generosity of wealthy people.

Islam sees no conflict between faith and works in the service of Allah. Both are essential. The Koran counsels active examples of kindness, forgiveness, and almsgiving, including both a voluntary giving and the *zakat*, a tax on the wealthy:

Piety does not lie in turning your face to East or West:
Piety lies in believing in God,
the Last Day and the angels
the Scriptures and the prophets
and disbursing your wealth out of love for God
among your kin and the orphans,
the wayfarers and mendicants,
freeing the slaves, observing your devotional obligations,
and in paying the zakat and fulfilling a pledge you have given,

and in being patient in hardship, adversity, and times of peril.
These are the men who affirm the truth,
and they are those who follow the straight path. (2:177)

Surely the men and women who spend in charity
and give a goodly loan to God
will have it doubled for them
and will receive a generous reward. (57:18)

O believers, some of your wives and children
are your enemies, so beware of them!
Yet if you forbear, overlook, and forgive,
God is indeed forgiving and kind.
Your wealth and children are surely meant as trial for you:
But with God is the great reward.
So fear God as much as you can,
and listen and obey, and spend in charity
for your own good.
He who is saved from his own avarice
will be successful.
If you lend a goodly loan to God,
He will double it for you, and forgive you.
God knows the worth of good deeds and is clement,
The knower of the unknown and the known,
all-mighty and all-wise. (64:14–18).

THE ANGLO-AMERICAN TRADITION

In England, the Statute of Charitable Uses of 1601 set up a formal legal system governing nonprofit organizations. That structure was adopted by the American colonies, where two traditions of philanthropy were to emerge. The religious approach was outlined by the New England clergyman Cotton Mather, in a 1710 essay entitled *Bonifacius: An Essay Upon the Good That is to Be Devised*. Mather said that in the name of religion, everyone should take a hand in helping the poor.

Meanwhile, Benjamin Franklin promoted a secular approach to philanthropy, based on his doctrine of wise stewardship of personal resources. In Philadelphia he organized a college, a lending library, and the American Philosophical Society.

The years prior to the Civil War saw the establishment of several notable philanthropic organizations such as the Children's Aid Society, to find homes in the West for orphans from the streets of eastern cities; the Cooper Union, to promote education for laborers in New York City; and the American Anti-Slavery Society.

The young American nation impressed foreign observers by the breadth of the charity among its citizens. D. Griffiths, Jr., a British traveler, wrote about the relatively few beggars he encountered, compared to English cities and towns. He explained their absence "by citing economic growth, an open countryside, and the compassion that those who were better-off showed for those rendered destitute by unforeseeable circumstances." Griffiths recounted how one "disabled Scotchman" received "board amongst the farmers, sometimes at one house, and sometimes at another." Likewise, he recorded that a Dutch family rendered poor by illness were "provided with doctor and nurse, and in fact with everything needful for them, until they recovered."

The famous French observer of American morals, Alexis de Tocqueville, wrote that Americans "display general compassion." He contrasted the voluntary private assistance that abounded in America, under its "free institutions," with the situation in Europe, where the "state almost exclusively undertakes to supply bread to the hungry, assistance and shelter to the sick, work to the idle, and to act as the sole reliever of all kinds of misery."

Indeed, Americans in the early stages of our history prided themselves on their altruistic response to many social problems, arguing that it was superior to the model in Britain, where a comparative few in the government attended to the needs of the poor. Charleston minister Thomas S. Grimke drew the contrast in 1927: "Formerly, the community was a mere bystander, a mere spectator, as to all that was going on. The government, a few ancient, well-endowed institutions, and a handful of individuals, were the only agents." In contrast, he said, "Now the people are everything, and do everything, through the medium of a vast multitude of organized associations."

One of the classic examples of the many charitable enterprises founded during America's transition to an industrial power was Goodwill Industries. It was started in 1902 by a Methodist minister who came up with the idea of giving immigrants work by having them fix up the wealthy's discarded household goods. Today, Goodwill operates fifteen hundred stores nationwide. Nearly $589 million per year is generated from donated goods, the revenues going to train handicapped workers.

The philanthropic ideal found a late-nineteenth-century champion industrialist Andrew Carnegie, who argued that with great wealth came great responsibility to help others. He built scores of libraries, schools, parks, and gymnasiums throughout the nation.

A shift came with Progressive Era philanthropists, some of whom turned their attention to large-scale social ills and the reform of institutions, more than dealing with individuals one by one. Still, in the vast array of nonprofit organizations that grew up during the first half of the twentieth century, every philosophical approach found expression. At least prior to the Depression, the nonprofit sector asserted itself as the primary provider of human services, health care, the arts, environmental protection, scientific research, and human-rights and social-issues advocacy.

But even with the vast increase in government involvement in social needs since the 1930s, nonprofits continue to perform vital functions. "There are currently more than 1 million nonprofit organizations nationally, with a combined annual revenue of $500 billion, 8 million paid staff (roughly 8 percent of the national service economy) and 89 million volunteers (about half the adult population)," reports Julie Vallone of the Nonprofit Policy Council. She points out that the nonprofit sector in recent years has grown much faster than the economy as a whole. "According to the head of the

Program on Tax Exempt Organizations at the U.S. Internal
Revenue Service, the assets of tax-exempt organizations increased
by over 150 percent, while revenues increased by over 227 percent
between 1975 and 1990. This compares to a growth in real GDP of
52 percent over the same period."

THE STATUE OF RESPONSIBILITY

I believe images convey meaning and seize public attention
better than just about anything else. That is why I have
embarked on my Statue of Responsibility project—as a means
of stressing the philosophical point that we, collectively, must
assume responsibility for our actions. The following newspaper
column describes my personal exercise in selling goodness:

"If you're an idea person, somebody with a gift for the
high-concept theme that can seize and stroke the imagination, prominent Hollywood publicist Michael Levine
wants to hear from you. Levine is at work on an unpaid
labor of love: his project to build a Statue of Responsibility
on the West Coast to complement the lady with the torch
in New York Harbor. He is asking for comments from people who share his vision of a monument to personal and
collective self-discipline. 'Without personal responsibility,
liberty leads to anarchy, which is what I think our culture
is moving toward,' says Levine.
    'My thought is that liberty is only possible when it's tied
to personal responsibility.' His observation boasts a distin-
guished pedigree. Alexander Hamilton offered an instructive warning about the fate of Athens: 'When the freedom
they wished for most was freedom from responsibility, then
Athens ceased to be free. And it was never free again.'
    "Aleksandr Solzhenitsyn, in his commencement address
at Harvard, said, 'It is time to promote human responsibility.'

One of the high-profile people who have endorsed Levine's project is M. Scott Peck, the psychiatrist and best-selling author of *The Road Less Traveled*, whose works suggest that mental wellness demands habits of self-control. To those who would belittle the idea of a statue as 'mere symbolism,' there is a formidable response, in copper and steel: the Statue of Liberty itself, and all the uplift it has imparted. There is nothing 'mere' about the most powerful symbols."

HAROLD JOHNSON,
The Orange County Register, August 23, 1995

THE MODERN ERA

Despite this great history, the robustness of the nonprofit sector may be somewhat deceptive in our modern era, and this is your challenge today. Julie Vallone cautions against overconfident assumptions that nonprofits can make up for the withdrawal of federal dollars from the social-services arena. "Roughly $1 trillion in cuts to nonprofit programs are expected [over the coming years]," she notes. "Legislators are making their decisions based on the idea that foundations and private contributions will fill in the gap, a myth that could prove very dangerous to the nonprofit community." She cites an estimate from National Catholic Charities "that in order for the ecumenical community to pick up the tab for these cuts, every church and synagogue in the country would have to spend an additional $2 million."

On the other hand, many leaders of nonprofit work argue that charities and nonprofits do a better job at service delivery than some government programs do. For example, the Institute for Nonprofit Organization Management at the University of San Francisco, reports that nonprofit hospitals in California operate with far lower expenses than government facilities. Expenses per admission at government hospitals in 1992 were $8,029, compared with $6,033 at nonprofit institutions. Moreover, "nonprofit long-term nursing and personal-care facilities have higher per-patient revenues and lower labor costs than their for-profit and government counterparts and lower rates of Medi-Cal and Medicare reimbursements than for-profits and government facilities," according to the Institute. "In 1993, these facilities had a Medicare reimbursement rate of 50 percent, compared with 66 percent at for-profits and 80 percent at government facilities."

An argument in favor of shifting more responsibility for social services to private charities was offered by Senator Dan Coats of Indiana. He called for new government efforts, in the form of special tax credits for charitable institutions, to get more money to the nonprofits and give them a bigger stake in solving the problems.

Americans have reached the end of their faith in bureaucratic solutions to human problems. Who, at the outset of the Great Society in the 1960s, would have predicted or accepted a 600 percent increase in violent crime during the following thirty years or a 500 percent increase in out-of-wedlock births?

Yet, it is precisely the urgency of these human problems that engages both our self-interest and our conscience. America, traveling another three decades down this road, will be unrecognizable and, for many of its citizens, uninhabitable. Public indifference to these trends would be dangerous for our society and our souls.

When counterproductive government programs are cut—as they must be—many of our problems as a nation will remain. Too many children will enter schools through barbed-wire fences and metal detectors. Too many will grow up without a family's stability and discipline and a father's love. Too many communities will be imprisoned by violence and fear. America's leaders must have something practical and compassionate to say about this suffering.

A compassionate response depends upon a basic shift in thinking. American politics has tended to focus on the role of the government and the rights of individuals. It must be refocused on a layer of institutions that stands between a distant government and isolated men and women: families, neighborhoods, grassroots community organizations, charities, churches, and synagogues.

These value-shaping institutions, in contrast to government, possess unique advantages in rebuilding communities and reconstructing broken lives. They can demand individual responsibility. They practice tough love. They often offer moral values and spiritual renewal. Government can't do these things—and I really would not want it to move in this direction. It can only write a check.

But people who are confused and suffering—a teenage girl in trouble, a young boy who wants out of a gang, a welfare mother who wants to change her life—need more than checks. They need the warm hand and hard advice of someone who really cares.

The difference in results brought by this type of private effort as opposed to government can be dramatic. Teen Challenge, a faith-based youth program with 130 chapters around the country, has a drug and alcohol rehabilitation rate of 70 to 86 percent, whereas government programs often have success rates in the single digits. Studies show that for children who participate in the Big Brothers/Big Sisters program for one year, the rate of first-time drug use is cut by 46 percent, school absenteeism is reduced by 52 percent and violent behavior falls by 33 percent. In my experience, no government program—federal, state or local—has a record this hopeful.

Where does this leave government? It does not release us from the duty of providing the basics of a safety net. But it does provide a direction for reform dramatically different from either the status quo or simple program cuts.

Wouldn't it be more compassionate and cost-effective

if government actively encouraged the work of other private, value-shaping institutions in our society—charities
and churches, neighborhoods and grass-roots organizations—instead of keeping these jobs for itself?

Senator Coats goes on to describe his proposals for "tax credits,
vouchers and grants to charities, community organizations, character-
education efforts, maternity homes and community-development
corporations to encourage their work among the disadvantaged."
Whether you agree with this philosophy, or with Senator
Coats's specific policy proposals for getting more resources to nonprofits, the fact is that you will need more resources as the government cuts back in coming years. And it is not clear that even
government tax incentives and other types of encouragement are
enough to stimulate a substantially larger pool of private donations.

CHARITY BEGINS IN THE DOGHOUSE

"It's amazing how much people love their pets. And how
much they enjoy being photographed with them. That's
the premise of *Best Friends of North Carolina*, a book filled
with 252 pictures of people and their pets. The book,
which sells for $60, is a fund-raising project for the Friends
of Animals Foundation, which disperses money through
adoption and cruelty prevention programs and by providing temporary food, shelter, or medial treatment.

"On page after page, people pose with their pets. Some
wrote little notes about their animal. There's Dean Smith
and his dogs Mazie and Kipper.... Local television personalities such as Kim Jenkins Dotson and her dog, Jessica.
Those involved in the project sought out a cross section of
people and pets. They accepted every photo submitted."

Greensboro (N.C.) News and Record

THE CHALLENGE FOR THE FUTURE

The challenge for charities demands revised thinking among charities and nonprofits as much as from government. Despite the success stories cited by Senator Coats and others, many Americans have developed skepticism about the nonprofit sector—and it is up to nonprofits themselves to turn those opinions around.

A 1996 Gallup poll conducted for *Independent Sector* found that giving increased 10 percent over 1994's level, after inflation was added in—with $1,017 contributed by the average family. But nearly one-third of respondents questioned whether charities use their money with integrity, a one-fifth increase in the amount of skepticism over 1990.

"Charitable giving is up," reports an April, 29 1997 Associated Press dispatch. "But giving with confidence is not. Americans harbor more than a grain of suspicion about the constant calls, mailings, and door-to-door seekers wanting a piece of their philanthropic pie." Actually, concern about questionable charity ventures is not new. It dates at least back to World War I, when some conscience-challenged fund-raisers kept money that they had raised supposedly to help soldiers on the European front lines.

Currently, suspect philanthropy is said to consume $1.5 billion per year. That may be a small proportion of the $120 billion or so that Americans contribute, but the stories about scams get remembered. Even some legitimate charities have run into troubles that have threatened to give the larger nonprofit sector some image problems. A former president of the United Way was charged with using money from the organization to fund lavish trips for himself, his wife, and female friends. The Marine Toys for Tots Foundation got a black eye in 1994 when it was revealed that its $10 million direct-mail fund drive had yielded no net gain.

As a charity provider, you therefore need to be aware of the fund-raising approaches that raise red flags among the public, and among watchdog organizations. You must avoid any practice that generates suspicion, such as a reluctance to share financial data.

Ironically, the case for promotion is actually strengthened by the woes that such charities and nonprofits have been experiencing. When you're doing good work and running a tight ship, it is in your best interest to make people aware of the fact. Indeed, when you *don't* market, you're more likely to fall victim to the public's suspicion. "If I've never heard of them, I would never send them a check until they send me some information," says Sara Melendez, president of Independent Sector. "I would want to see how they are spending the money."

THE CALL TO ETHICS IN SELLING GOODNESS

Instilling trust in prospective donors ought to start with an honest, open, rigorously ethical approach to everything your nonprofit does. That includes your marketing efforts. In learning to think like a publicist, you will be acquiring the wrong lessons if you believe that it means learning to be good at flimflam.

I know from experience that most people think that cheating, lying, or at least bending the facts into unrecognizable form are part and parcel of the art of PR. But that is not my experience with successful publicity professionals whose careers and businesses have staying power. Quite the contrary, most professional PR agents—certainly the quality leaders in the business—are principled people.

This doesn't mean that hype isn't permissible in the trade. Injecting emotion and humor into your pitch, in certain circumstances, to certain parties, can be an absolute necessity to convey your enthusiasm about your belief in your message. For instance, telling a hiring agent that a young new comic you're representing "could make Mona Lisa break out in a toothy grin!" may sound like hyperbole, but everyone in the business understands the metaphor and the fact that you honestly think the guy is funny. Some people simply want to use a little bit of embellishment here and there, as it injects life into the presentation.

But hype and dishonesty aren't the same things. Putting some ornaments on the truth is different from dismantling the truth or hawking untruth.

Which one you use is up to you. But remember that conscience is not our own creation. It's a voice that's there even when we might prefer not to be so rudely interrupted in our thoughts. I urge you, in your practice of the publicity arts, not to cross lines that will stimulate that inner voice to scold you in the quiet hours. For one thing, your mental energy is needed for productive things like brainstorming for innovative promotional ideas; it's too valuable to squander on internal wrestling matches with your conscience that could be avoided by staying within the boundaries of ethics.

Ethics is more than a strategy for ensuring your self-esteem. It is also a very practical promotional tool, and an easy strategy for avoiding avoidable problems. Most people are far too smart to be taken in by lies or attempts at manipulation. You will only hurt your cause with potential donors by trying to promote it with such tricks. In contrast, a promotional approach that stresses forthrightness and integrity will gain the respect of precisely the kinds of people you most need as supporters—those who themselves have strong codes of behavior. Indeed, I have found that the kind of successful people who are most likely to become long-term donors tend to put heavy emphasis on codes of conduct in their own personal and business lives, and they look for a similar philosophy in organizations seeking support.

One of the country's most generous benefactors to charities offered me a few comments that illustrate the type of illicit behaviors that should not be practiced. He noted some of the tricks of the nonprofit trade that donors consider dirty, such as breaking up into ten different funds so that each one can make a separate request, or deliberately claiming to be in a financial crisis so that those who will give more under such conditions might give larger gifts. Such tricks turn him off, and any group that tries to bamboozle him won't be seeing his name on any checks.

Roberta Green Ahmanson, wife of California philanthropist Howard Ahmanson, and chief operating officer of their philanthropic organization, Fieldstead and Company, stresses that responsible donors do not tolerate the twisting or hiding of important facts by charities seeking their support. A former religion reporter and a devout Christian, Ms. Ahmanson rephrases the general attitude among serious donors in terms of her own religious commitment: "The donor is responsible to God for how the money God has put in his control is spent. Donors have responsibilities. They must see where the money goes, how is used, what purpose it serves. That doesn't make the donor better or morally superior. It does make him or her responsible to follow the money."

GLITTER IN THE GOLDEN STATE

The story of charities and nonprofits in California, the nation's most populous state and in many ways a trendsetter, offers an instructive picture.

✦ California currently boasts 120,000 nonprofits; that number represents a 66 percent increase since 1980.

✦ The 750,000 people employed by the state's nonprofits represent 5 percent of California's labor force.

✦ Fifty billion dollars were received and spent by the state's nonprofits in 1992. That is nearly 6 percent of California's gross state product.

✦ Despite those large aggregate numbers of employees, 75 percent of the state's nonprofits have no paid workers at all—relying instead entirely on volunteers for administration as well as operation.

Getting Accountable

What this means is that every organization needs to be accountable to the public and to its donors for its actions. Accountability means keeping straight books. It means doing what you purposed to do. It means keeping the donor up-to-date. It means being honest about problems in the project. It means being honest about the financial status of the organization. It means counting donations in kind as just that, not adding their dollar value to the bottom line of income to make the overhead look like a smaller percentage than it is. Honesty in promotion is essential not just to honor the intelligence of donors, but to avoid being targeted as liars by the ever-cynical media.

In a larger sense, ethics are essential because they are the glue that hold society together and allow us to lead tolerable, peaceful lives. A breakdown in ethics can lead to horrific episodes—such as the violence and looting during the 1992 Los Angeles riots. Nonprofits are supposed to be about strengthening the humane foundations of society. They should be citadels of ethical commitment, in the way they carry out their work—and in the way they promote it.

Noted writer and leadership expert Stephen Covey, who wrote *The 7 Habits of Highly Effective* People, and *Principle-Centered Leadership*, argues that ethics are central to personal and organizational success. Principle-centered leadership "means your life is integrated around a fixed set of principles," he says. "You apply those principles interpersonally and organizationally in your management responsibilities so people come to trust you."

Covey's famous book goes on to say that he defines principle-centered leadership as seven habits at four levels: *personal, interpersonal, managerial,* and *organizational.*

✦ *Habit one*—Be proactive and take responsibility.
✦ *Habit two*—Begin with the end in mind. All things are created twice, first in your mind, then in reality.
✦ *Habit three*—Live by that vision; have integrity.
✦ *Habit four*—Respect others and seek to benefit them as well as yourself. It's win-win. It's the golden rule.
✦ *Habit five*—Seek to understand instead of being impatient to be understood.

✦ *Habit six*—Value differences. In an organization, conflict and tension are healthy and normal. They should be celebrated because they can produce better, more creative products.

✦ *Habit seven*—Renew yourself. You must constantly recharge your own batteries.

I distill the ethical issues down to four simple "goodness guidelines":

1. Never deliberately lie.
2. Do not claim something about your project that cannot be substantiated in some credible way.
3. Do not mislead donors or the media about your organization's merits or activities or results.
4. Do not make promises that can't be kept.

The Publicist's Professional Code of Ethics

To give you an idea of the guidelines that top public-relations people submit themselves to, I include here the "Code of Professional Standards for the Practice of Public Relations," as adopted by the Public Relations Society of America's Assembly in 1988.

Not all these precepts are applicable to people promoting their charities, but they can give you an idea of how to think about ethics in a professional context.

1. A member shall conduct his or her professional life in accord with the public interest.
2. A member shall exemplify high standards of honesty and integrity while carrying out dual obligations to a client or employer and to the democratic process.
3. A member shall deal fairly with the public, with past or present clients or employers, and with fellow practitioners, giving due respect to the ideal of free inquiry and to the opinions of others.

4. A member shall adhere to the highest standards of accuracy and truth, avoiding extravagant claims or unfair comparisons and giving credit for ideas and words borrowed from others.

5. A member shall not knowingly disseminate false or misleading information and shall act promptly to correct erroneous communications for which he or she is responsible.

6. A member shall not engage in any practice which has the purpose of corrupting the integrity of channels of communications or the processes of government.

7. A members shall be prepared to identify publicly the name of the client or employer on whose behalf any public communication is made.

8. A member shall not use any individual or organization professing to serve or represent an announced cause, or professing to be independent or unbiased, but actually serving another or undisclosed interest.

9. A member shall not guarantee the achievement of specified results beyond the member's direct control.

10. A member shall not represent conflicting or competing interests without the express consent of those concerned, given after a full disclosure of the facts.

11. A member shall not place himself or herself in a position where the member's personal interest is or may be in conflict with an obligation to an employer or client, or others, without full disclosure of such interests to all involved.

12. A member shall not accept fees, commissions, gifts or any other consideration from anyone except clients or employers for whom services are performed without their express consent, given after full disclosure of the facts.

13. A member shall scrupulously safeguard the confi-

dences and privacy rights of present, former and prospective clients or employers.

14. A member shall not intentionally damage the professional reputation or practice of another practitioner.

15. If a member has evidence that another member has been guilty of unethical, illegal, or unfair practices, including those in violation of this Code, the member is obligated to present the information promptly to the proper authorities of the Society for action in accordance with...the bylaws.

16. A member called as a witness in a proceeding for enforcement of this Code is obligated to appear, unless excused for sufficient reason by the judicial panel.

17. A member shall, as soon as possible, sever relations with any organization or individual if such relationship requires conduct contrary to the articles of this Code.

This code may seem pretty stern, detailed, and demanding, but real professionalism is about living by standards. Selling goodness should be, too.

How Does Your Organization Rate Itself?

There are two groups that rate charities according to specific standards: the National Charities Information Bureau (NCIB) and the Better Business Bureau's Philanthropic Advisory Service. Their criteria offer a useful measuring stick to see how well your organization has structured its finances and operations. If your group holds up well against these checklists, you have something to boast about in your PR campaign.

THE COUNCIL OF BETTER BUSINESS BUREAUS

The Standards for Charitable Solicitations of the Council of Better Business Bureaus (CBBB) pertain to how open an organization with the public and how it actually uses its funds.

Their criteria include:

Public Accountability

   1. Soliciting organization shall provide on request an annual report. "The annual report...shall present the organization's purposes; descriptions of overall programs, activities and accomplishments;...information about the governing body and structure; and information about financial activities and financial position."
   2. Soliciting organizations shall provide on request complete annual financial statements.
   3. Soliciting organizations' financial statements shall present adequate information to serve as a basis for informed decisions.
   "Information needed as a basis for informed decisions generally includes but is not limited to:
   ✦ significant categories of contributions and other income;...
   ✦ detailed schedule of expenses by natural classification (e.g. salaries, employee benefits, occupancy, postage, etc....
   ✦ accurate presentation of all fund raising and administrative costs...."
   4. Organizations receiving a substantial portion of their income through the fund raising activities of controlled or affiliated entities shall provide on request an accounting of all income received by and fund raising costs incurred by such entities.
   "Such entities include committees, branches or chapters which are controlled by or affiliated with the benefiting organization...."

Use of Funds

   1. A reasonable percentage of total income from all sources shall be applied to programs and activities directly related to the purposes for which the organization exists.
   "A reasonable percentage requires that at least 50% of total income from all sources be spent on programs and activities directly related to the organization's purposes.
   2. A reasonable percentage of public contributions shall be

applied to the programs and activities described in solicitations, in accordance with donor expectations.

"A reasonable percentage requires that at least 50% of public contributions be spent on the programs and activities described in solicitations,..."

3. Fund-raising costs shall be reasonable.

"A reasonable use of funds requires that fund raising costs not exceed 35% of related contributions."

4. Total fund raising and administrative costs shall be reasonable.

"A reasonable use of funds requires that total fund raising and administrative costs not exceed 50% of total income."

5. Soliciting organizations shall substantiate on request their application of funds, in accordance with donor expectations, to the programs and activities described in solicitations.

6. Soliciting organizations shall establish adequate controls over disbursements.

GIVE GOODS, GET TICKETS

"Los Angeles business and industry are being solicited to open their warehouses—rather than their checkbooks—for an innovative charity event designed to provide goods and services to the county's homeless. Tickets to the inaugural Merchants and Manufacturers Dinner...may be secured by donating surplus or slow-moving goods to the Shelter Resource Bank. A program of the nonprofit Shelter Partnership, the Resource Bank obtains quantity donations of everything from mattresses and clothing to baby strollers and refrigerators, then distributes them among more than 150 Southland homeless shelters and human service agencies.

"This event offers businesses an easy and effective 'one-stop philanthropic vehicle to address homelessness,' notes Nordstrom vice President Betsy Sanders, who is co-chairing

> the evening.... Sanders points to significant tax advantages
> (up to twice the donor's cost of goods), plus savings on ware-
> housing and other storage-related costs which make this an
> attractive corporate donation. Such firms as Levi-Strauss,
> Kimberly Clark, Redken Labs and Nike have already given
> products in Shelter Resource Bank's first year of operation.
>
> *Business Wire*, February 26, 1990

THE BEST OF THE BIGGEST

The matter of how much money a charity spends on programs, as opposed to fund-raising and overhead, is taken very seriously by rigorous observers of the nonprofit sector. In November 1996, for instance, *Money* magazine ranked the twenty-five top-grossing charities according to the percentage of their income spent on programs over the previous three years. Here is that listing

RANK/CHARITY	TELEPHONE	TYPE	SPENDING AS % OF TOTAL INCOME
1. American Red Cross	703-206-7090	Human services	91.5
2. Catholic Charities USA	703-549-1390	Human services	87.7
3. Salvation Army	703-684-5500	Human services	85.5
4. Campus Crusade for Christ	407-826-2000	Religious	83.9
5. YWCA of the USA	212-614-2700	Human services	83.8
6. Goodwill Industries	301-530-6500	Human services	83.4
7. Nature Conservancy	703-841-5300	Conservation	83.0
8. Planned Parenthood Federation	212-541-7800	Human services	80.5
9. Habitat for Humanity	912-924-6935	Relief, development	80.4
10. Christian Children's Fund	804-756-2700	Relief, development	80.3

Rank/Charity	Telephone	Type	Spending as % of total income
11. National East Seal Society	312-726-6200	Health	79.8
12. Boys and Girls Clubs of America	404-815-5700	Human services	79.7
13. Focus on the Family	719-531-3400	Religious	78.6
14. World Vision	206-815-1000	Relief, development	78.5
15. March of Dimes	914-428-7100	Health	77.2
16. Girl Scouts of the USA	800-478-7248	Human services	76.8
17. Metropolitan Museum of Art	212-535-7710	Cultural	76.8
18. American Heart Association	800-242-8721	Health	76.6
19. American Lung Association	212-315-8700	Health	76.6
20. Boy Scouts of America	214-580-2000	Human services	76.5
21. Muscular Dystrophy Association	520-529-2000	Health	76.5
22. American Cancer Society	800-227-2345	Health	70.2
23. Disabled American Veterans	606-441-7300	Human services	58.5
24. ALSAC–St. Jude Children's Hospital	800-877-5833	Health	54.9
25. Shriners Hospitals	800-241-4438	Health	54.9

You can be sure that major charities that show up well on such rankings don't hesitate to promote the fact. In fact, a press release in early 1997 from the Red Cross was headlined, "American Red Cross earns top rankings from consumer watchdog groups and

Money magazine; Dole credits volunteers, donors, staff." The release quoted Red Cross president Elizabeth Dole: "Each of our dedicated 1.4 million volunteers should take great pride in helping people through an organization that consistently ranks at the top in efficiency and accountability while maintaining the highest level of humanitarian service."

Although your own nonprofit organization may be small and just taking flight, the same attention to frugal and efficient management—and accountability to the public—will help you reach your goals by building credibility with potential donors. This assumes, of course, that you vigorously promote the fact that your group has these virtues.

Summary: Goodness Guide

1. Charitable giving is a tradition dating at least back to the ancient Greeks. And public promotion of one's charitable generosity was a tradition as early as the days of classical Rome.

2. Surveys in recent years suggest a rising level of public skepticism about how nonprofits spend their money.

3. To overcome such doubts among potential donors, check your organization's practices against the criteria for responsible charity management issued by such watchdogs as the Philanthropic Advisory Service of the Council of Better Business Bureaus, and the National Charities Information Bureau.

4. Among the criteria that help establish credibility: having an independent board that meets at least twice yearly; spending at least 50 percent of your income on programs, and spending no more than 35 percent of revenues on fund-raising.

5. Make the financial details of your organization available to anyone who requests to see them.

6. If your organization meets those watchdog criteria that might apply to a nonprofit your size, take a cue from the Red Cross and boast about that fact in your marketing campaigns.

Dealing with Crisis

*Our problems are man-made; therefore they can be solved by men.
And man can be as big as he wants.
No problem of human destiny is beyond human beings.*

JOHN F. KENNEDY

WHEN the red light lit up on the television camera that was trained on me, I was beamed into the homes of millions of late-night television viewers around the nation. This evening I was the live guest on ABC's *Nightline*. I had been asked to come on the news and interview program to discuss the prospects for rehabilitation of a very prominent person who had just been found liable by a civil jury for a very sinister crime.

To the question, could O.J. Simpson win his way back to public affection, my answer was clear: There was as much chance of O.J. being redeemed as there was for Charles Manson being named Baby-Sitter of the Year. The deed for which Simpson had been declared liable was too dark, and his insistence on denying the overwhelming weight of the evidence too audacious. He might be able to gain, over time, some public recognition that he did have a conscience, but only through a very public admission of his wrongs and penance for them. Neither of which appeared very likely, I pointed out. I also added that no PR campaign could make Simpson a viable spokesman for corporate America again, or someone that mainstream Hollywood producers would consider casting. The only legitimate opportunities before him, I suggested, were of a personal nature: the opportunity to show humility and somehow try to cleanse his soul and psyche.

As this example shows, there are situations so disgraceful and repugnant that they are beyond the abilities of public-relations professionals to change public perceptions. Situations such as the one Simpson created for himself, are a mess from which any self-respecting, ethically rigorous PR professional would want to stay clear.

But not every potential public-relations disaster is beyond being reversed in the public mind. And other than especially dark moments for humankind such as O.J. Simpson's, many difficult and challenging incidents can be turned into something positive that benefits everyone involved. Indeed, the modern profession of public relations came into being in the United States largely in response to the bad press that corporate chieftains, such as John D. Rockefeller, were getting from investigative or "muckraking" journalists around the turn of the century. Rockefeller's refusal to talk to the press after deadly disasters at mines owned by his company, earned him the hatred of the nation. That animosity was largely defused beginning a few years later, when Rockefeller hired PR agent Ivy Lee. This pioneer of the profession got Rockefeller's corporate empire to begin cooperating with the media. And his creative mind conjured up promotional strategies to garner good press for Rockefeller as an individual. Most famously, Lee counseled the old capitalist to give away dimes whenever a crowd—and press photographers—were present.

No organization is immune to mistakes, blunders, errors, or hidden criminal activities among its membership, affiliates, business partners, and others with whom it has contact. That is why this chapter will teach you how to handle what is commonly called "crisis PR."

CRISES HAVE A LONG SHELF-LIFE

Developing strategies to handle crisis are of tantamount importance to the PR professional, because the worst part about a crisis is not in the immediate moment but in the long shelf-life that they continue to have years and years afterwords. For example, a recent survey asked one thousand Americans to name any corporate blunders that came to mind. Some could recall crises that had been out of the news for years, while nearly everyone could name at least one relatively recent corporate fiasco. The most-remembered crises included

1. The Exxon Valdez oil spill (named by 51 percent of those surveyed);
2. The savings-and-loan scandals (25 percent);
3. Sears unnecessary auto repairs (23 percent);
4. General Motors layoffs and fuel-tank problems (22 percent);
5. Dow Corning silicone breast-implant troubles (15 percent);
6. IBM layoffs (13 percent);
7. Food Lion supermarkets food-handling controversy (11 percent); and
8. The Tylenol tampering incidents (11 percent).

While crises like these are more likely to happen in big business, charities and nonprofits must learn crisis-management techniques as well. Fortunately, while it is a challenging art, it is arguably less so when the "client" that has run into public-relations trouble is a fundamentally worthy individual or organization (such as your nonprofit is likely to be). In such a case, much of the publicist's task involves basically reminding the public of the client's solid, ethical core so that people will frame their perceptions with that essential point in mind.

How to Prepare for the Stormy Day

The bombing at the World Trade Center in 1993 is an excellent example of how one organization learned, as the event unfolded, to handle a crisis with dignity and respect. It is a case worth studying. As you might recall, this bombing created havoc in one of the largest buildings in the world, killing six people and injuring thousands. By droves, thousands of dazed office workers staggered out of the building, into the glare of media lights. Hundreds of reporters wanted to know what was going on in the building, what had happened, who was responsible. The media-relations people for the Port Authority of New York, the owner of the building, didn't have answers.

But did they clam up or claim that they couldn't say anything until they spoke to their lawyers? No. The Port Authority (PA) faced a potentially irreparable loss of credibility, so this was no time to feed suspicion and distortion by playing the strong, silent type. "What's important to remember is what we did not do," Peter Yerkes, media-relations supervisor of the agency, told the *Public Relations Journal*. "We didn't hunker down. The press had access to virtually all the information the PA had. The only exception was information related to law enforcement officials."

To keep the lines of communication open, Yerkes and his colleagues created a media-relations command post from which they stressed over and over again the message: "We don't know what happened, but, obviously, it was an explosion of tremendous force that ripped our communications system apart." From the first, it was decided to hold daily press briefings and to provide access to the blast site. Yerkes, a former journalist, explained to *PR Journal* how crucial it is to disseminate information to reporters: "If no one was willing to tell me [when I was a journalist] what was happening, I would either conjure up the worst possible image in my own mind or talk to people who would give me what purported to be information, although it might be very inaccurate. It served our best interest to show the devastated bomb site."

In the end, little misinformation went out through the media. Over time, the focus of coverage eventually turned to the routine of repair efforts. Responsible reporting prevailed over rumors that might have been destructive to the PA's image and broader social stability. The strategy of openness had proved its worth.

There are several lessons to be gleaned from this case history. First, it helps if you plan right now to implement a strategy of openness in the event of a crisis occuring to your organization. Make a commitment to honesty and integrity in dealing with the press rather than initiating a campaign of lies and self-protectionism.

Secondly, develop a long-range crisis plan that accounts *now* for the many decisions you won't have time to make in the midst of a crisis. Photocopy the box below which contains ten steps you should take *immediately* to have your crisis plan ready for action should you need it.

CRISIS PLAN: TEN STEPS TO TAKE BEFORE A CRISIS

1. Name a crisis PR team, which includes the top officials in your nonprofit, among others.

2. Brainstorm about possible crises that could occur to your organization. Imagine at least a dozen scenarios that would be potential publicity nightmares, and have members of your organization talk about how they would handle media relations in each case.

3. Designate a place where this decision-making team will meet during a crisis.

4. Have your media list in order, so that you can make proactive phone calls to your media contacts if a crisis arises. You will offer, in those phone calls, to share any information you have, so that they know as much as you know.

5. Among your crisis-management team, designate who will be responsible for data-gathering during the peri-

od of trouble. That person will continually update everyone on all relevant information.

6. Designate a primary spokesperson and a substitute.

7. Set aside some money to pay for special media-response needs in the event of crisis.

8. Keep a basic fact sheet about your organization on hand for dissemination during any crisis. Make sure it is updated at regular intervals. It should include the mission of your nonprofit, the budget, and the names and affiliations of board members, managers, and key volunteers. Also—the names of people who have been helped by your group and can be relied on for positive testimonials.

9. In the (hopefully) unlikely event that you'll actually have to implement this plan, conduct yourself with courtesy and patience in all conversations with the media. Do not let words of panic, or frustration, escape your lips. If the incident warrants it, a press release expressing your agency's concern should be produced and disseminated immediately.

10. Make the top officials of your nonprofit available to the media. Return media phone calls promptly. "Can I be of any further help?" should be a standard question to any reporter.

A CRISIS BRINGS JUDGMENT DAY

Making decisions in the face of crisis is admittedly very difficult. Some companies facing a major crisis have tried to pursue an honest and candid response, but failed for lack of true sincerity. For example, when Foodmaker Inc., the parent company of Jack-in-the-Box, was faced with a food-poisoning public-relations nightmare several years ago, the company's chairman went on commercials to say the firm was praying for the recovery of those who had fallen ill. This was a good response, but not good enough. The public was angered because there was not a perception of deep concern from the company. I, for one, would like to have had the executive say they were praying for *and paying* for the victims. The lesson here: The public knows sincerity when it sees it. Don't think they are blind or deaf. Here are some essential guidelines that you should commit your staff to follow to avoid this type of mistake:

✦ Don't head for the cubbyhole. Deal with the crisis forthrightly and candidly. How you and your colleagues respond will be a defining moment personally and for your organization.

✦ Not even a white lie is acceptable. Untruths risk earning your organization lingering mistrust in the media and the community.

✦ If people have been killed or injured through actions by your organization, express as much sorrow and sympathy as you can, even on occasion offering money to those in need if such an offer can be accomplished without being interpreted as an expression of culpability.

✦ Respond to all questions from the media, but don't necessarily answer them all. Don't answer hypothetical questions, for instance, and don't speculate. Deal only with facts.

✦ Don't volunteer negative information.

✦ Speak in precise sentences. Undisciplined rambling can lead to saying something you might regret.

✦ Don't go off the record.

✦ Use simple terms that everyone can understand, even if they have no knowledge of your organization's area of expertise. No insider's jargon.

With this kind of commitment to helpfulness, honesty, and candor, your organization's fundamental sincerity and integrity can be reinforced, and it can emerge from a crisis with reputation enhanced. You've probably heard that the Chinese character for crisis is also the character for opportunity. A well-planned crisis media response can actually build your reputation and create a positive outcome for your nonprofit.

THE $50,000 PR QUESTION

Sometimes PR consultants to businesses in trouble have come back with surprising prescriptions. Certainly that's one way to describe the plan that PR giant Ben Sonnenberg hatched for the Ford Motor Company when it hired him in the late 1950s to help it get beyond the flood of bad press and public opinion unleashed by the Edsel. Sonnenberg took three days to come up with his plan, and asked for $50,000 in compensation. The assembled Ford executives were all anticipation as he opened his mouth to deliver his advice. "Do nothing," he said. He then took his money and left.

STRATEGIC THINKING FOR GOOD TIMES AND BAD

Hopefully, the need to deal artfully with a time of trauma will never confront you and your nonprofit. But planning for such an unwelcome possibility is a good exercise in developing strategies for effective marketing in good times and bad. These are the strategies I have stressed throughout this book:

✦ Build an ongoing relationship with people in the media, don't wait until you "need" them to contact them.

✦ Earn a reputation as an expert in the field that your nonprofit addresses; make yourself a reservoir of reliable, factual information so that journalists will call you even when they're not doing a story on your particular organization.

✦ Master the skills of effective press releases and media kits.

✦ Become artful at the interview, able to respond concisely and colorfully, packing a lot of meaning into a sound bite.

✦ Develop a loyal following of individual donors and business partners for your nonprofit who will sustain it through times good and bad, and will help carry the marketing plan by

spreading good word-of-mouth about the organization.
+ Build your organization's reputation for integrity by making
sure it has an outstanding board or management, and efficient
spending. And brag about these qualities in press releases.
+ Build goodwill by speaking frequently in front of trade, community, and service organizations.
+ Further create goodwill with innovative fund-raisers and special
events that create excitement and "buzz" in the community.
+ Become an effective networker at social and business events.
+ Follow up anyone's expression of support for your nonprofit
with a formal expression of thanks.

As the government retreats from social-service involvement,
the need for private-sector activism on behalf of cultural and
social renewal becomes greater than in many decades. As someone
committed to nonprofit altruism, you are on the front lines of an
exciting, historically momentous campaign. You're spreading goodness with the effectiveness that only the nonprofit sector can do.
What a privilege you have been given—to be able, at the same
time, to sell goodness to society, to market altruism to those who
haven't yet tasted its joys, so that good works can multiply and
grow and thrive.

SUMMARY: GOODNESS GUIDE

1. Create a plan for media response in the event that some
kind of crisis hits your nonprofit.

2. Designate a team of workers and officials of the organization
who will handle the response decisions, and a command post
where they will meet. One member should be responsible for gathering facts during crisis, and another for being the point person
with the media.

3. Adopt a rule of candor, diplomacy, and accuracy in statements to the press.

4. Be proactive in a crisis, phoning the media before they phone you, to share the latest information.

5. Make top officials of the organization available to journalists.

6. Set funds aside for special media-related expenditures in the event of a crisis.

7. Have a fact sheet about your organization on hand.

8. In all things, work to vindicate and enhance your nonprofit's reputation for sincerity and genuine concern for people.

A CALL TO ALMS

THE need for nonprofits to cultivate an agile approach to promotion perhaps has never been more crucial than right now. The din and clutter in the mass media is louder and has a greater variety than ever, so getting your message out requires more imagination than ever before.

The good news is that America is fertile terrain for nonprofits to seek donors and voluntary helpers. Giving and volunteering have always been part of the nation's culture. But it claims a new urgency today, as the public sector begins to step back from the delivery of social services. As government tightens, the pinch on tax-funded social programs increases. The welfare-reform law enacted in 1996 is symbolic of the trend: It will eventually impose time limits for welfare on all able-bodied recipients.

The success of this approach depends partly on a vigorous business community expanding to create more jobs. But the private charitable sector confronts new tasks as well. It will be called on for training, support, and emergency financial aid in many cases where government was previously the provider.

A scaling-back of government support is also taking place in the arts and humanities. Here, too, the private and nonprofit sectors will have to step up their efforts.

This new reliance on non-public resources was given a defining expression at the Presidents' Summit for America's Future, which convened in Philadelphia in April 1997. Led by General Colin Powell, and with President Clinton and former presidents Bush and Ford in attendance, along with Nancy Reagan representing her husband, the event was "a call to alms," as the *Wall Street Journal* put it. Its aim was to summon public-spirited Americans to a new level of volunteerism.

General Powell envisions a leadership role for corporate chieftains in this revitalized emphasis on private-sector solutions to social needs. "I want it to become part of their daily corporate life that they worry about the communities in which their plants are located and their headquarters are located," he says. "The leadership capacity that exists in corporate America to build wealth and make products, that same capacity can be brought to bear in the problems of American communities."

But small nonprofits have a crucial part to play as well. That is why there was never a more important time for charity workers to learn the basics of selling goodness.

Indeed, the Presidents' Summit itself was an exercise in selling goodness. It was a proudly promotional event—intended to generate the massive amounts of publicity it got.

It was also a wonderful argument for the theme of the manifesto in this chapter: the moral case for promotion. Public awareness is now heightened, as the issue of volunteerism becomes part of the nation's table-talk. The charitable sector got tangible benefits. A number of corporations, answering the general's challenge (and no doubt recognizing the publicity potential) have pledged new efforts to help nonprofits. And charities from around the nation convened in discussion sessions where they exchanged valuable ideas on how to cultivate donors and volunteers.

CHEERS FOR VOLUNTEERS

"Thoughts of unchecked idealism have a way of giving naysayers the shivers. So it's no surprise that a three-day, star-studded, all-stops-out extravaganza (the Presidents' Summit) designed to mobilize volunteers nationwide drew cynics as well as saints. Too bad that such negative energy couldn't be made positive and applied to the task at hand—encouraging volunteerism as a natural part of life.

"Whether choosing to read to children, build homes for the poor or serve soup to the hungry, the value of volunteerism is in its return. Having a caring adult in a child's life increases the odds that the youngster will stay out of trouble, stay in school and make the most of his or her potential. Getting children of any circumstance involved in volunteering themselves pays off, too. Those who are raised to think of the needs of others are bound to be better citizens.

"This country was fought for by volunteers. Its democratic doctrines were drafted by volunteers. Presidents have traditionally espoused these values and encouraged the 'points of light' for which America shines.

"It's easy to find reasons why something is not possible. It takes leadership and vision to chip away at obstacles and work together to overcome them."

The Hartford Courant, April 29, 1997

ADVOCATES OF NONPROFITS, TAKE HEED

Washington-based journalist Carl Rowan captured the excitement in a passionate column:

[This event] could turn out to be as important to America, socially and economically, as the GI Bill of Rights....

[T]he most notable thing about the event is that

President Clinton and former Presidents Ford, Carter, and Bush are joining Powell and at least half the nation's governors in a plea to corporations and individuals to volunteer money and time to broaden the opportunities and fulfill the basic dreams of 15 million disadvantaged American children.

America's leadership is saying loudly that the youngsters now trapped in poverty, sickness, crime, sex and drug abuse are not hopeless, uneducable burdens doomed by God to be worthless.

It is a remarkable leadership stance in a time when millions of Americans have swallowed the Bell Curve bull that governmental and charitable programs to lift the so-called underclass are colossal wastes because those in the underclass are inherently inferior, intellectually, morally and otherwise.

It is of monumental importance to have the nation's leaders reject such slander, and to say that not only can we help make deprived youngsters proud contributors to this society, but we must do it to avoid the raging anger produced by scorning and oppressing them.

I liken the initiative to the GI Bill because that program, which provided for federally financed education after World War II, lifted million of former soldiers and sailors, whose families lacked learning and money, into middle- and upper-class status. I am one of the former GIs who benefited.

The second great thing about the movement for increased volunteerism is that its leaders are not pretending that it can be a substitute for government social programs. Powell is emphatic in saying that the billions of dollars of volunteerism that he is calling for can never be a substitute for government financing of education, medical, welfare and other social programs.

The third point to note with pride and hope is that more than 150 corporations and many universities, civic groups and individuals already have responded positively to appeals by Powell and the presidents. They have agreed to build safe playgrounds and after-school havens for children with working parents, give free health coverage to children who don't have ordinary access to it, provide Internet training, offer scholarships and give education on drugs and training in personal safety.

If the program comes to full fruition and maintain enthusiastic support for the long run, America clearly will become a wondrous place—not just for long-deprived children, but for all of us.

To be sure, the Summit came in for its share of criticism. Some saw it as a flash-in-the-pan event unlikely to generate long-term changes. Others imagined it as promoting some kind of compulsory "volunteerism," even though General Powell explicitly rejected such a policy. If both criticisms were off the mark, they were further testimony to the Summit's power as a promotional event.

Yes, the Philadelphia Summit had its strong critics, but it also enjoyed strong advocacy by people such as columnist Arianna Huffington:

A Damning Moment

For years, liberals have denounced conservatives as heartless. For years, conservatives, like myself, have responded that liberals were equating compassion with government action. For years, liberals have claimed that we had no real plans to help the poor. For years, conservatives have argued back that we care just as much but advocate nongovernmental—and more effective—ways of helping them. Indeed, caring for the poor, conservatives have insisted, is a moral imperative of citizenship.

It pains me to say so, but the conservative argument may turn out to be a sham. We are in the midst of a damning moment in the history of modern conservatism—crystallized in the reactions to the presidents' volunteerism summit. Whatever the summit's shortcomings, it was the kind of thing conservatives are supposed to be for. It emphasized private-sector responses to social problems. No taxpayer money was spent, and not a single legislative initiative was endorsed by the summiteers. And it was chaired by Colin Powell, a by-the-bootstraps success story.

Yet conservatives were apoplectic. "Citizen service," Rush Limbaugh sneered, "is a repudiation of the principles upon which our country was based." He went on to clarify: "We are all here for ourselves." Thomas Sowell, a conservative intellectual, similarly attacked the ideas that "those who produce the things we all live on are supposed to 'give something back' to those who produce nothing." Even more desiccated was Florence King's argument in the *National Review*. She went to peices over the prospect of each of us "being assigned our own personal illiterate to tutor." King, a patron saint of the Leave Us Alone Coalition, a group whose creed is: Cut our taxes, reduce government, and all will be well—including for the poor. And if not, what the heck?

Lady Bountiful

But has not conservatism, from Edmund Burke on down, been grounded in the Judeo-Christian notion that to whom much is given, from him that much more shall be expected? Alfred Marshall called this principle "economic chivalry"; Russell Kirk defined citizenship as the "willingness to sacrifice private desires for public ends." Pick your own conservative heavyweight. The point is that freedom is not sustainable without a sense of social responsibility.

Liberty is not an end but the best available means to the Good Society. What makes this moment so perilous for the conservative movement is the intellectual confusion that permeates the thinking of its best and brightest: the confusion between government programs and the bully pulpit, between promoting civil society and expanding state power, between obligations and entitlements. An article by Marvin Olasky in the *Wall Street Journal* was called "The Entitlement Summit." So, according to the new conservative gospel, a call to the private sector to provide 2 million mentors for at-risk kids is a liberal entitlement to be denounced?

Conservatives will never be able to reduce the role of government until they have convinced the public that there are other ways to care for those in need. For now, they merely glorify a shrunken view of self-interest and, indeed, of human nature. As Bob Novak put it: "What time have [Americans] got to go out and be Lady Bountiful, like Nancy Reagan wants them to be?" Nancy Reagan accused by the right of being too compassionate? That *is* news.

Born in opposition—first to communism and then to the welfare state—conservatives have had little practice doing anything except opposing things. With the summit, this contrarian tendency combined with horror over Bill Clinton's involvment. In article after article, conservatives simply edited out Presidents Bush, Reagan, Carter, and Ford, calling the event the president's summit, not the presidents' summit. But conservatives could loathe Clinton without casting aside the idea of civic responsiblility.

Mercifully, there is another strand of conservatism. Two dozen elected officials have formed the Renewal Alliance to help empower communities to do the work of social renewal. In a letter to Powell, they enthusiastically endorsed his "call to action." Have members of the alliance, including Representatives John Kasich and J. C. Watts, talked to Limbaugh lately? It's time to decide: Is the conservative movement going to be defined by the social Darwinism and carping small-mindedness of Limbaugh and the Leave Us Alone Coalition or by the generous civic-mindedness that was central to America's founding?

Let's hope that a few copies of *Selling Goodness* are on hand— or at least the PR Moral Manifesto—to help guide them in their good work, and point us in the direction of salvation.

BIBLIOGRAPHY

Adams, Kathleen, Bruce Crumley, Tammerlin Drummond, Janice Horowitz, Nadya Labi, Lina Lofaro, Emily Mitchell, Megan Rutherford, and Alain Sanders. "Notebook." *Time* (March 10, 1997).

Ailes, Roger. *You Are the Message.* New York: Doubleday, 1988.

Anderson, Greg. *Living Life on Purpose.* San Francisco: Harper, 1997.

Averill, Joni. "Millinocket Group Seeks Entries in Baby Contest." *Bangor Daily News* (June 8, 1995).

Barry, Dave. "Revenge of the Dorks" *Miami Herald* (April 3, 1994).

Behrens, Leigh. "Storytelling Finds a New Audience at the Office." *Chicago Tribune* (November 3, 1991).

Belkin, Lisa. "One Charity's Power" *Orlando Sentinel* (February 9, 1997).

Bernstein, Peter, and Christopher Ma, editors. *The Practical Guide to Practically Everything.* New York: Random House, 1996.

Blumenthal, Karen. *Wall Street Journal* (November 20, 1995).

Cohen, Aaron. *Las Vegas Business Press* (January 11, 1993).

Connors, Tracy D. *The Nonprofit Organization Handbook.* New York: McGraw Hill, 1988.

Covey, Stephen. *Principle-Centered Leadership.* New York: Simon and Schuster, second edition, 1991.

Covey, Stephen. *The Seven Habits of Highly Successful People.* New York: Simon and Schuster, 1989.

Creamer, Anita. "Female Conflicts in the Age of TV." *Sacramento Bee* (May 28, 1994).

Cruz, Mike. "Derby Day at Dachshund Downs." *Orange County Register* (June 6, 1996).

"Unbounded Cheers from Volunteers." *Hartford Courant* (April 29, 1997).

Eigen, Lewis D., and Jonathan P. Siegal. *The Manager's Book on Quotations.* New York: Amacom, 1989.

Farnham, Alan, and Joyce E. Davis. "How to Nurture Creative Sparks: Teaching Creativity Tricks to Buttoned Down Executives." *Fortune* (January 10, 1994): 95, 98.

Fiffer, Steve. *So You've Got a Great Idea.* New York: Addison-Wesley, 1986.

Fulkerson, Jennifer. "The Secret Life of Donors." *American Demographics* (August, 1995).

Gill, Ardian. "How to Ignore Charitable Appeals with a Clear Conscience." *Wall Street Journal* (February 18, 1997).

Graham, Billy. *Just as I Am.* New York: Harper Collins Worldwide, 1997.

Hodgkinson, Virginia A. Ph.D., and Murray Weitzman, Ph.D. "Independent Sector Study." 1996.

Huffington, Ariana. "On Politics." *US News Online* (May 19, 1997).

Hull, Betty. "Terror in the Tower: A Media Relations Professional Tells His Story." *Public Relations Journal* (December 1993).

Iwata, Edward. "Businesses Find a New Tool: Creativity." *Orange County Register* (May 19, 1995).

Jabs, Caroline. "On Line Volunteering." *Home PC* (October 1, 1996): 124.

Jacoby, Jeff. "Kids Learn Nothing From TV—Not Even From 'Sesame Street.'" *Boston Globe* (April 17, 1997).

Johnson, Harold. "Erecting a Moral Beacon in the West." *Orange County Register* (August 23, 1995).

Jones, Lynn. "Gen in Gen-X Means Generous." *Direct* (March, 1996).

Kawasaki, Guy. *Selling the Dream.* New York: Harper Collins, 1991.

Kushner, Rabbi Harold. *When Bad Things Happen to Good People*. New York: Schocken, 1981.

Leavy, Bob. "The Ball You Won't Have to Attend." *Washington Post* (April 12, 1988): D23.

Lewis, Nancy. "It's 1-2-3 Pull-a-Plane." *Norfolk Virginian Pilot* (September 29, 1996).

"Majority of Primary Care Physicians Unaware of Difference in Heart Disease in Men and Women; Many Cases of Heart Disease in Women Undiagnosed." *Heart Info Network* (November 21, 1996).

Mattingly, Terry. "Some Tips on How to Improve Religious Coverage." *Knoxville News-Sentinel* (August 5, 1995).

McCafferty, Dennis. "Creative Charity Helping to Close Gap on Hunger." *Atlanta Journal and Constitution* (December 14, 1991).

Miller, William H. "More than Just Making Money." *Industry Week* (August 2, 1995).

Money Magazine (November 1996). Tabled information came from website *http://www.nptimes.com/Nov96/nov100.html*.

Myers, Marc. "Interview with George Weinberg." *Bottom Line/Personal* (September 15, 1996).

Nichols, Judith E. "Revisiting the Baby Boomers at Mid Life." *Fund Raising Management* (July 1996).

Norman, Michael. "Why the Left-Handers Gathered in Great Neck." *New York Times* (April 4, 1985).

Ode, Kim. "The Mother Teresa of Minneapolis." *Good Housekeeping* (April 1994): 8.

Oldenberg, Don. "Experts Provide a Sampling of Tips for Self Promotion." *Washington Post* (June 13, 1985).

Pearlman, Ellen. "Surfing the Net, and Serving Communities in Need." *Home PC* (October 1, 1996): 17.

Prager, Dennis. *Think a Second Time*. New York: Harper Collins, 1995.

Public Relations Society of America's Assembly. "Code of Professional

Standards for the Practice of Public Relations." 1988.

Richardson, Anwar. "Guardians Serve, Protect, and Sack." *Tampa Tribune* (March 22, 1997).

RoAne, Susan. *How to Work a Room*. Los Angeles: Audio Renaissance, 1988.

Rowan, Carl. "The Presidents' Summit on Volunteerism." *Houston Chronicle* (April 27, 1997).

Saben, Ariel. "Barristers Learn how to Fish and Not Come Out Smelly." *Recorder* (December 5, 1994).

Schultheiss, Sally. "Food from the Heart." *In Style* (October 1996).

Selifman, Martin. *Learned Optimism*. New York: Alfred Knopf, 1991.

Sharn, Lori. "Black Philanthropy Is Growing." *USA Today* (March 6, 1997).

Smith, Dean. "A Book About Love." *Greensboro News and Record* (March 1, 1997).

Stettner, Morey. "How to Master the Fine Art of Small Talk." *Investor's Business Daily*.

Stonecipher, Harry. *Editorial and Persuasive Writing*. New York: Communications Arts Books, 1979.

Templeton, Sir John Marks. *Discovering the Laws of Life*. New York: Continuum, 1994.

"Thumbs Up, Thumbs Down." *Fresno Bee* (May 2, 1997).

Trevitt, Tom. "Unique Good Raising Event Lets Businesses Help Homeless, Reap Tax Advantages." *Business Wire* (February 26, 1990).

Van Ekeren, Glenn. *Speaker's Sourcebook II*. New York: Prentice Hall, 1994.

"Where Can You Find New Donors?" *Nonprofit World* (May/June 1995).

Whiteside, Thomas. *The Blockbuster Complex*. Connecticut: Wesleyan University Press, 1981.

INDEX

All page numbers in italics refer to tables.